SUMMERS IN SQUID TICKLE

ALSO BY ROBERT FINCH

The Outer Beach: A Thousand-Mile Walk on Cape Cod's Atlantic Shore

A Cape Cod Notebook 2

A Cape Cod Notebook

The Iambics of Newfoundland: Notes from an Unknown Shore

Special Places on Cape Cod and the Islands

Death of a Hornet and Other Cape Cod Essays

Outlands: Journey to the Outer Edges of Cape Cod

Cape Cod: Its Natural and Cultural History

The Primal Place

Common Ground: A Naturalist's Cape Cod

COAUTHORED AND EDITED BOOKS

*The Smithsonian Guides to Natural America:
Southern New England: Massachusetts, Connecticut, Rhode Island*
(coauthored with Jonathan Wallen)

A Place Apart: A Cape Cod Reader

The Cape Itself (with photographs by Ralph MacKenzie)

The Norton Book of Nature Writing (coedited with John Elder)

SUMMERS IN SQUID TICKLE

A Newfoundland Odyssey

ROBERT FINCH

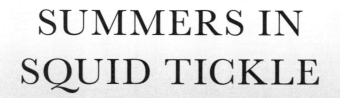

W. W. Norton & Company

Independent Publishers Since 1923

Copyright © 2025 by Robert Finch

All rights reserved
Printed in the United States of America
First Edition

For information about permission to reproduce selections from this book, write to
Permissions, W. W. Norton & Company, Inc., 500 Fifth Avenue, New York, NY 10110

For information about special discounts for bulk purchases, please contact
W. W. Norton Special Sales at specialsales@wwnorton.com or 800-233-4830

Manufacturing by Lakeside Book Company
Book design by Patrice Sheridan
Production manager: Ramona Wilkes

ISBN 978-1-324-05131-2

W. W. Norton & Company, Inc., 500 Fifth Avenue, New York, NY 10110
www.wwnorton.com

W. W. Norton & Company Ltd., 15 Carlisle Street, London W1D 3BS

10 9 8 7 6 5 4 3 2 1

FOR KATHY,
who was always there.

FOR THE GOOD PEOPLE OF SQUID TICKLE,
*whose generous friendship and willingness to share their lives
made this a rich and rewarding experience.*

Here is a life not mine. I am enriched.
—JOHN HAY

Home is where you know what things mean.
—GORDON PINSENT

SUMMERS IN SQUID TICKLE

PROLOGUE

Between Dreams

IT IS AN OLD DREAM, TO ESCAPE HISTORY; IT IS THE DREAM that led my race to this continent, which populated and settled it. We created our own history here, and in doing so, curiously bypassed and largely ignored this large, obdurate piece of geography in our rush westward. Newfoundland exists not only at the edge of the continent, but at the edge of our consciousness as well, on the periphery of our history and memory. It has always been a temporary place, a migratory and mutable land that was first visited by Europeans a thousand years ago, that was claimed as the first bit of the British Empire over four centuries ago, that languished in civil limbo for centuries while its fishermen fed the hungry hordes of Europe, enjoyed a brief and always troubled period of independence as a separate nation, fell into financial disgrace and British receivership between the two world wars, and finally jumped into the economic lifeboat of Canadian provincehood in 1949.

SUMMER 1995

AFTER FIVE DAYS OF DRIVING AND A HUNDRED-MILE FERRY crossing, I've arrived at my destination in the village of Burnside, a tiny outport tucked deep into the inner recesses of Bonavista Bay on the island's northeast coast, one of the oldest-settled and longest-fished areas in Newfoundland. The landscape is one of low ridges and archipelagos of rocky islands. These hills are the last outpost of the once-mighty and ancient Appalachian range that stretches from northeast Alabama to the tip of Newfoundland's Northern Peninsula, the ground-down essence of the continent. Here at the edge of the sea, they appear low and half submerged, like the backs of giant black whales frozen in the act of sounding.

Though no longer lofty, at close range these mountains are still impressive and assertive, rising in sheer cliffs hundreds of feet high above the beating surf, bare rock capped by a thin layer of soil and long grassy turf, spilling dozens of small cascades over and down narrow ravines into the sea.

I arrived in Burnside heartsick and heartsore, full of guilt and a pain I could find no release from. I had shattered one life and had not yet built another. I was far from home, and yet felt I had no home. I was in a liminal state of being—in Joseph Campbell's phrase, "between dreams"—though it felt more like a nightmare than a dream. In other words, I was totally unfit to open myself up to a new place and a new set of people.

Yet I knew I had to go, had to get away and try to heal myself in a new place, an unfamiliar world, where the old ghosts could not follow me, or if they did, might become lost in new surroundings. Newfoundland seemed like a good place to go.

Burnside is a small coastal village, or outport, with perhaps forty or fifty year-round residents, down from three hundred and fifty a generation ago. I'm staying in the western part of the town, which was traditionally known as Squid Tickle. Like many of the names in Newfoundland that strike the visitor as humorous or quaint, Squid Tickle is straightforwardly descriptive. In the center of the town there is a narrow water passage, or "tickle," separating the Burnside mainland from Squid Island. In the old days there used to be heavy runs of squid in the tickle in late summer, which the local residents gathered and dried.

The house I am staying in belongs to Mark and Fraser Carpenter, two friends who had left Cape Cod and immigrated to Newfoundland eight years ago. In a staggering burst of sustained energy, they built the house themselves in four months, from October to January, living in a camper in the back of a Mazda pickup truck. They worked from sunup to sundown, and when they woke up in the morning their sleeping bags were frozen solid with their sweat.

Over the next seven years they operated a tour boat business in the nearby Terra Nova National Park. Last year they sold the business and were now on a voyage into Arctic waters on the *Joshua*, a forty-foot sloop whose steel hull they had welded themselves in their driveway and hauled on log rollers down the dirt streets of the town to the harbour.

Their enterprise and capacity for work had given them almost legendary status in the town. They generously offered me the use of their house while they were gone.

The house is a modest one-and-a-half-story Cape set on pilings with a crawl space enclosed by boards, built of native spruce and pine lumber that Mark and Fraser cut from the nearby islands. Its Cape Cod design, uncommon here in Newfoundland, immediately gave me a sense of familiarity and some comfort in strange surroundings.

When I first arrived, I literally had to burrow into the house. Since winter gales here will pry open even locked doors, Mark and Fraser had nailed shut their front door and all the windows from inside when they left, exiting through a trapdoor in the pantry and then stacking the crawl space with several cords of "junks"—cut-up spruce and birch stove logs. It took me nearly two hours to toss out enough wood to make a tunnel through which I could crawl to reach the hatch. When I did and poked my head up like a groundhog into the dim kitchen, I found a sweet house, tightly built, with homemade curtains pinned shut across the windows, painted wainscoting, and maps of all kinds covering the walls.

The house fronts a protected cove, shielded from the open water by the western arm of Squid Island. Rock ledges, fringed with rockweed and knotted wrack, are visible at low tide. To the west across Fair and False Bay is a series of low wooded islands backed by a rugged, rocky ridge known as the Bloody Bay Hills. They are not tall enough to be true mountains (none of the hills around here are), but their ruggedness gives them a dimension beyond their actual size.

Before they left, my friends had shut off the power and drained the plumbing, and for the time being I decided to do without them. There was a stone-lined "dug well" just outside the front door that I drew water from in a pail and carried into a large washing tub in the bathroom. This water I used for washing and rinsing dishes. Occasionally I also used it to flush the inside toilet, though most of the time I used the outhouse—or "shithouse," as most people here unceremoniously refer to it—which has a wonderful view of the water and the northern lights.

For cooking and drinking I obtained water in plastic jugs from a hose at the community center building, formerly the local school, just up the road. Ron Crocker, who runs the Burnside Store, offered to let me put several five-gallon plastic jugs of water in his deep freezer, which I then rotated in my refrigerator every four to five days, thus giving me a functioning icebox with little fuss or mess and no dripping. For light I had a Coleman propane lamp, a kerosene lamp, and candles, which were quite adequate when I arrived, since it grew light by 5 a.m. and didn't really get dark until after 10 p.m. There was a large woodstove in the kitchen and tons of stove wood under the house, though I rarely had to use it that summer.

One evening a few days after I moved in, I was sitting at the table when I saw through the triptych windows three greater yellowlegs, moving in a group, like friends, picking among the shallows and the knotted wrack in front of the house. *Visitors from home*, I thought, *heading south*. All at once I had a panicked sense of the summer passing, of being assaulted with a thousand things to see and learn and do and having no time to do them in, not even the ability to remember what they were. I found myself going about the house making frantic, fragmentary lists, then forgetting where I put them. Although I had barely arrived here, I felt it was nearly time to go, and I had done nothing.

As usual, this inner state was partly a product of outer weather. Here, midway through the human summer, the wild weather and the clear, slanting northern light and the migrating shorebirds all conspired to give me the sense of late September. But it was only the middle of July, and I had nearly another two months to stay. It was time to set about fashioning the rituals and the connections that would take me through the days.

Now, after two weeks here, my days here go something like this: I rise about six thirty or seven, make a cup of tea, and take a walk through the village. Usually this early, I don't meet any neighbors, since the few active fishermen in the village were up and gone hours ago, and most of the rest are either summer visitors like me or retired.

I pass by the wharves, examine some of the old empty houses, explore some of the rocky points, and enjoy the stunning profusion of wildflowers along the roadsides and in the fields here. Blankets of irises grow everywhere in ditches and low places along the roadsides, and lilacs are still in full bloom in front of several houses. With one sweep of my pocketknife, I gather up a rich bouquet of brilliant lupine, sheep laurel (called "goo-witty" here), daisies, cow vetch, beach pea, wild roses, wild geranium, and bluebells.

After breakfast I usually sit at the kitchen table and write for several hours. When I'm working, I tape a sign on the front door that says "WRITING. PLEASE COME BACK AFTER 12. THANKS." I've had to do this since the common practice in Newfoundland is just to walk into a neighbor's house without knocking and "yarn" for a while. But when I am simply writing letters, or reading, or practicing my typing, I remove the sign and leave myself open to opportunistic interruption.

Visiting has always been the prime social activity in Newfoundland outports, and Burnside is no exception. Unlike most small towns in the States, there are no public gathering places here. People do not congregate and linger at the post office or the general store—they come and post their mail or pick up groceries and leave. Coffee shops are still rare in the outports, where tea remains the preferred hot beverage. At any rate, in a society where men traditionally set off in small boats at 3:30 or 4 a.m., "bilin' up" water for tea in a small stove as they rowed or motored to their fishing berths, such places had no function. When the men were away in summer on the Labrador, the women visited one another at their houses, and when the men were home, in winter, they worked together cutting firewood in the woods or mending nets in the "stores"—small sheds built on the individual wharves for "storing" fishing equipment.

Though I was a CFA, or "come from away," I soon found I had an entrée into the social life of the town simply by living in Mark and Fraser's house. They were two people known and admired by most of the residents. In addition, they had told most of their friends about me, and left me a detailed map of the town with names and notes about the residents of the houses. Thus, I had a mental picture of the community even before I had met its inhabitants.

I make a daily circuit walk along the hardened dirt roads of the town: up past my next-door neighbors, Bert and Laura Burden, left at the corner and down to the Oldford family's stage and wharf along the shore, then right on a muddy path around the shore to the small plank bridge across the tickle to Squid Island, then right again to Jim and Jessie Moss's house and the village post office.

The Burnside post office is a small one-room wooden building profusely planted with flowers all around it. The postmistress, Christine Moss, is Jim and Jessie's niece-in-law, and lives in the house next to the post office with her fisherman husband, Howard. One enters a tiny vestibule and pushes a buzzer, which brings Christine out of the house, brushing by you into the "office" proper, where she opens the counter window and, with a smile and a toss of her hair, says, in a cordial tone, "Now, my dear, what can I do for you?"

Back over the tickle, I turn left and follow the shore road up a slight hill past the Burnside Heritage Museum, which the older people in town call "the Hindian place." The Burnside Heritage Project is the major enterprise in town these days, an archaeological research project, funded by the federal and provincial governments, that began about six years ago and, with Laurie MacLean as its director, has made several major finds of prehistoric Innu and Inuit sites in the area. Most of these sites are reachable only by water, and Laurie hopes to develop the project as a tourist attraction, running regular tour boats to the sites, building a proper museum, running school programs, and so forth. Tourism in general seems to be the hope of the future in Newfoundland now that the fish are gone, and about the only chance of keeping the young people here.

Past the Heritage Project buildings the road curves around to the right and down to the ferry wharf. On most days the only vessel using it is an old wooden-hulled six-car ferry with a loud, clattering, smoky engine that serves St. Brendan's, the only remaining island community in Bonavista Bay, some eight miles north of Burnside. It usually runs four to six times a day throughout the year, until pack ice locks up the bay for the winter.

At the ferry wharf the road splits three ways: the left road takes me to the eastern part of the town, known as Hollett's Cove; straight ahead is the highway to Eastport, the nearest town of any size, paved only a few years before.

Turning right and heading back up the hill, I pass on the left "the new cemetery"; then, on the right, the tall, red-peaked roof and steeple of St. Alban's, the Anglican church and the most imposing structure in the town; on the left is the small community building (formerly the village school); and then the "Burnside Store—Thrifty Grocer," the only store in town, run by Ron Crocker and his parents, Lonz and Ida.

Ron is a beefy man in his early forties, with thick glasses and a short dark beard, and has the ample appearance and jovial manner of an Elizabethan innkeeper. He commonly greets me with some friendly insult ("Here's the Yankee boy!") and conveys the latest news of the town—who is sick, who is visiting, who has a boat for sale, etc.—with my groceries.

After leaving Ron's I continue down the hill, forking left at the corner by Cleaves Oldford's house, a large yellow structure with an old-fashioned tepee of long, thin spruce trunks stacked in his yard; then past a common wood-cutting yard on the left with a ring of larch (called "sycamore" here) trees and Ski-Doo trails leading out between them into the marshes, or "mishes," and the wooded country beyond; then left at the fork onto my road, past Bert and Laura's again on the right, to the small "old cemetery" on the rise just across the road from my house.

The last house on the road is also the largest in Squid Tickle: an imposing twin-turreted, green-roofed dwelling that sits on top of a rocky point overlooking the bay and dominating that end of the town. Known as the Hiscock House, it looks as if it should belong to the richest man in town, the local fish merchant perhaps, though in fact it has been unoccupied for nearly twenty years.

The nights are cool, and I sleep in the snug ship's bed in the corner of the bedroom under a down comforter, my head level with a window that looks out on the water. In the morning I start a small fire in the stove to take the chill out of the kitchen, make tea and cook eggs or polenta on the propane camp stove. The world looks clean and new and fresh outside with tall purple irises blanketing the swales and the fringes of the shore and azaleas like banks of rose flames along the roadsides and the fresh new lime tongues of cottonwood leaves fluttering like a cool green stream at the edges of the clearings.

It is a lovely morning now, the wind out of the northeast, the temperature near 70 degrees Fahrenheit. Across the bay clouds sail like fleecy flotillas over the gnarled racks of the Bloody Bay Hills, and the dark ledges in the water around the house are fringed in *Ascophyllum* the color of spun gold.

A fiberglass sloop sails silently by my windows, a rare sight in these waters where few sailboats are seen. Through my binoculars I can see an elderly man at the helm, with a shock of white hair and a white mustache, wearing wire-rimmed glasses and a grey-checked porkpie hat, and an old Irish setter standing in the bow. I know nothing about him, though his dapper appearance marks him as "from away," but I feel an affection for him and his dog, for his apparent self-containment in spite of a sense of loss about him, and I envy the way these two old animals have chosen to spend some of their last years together, contentedly and peacefully sailing over these empty waters.

The first Sunday after I arrived, I went to the 9 a.m. church service at St. Alban's Anglican Church. The whole of Bonavista Bay is predominantly Anglican, with a lesser number of United Church—"UC"—or Methodists, and a smattering of Catholic, Salvation Army, and Pentecostal congregations. For a community of such modest size as Burnside, St. Alban's is imposing. It sits on a prominent rise in the center of town, a large wooden structure with a red roof, white clapboards, and a tall steeple. Inside, the ceiling is impressively vaulted and beamed to resemble the inverted hull of a ship, sheltering pillared rows of wooden pews that were obviously meant to hold several hundred worshippers.

Today, however, there are only a couple of dozen people in the congregation, mostly elderly couples. In the small vestibule I notice a plaque commemorating the church's Young People's Association, which was formed in 1960 and disbanded in 1982. The choir itself seems to have dissolved as well, as the three pews in the chancel sit empty during the service.

The rector, Marilyn Morse, is a tall woman with short brown hair and a loud, booming outport voice that eschews the microphone on the pulpit and demonstrates admirably the acoustic qualities of the church. The lay reader is a large and impressive-looking man with a thick bull neck, dressed in a white surplice, who reads the text from Scripture with a thick local accent in a deep, growly voice that sounds accustomed to authority, ending with "De word a de Lord."

The sermon is a straightforward lesson on the parable of the Good Samaritan. The organist, a thin, angular woman with long dark hair and an Appalachian face, wearing a flowered print dress straight out of the 1940s, squeezes three unfamiliar hymns out of an old-fashioned pump organ, accompanied by the high, sliding, dragging, wheezing voices of the congregation.

The readings and the liturgy are all from the revised *Book of Alternative Services*, and the responses are spoken in a muddled, hesitant drone; but when we get to the Lord's Prayer, everyone ignores the written text and recites the original King James Version in unison with sudden energy and conviction. My guess is that the change from the original language of the *Book of Common Prayer* was a disorientating experience for this aging congregation, most of whom no doubt absorbed the responses unconsciously as children.

As we go out the rector greets me with a smile and shakes my hand vigorously. "Long time, no see," she says. I am nonplussed and blurt out, "Yes!" Later in the day, at the Burnside Store, I mention this to Ron Crocker.

"That's because you looks like Harold Hiscock. He's got that blue bungalow down by the tickle—comes up here from St. John's in the summer sometimes. Yis, b'y, he's got a beard just like you. You've got more hair on top now—but not much. He's got more of a bald spot in back, wears round glasses like this"—he holds up his fingers in circles around his eyes—"but put yourselves together and, yis b'y, I'd say you was brudders."

The shoreline, or landwash, around my house is mostly shale ledges, steeply tilted at a twenty-to-thirty-degree angle. In places great blocks of it have fallen out of the cliff face, like a drawer sliding out of an upended bureau. Its dark, flaking surface is covered in creeping juniper, crowberry, partridgeberry, and little tufts of grass in the narrow clefts. Here, a large chunk about five feet long has obviously slipped from the ledge it now lies against. I see the angular, concave mold it left in the rock and wonder, When did this happen? Five years ago? Fifty? Five hundred? Five thousand? I have as yet no sense of geologic pace on these strange shores. The geologic time scale I learned on the swiftly shifting sands of Cape Cod does not apply at all here.

Last evening, I was invited to my first meal here by Jim and Jessie Moss, a lively couple in their seventies who had been close friends of the Carpenters. Their house, a small, neat, two-story traditional flat-pitched-roof structure, sits on the shore just across the tickle on Squid Island. Jim's older brother, John, who is eighty-two, was there as well. He lives in a similar and even smaller house next door behind that of his son, Howard, and Christine, the postmistress. I could only catch snatches of the conversation, which seems to be carried on in an accent thicker than most I have encountered here, a kind of continuous low growl with few discernible consonants.

Both Jim and John were born on Flat Island, a once-populous archipelago fishing community some six or seven miles northeast of Burnside. At one time, Jim said, there were two churches on Flat Island, one Anglican, one UC. The former had seven hundred seats in it—"Y's b'y!"

Both Jim and John went trap fishing on the Labrador coast in their youth, and it was off Labrador that Jim met Jessie, who was a cook on another fishing vessel run by her family. They came from Fair Island, another island settlement north of Flat Island.

Like hundreds of other small Newfoundland outports, Flat Island was gradually abandoned in the 1950s during the great resettlement program instituted by Joey Smallwood, Newfoundland's first premier after Confederation with Canada in 1949. Jim's and John's families were among only twenty families that remained during the last winter, in 1958. The following spring the Mosses floated their houses on oil drums from Flat Island to Burnside and hauled up onshore where they sit now. All but a few of the houses in Burnside, it turns out, were either brought here or built after 1912, the year that a massive fire destroyed most of the town.

The day ended calmly out over the water, and after supper I went over to the old cemetery that sits up on a little rise just across the road from the Carpenters' house. As I walked through the graveyard, a veritable garden of wildflowers, largely untended, my spirits suddenly rose at the sight of all these flowers growing from the bodies of the long-dead. A new crescent moon hung in the sky over the Hiscock House on the hill. It, too, gave my soul a little lift of hope—that things come round.

As I turned to go back to the house, a grey sedan pulled up. In it was a large man, bald with a white fringe, his dark skin tight over his scalp, face, and bull-like neck. He appeared to be in his mid-seventies. I recognized him as the lay reader in the church last Sunday. He is the strongest-looking man I have seen here.

Leaning over to the passenger side, he said, "You've got lots of neighbors there." I gave the expected reply, "Yeah, but they're all quiet." He laughed, and then introduced himself as Fred Oldford, who lives in the brick house behind Ron's store with his wife Betty and daughter Shirley. He asked me what I was doing for water. I told him I hauled it from the stone well in the yard or got it in plastic jugs from the community faucet at the old school building.

"Colored, isn't it," he said, "full of arn," and offered to let me use his well, of which he is quite proud. "It's artesian—a hundred and twenty feet deep, and clear as a bell."

The following morning, when I was typing upstairs, Fred walked in, unannounced, ignoring my sign on the door, hauling himself up the narrow ship's stairway with his muscular arms and sitting in the stairwell, huffing and puffing. He told me he's had a year of sickness, flu last winter, and angina that put him in hospital for eight days that spring, followed by pneumonia, and now more flu. I repeated the old quip about growing old not being for the timid.

"Well," he snorted, "it might not be for the timid, but I'll tell you, b'y, it's not for those that could work and now can't."

He had come because he thought I might want a boat to use while I was here and offered to let me use a small fiberglass dinghy he keeps down at his family's wharf.

"But I don't want to disturb you if you're writing. You've got to write when you're inspired—you can't do it just whenever you want. I write myself, some—mostly poetry—it comes to me, usually when I'm in the garden. I like the old-fashioned kind, the kind that rhymes, not the stuff they writes nowadays."

The next morning Fred took me to his boat down at the Oldford wharf, which is used by Fred, his older brother Cleaves, and younger brother Con. At the head of the wharf is the inevitable "store," a small one-and-a-half-story wooden building—not to be confused with the local general store—traditionally used for the storage of fishing gear and winter mending of fishing nets. While most houses here are replaced as casually as cars, stores and other outbuildings associated with fishing seem to be preserved with an almost religious devotion and are frequently the oldest structures in town. Fred's, like nearly every other store in Newfoundland, is painted ochre red.

Most of the boats in town are still wooden, and most of those were built by their owners. I helped Fred push his wooden trap boat down the slip and then slid the rowboat around it. "They's all I have left, after selling me trawler," he said with some disgust. A man's stature here seems reflected in the number of boats he keeps, and as he relinquishes them, one by one, keeping ever-smaller ones, he seems to contract in his own eyes.

Fred sent me off ceremoniously by going up onto his stage and tossing me a yellow life jacket: "Here, that's for legalities. Just tie her up at the wharf when you get back and I'll take care of her."

I was out for about an hour, pulling westerly against a fresh breeze, snaking among the upended ledges of shale that looked like burnt timbers, the hulls of sunken ships, or the charred pages of an ancient, giant book, fringed with rockweed and fucus at low tide. The waters are beautiful, cold, and very, very empty, and there are no children here. These are the two things that impress me most strongly. The silence of the early morning is peaceful but appalling. When I walk out on one of the wharves, the waters are empty not only of fish, but of the darting minnows, scuttling crabs, crawling periwinkles, and stationary clams and mussels that one sees almost anywhere in the shallows on Cape Cod. Even the terns and seabirds are scarce by comparison. Most of the wooden stages and stores are empty, too. It is as though both human and ocean life have absconded from this place.

The northeast coast of Newfoundland is one of the oldest and most densely settled parts of the island and traditionally one of the richest fishing grounds. But overfishing over the past several decades led to a collapse of the cod stocks, which in turn resulted in a moratorium on commercial cod fishing in 1992. Thus, there is no commercial fishing now, and there may never again be, in which case most of the hundreds of small outports that still dot this rocky coast may dry up and blow away in not too many years. This is the thought that seems to be on everyone's mind, though it is not spoken of much, as there seems to be nothing to do but wait and see if the fish come back.

The children are another story. Burnside, like many of the outports, is already a largely geriatric community. There is only one family with school-age children left in Squid Tickle, and they are planning to move to Eastport, where the regional school is. Most of the young people have moved away—to Gander, St. John's, or the Canadian mainland—in search of work. Linda Oldford, Fred's younger brother's daughter, and her husband Cyril have settled permanently in Gander, though they have kept Cyril's family house here. Essie, the woman who helps at Ron's store, has a son on the mainland she hasn't seen in eight years. And Howard and Christine Moss's two boys, Michael and Christopher, recently out of high school, may have to go to Alberta soon (where there is now a large Newfoundland labor contingent in the oil sands fields in Fort McMurray) if they can't find work here.

This has always been a pattern in Newfoundland, which has suffered from chronic poverty through most of its history. In times of no fish or poor markets, the men would "go away," to Canada or the States, to find work, and send money home, much the way immigrants from Central America do today. Sometimes they would be gone for years. When times improved, they would return to their families and to fishing. And always they would return when they could no longer work, to be cared for by their families and to die in Newfoundland.

But now, even if the fishing does come back, few believe the life of these outports will survive as it has for centuries. For one thing, a revived fishery is likely to be much more streamlined, high-tech, and government-regulated, and, most essentially, no longer family-based. In actuality, only a small fraction of Newfoundland's population—some twenty thousand or so—were dependent upon fishing or fish-based employment at the time of the groundfish moratorium, though these often constituted a majority of the people in the smaller outports. It is more that the *identity* of Newfoundlanders has, since its beginnings, been that of fishermen, and even when the majority of the population no longer made their living directly from the sea, it was that ongoing connection with it, the seasonal rituals of going out for herring, lobster, caplin, mackerel, flounder, haddock, halibut—but always, and most importantly, cod—that kept the fibers of community life and the connections between generations together.

Even though only two or three men in Burnside still actively fish, one can see how the psychology of fish continues to pervade the community, particularly the older men.

I often see Fred, and some of the other older men in the town, cruising the roads in the evening in their cars, going slowly, about trolling speed, for no apparent purpose. At first I thought it was just the restlessness of old men who no longer get around well on their legs, perhaps out looking for someone to tell their stories to. But lately I have been thinking it may be archetypal, vestigial behavior, from the days when they walked the paths or climbed the rises in the town looking for fish, spotting shoals of cod or mackerel swimming offshore.

It is quiet, so quiet today on this road, with still no one in any of the houses beyond me, and not a peep from Bert's house next door. After lunch a pickup pulls up in the cemetery drive. I walk over and find a short, rotund man in a feed cap and blue plaid shirt mowing some of the plots down in back. He introduces himself as "Rage," or Reg, Lane, a sixty-nine-year-old semiretired lobsterman and self-described "lifelong bachelor," who lives in a house set back from the road behind the church, an area of town that, he tells me, was once "all Lanes." He has no family here anymore and is one of only two people left in the town who still tend these old plots.

"The new cemetery—y's b'y, the church elders see to that. I takes care of the Lanes here, the Chaytors, and some Ralphs." He points to a nearby overgrown plot with one recently dug grave in it: "He used to take care of that one, but he fell by last year." So, one by one, it seems, these grave sites lose, or rather, acquire, their caretakers, until finally there will only be benevolent neglect.

I ask him to drop by when he finishes for a cup of tea, which he does, and I give him one of the tea biscuits Laura Burden gave me earlier in the day. His manner is shy and polite, as those of people who have lived alone a long time in silence often are. He talks through his nose more than his teeth, but I am beginning to decode these thick accents a little. When he speaks of "Ants Arbour," I realize this is not some insect tree but "Hant's Harbour," the name of the eastern section of town beyond the ferry dock.

He lived with his mother until she died ten or twelve years ago. A woman in town said to me, "I'm not sure any woman would have him now. His house is so spotless and meticulous, there wouldn't be anything for her to do!" Another man told me that Reg was "born deaf, has been that way ever since he were a child—and his sister, also deaf and dumb, married another deaf and dumb, and sure enough their son talks like a politician."

Reg, like most of the local men of his generation, went down to the Labrador in his youth, first under sail, then later with motors. They would go down in early July, he says, or sometimes in June if the ice had gone out early.

"Going to the Labrador" was a constant feature of outport life on the northeast coast for nearly a century. Even the younger men in Burnside used to go to the Labrador, until the fishing there gave out.

Howard Moss, a man now in his mid-forties, went nearly every year until 1991, when they got no fish at all.

"The first time I went out we worked thirty-one hours straight catching cod and turbot without so much as going off the deck down for a cup of tea. I thought to myself, 'If this is what it's going to be, I don't think I can stick it,' but after we was done the captain told me that was the first time they'd done that—and then we had to unload and clean the gear. After that we cooked up a big pot of fish and brewis* and turned in—and I'll tell you, nobody got up that day."

The stars are brilliant overhead, the water lapping softly beyond the house, answered by a kind of tinny, vibrating whistling in the wires

---

* pronounced "brews"

overhead, both voices moved by the wind. Against the dark bay phosphorescent lines of blue lap gently against the rocks, as if they had stolen some light from beyond the hills and smuggled it here, rocking in the water. The sky is still unpolluted, and the stars a great presence.

It is August, and summer visitors and seasonal residents are beginning to show up in Squid Tickle. Last night the three or four houses to the west of mine were lit up like jack-o'-lanterns with recently arrived families. At last, there are children in the village. Yesterday morning there were five, between six and ten years old, playing in Cleaves Oldford's yard at the corner. And in the evening, there was another batch playing on the wooden bridge over the tickle, riding bikes across the clattering planks, jigging for cunners, and just hanging out. The old folks, seeing them, must remember what it was like here a generation ago.

I have been spending more time with Fred and his family lately, and he appears to have consciously taken me under his wing. He is definitely a prominent figure in the community and a man of many parts, having been in his time a fisherman, boatbuilder, lumberjack, sawmiller, store owner, and taxi driver. Even now, in "involuntary retirement," he holds many positions in the town: rector's warden, Heritage Project board chairman, member of the garbage collection committee and Eastport Peninsula Development Association. He and his wife Betty used to run the Burnside Store before they sold it to Ron Crocker. Betty came here from Fogo Island as a teacher in the late thirties or early forties. They have two daughters: Donna, a nurse in New Brunswick, and Shirley, a very pleasant woman of about forty, who grew up here, obtained a doctorate in geology at Memorial University of Newfoundland in St. John's, and worked as a geophysicist for an Alberta petroleum company for nearly twenty years before retiring on a disability and returning to Burnside a few years ago to help care for her aging parents.

Yesterday morning Fred dropped by and asked if I'd like to go out on the bay with him, Shirley, and her dog, Jock, a small long-haired terrier also of amiable disposition. We set off in Fred's motor launch and spent several hours cruising among the reaches, coves, and islands of Fair and False Bay. We cruised down forested canyons on broad blue highways of water. I was surprised to see dozens of cabins tucked away on the islands and in the coves we passed, none of them visible from town. Most, said Shirley, were built by the children of locals, who have moved away and visit in the summer.

"There's three generations now come back to spend summer with their grandparents. This was a community that cared about the education of their young people, and the profit of it was, we got a good one and moved away."

We passed Magic Arm and Mishes Cove, the Pretty Islands and Long Reach Island, and finally reached the long, high, rocky peninsula of the Bloody Bay Hills that points its stony digit out into the wide pathway of Bloody Reach. We stopped briefly at Bloody Bay Cove, the entrance to the Quarry Site, one of the two major archaeological sites in the bay. Fred says the Quarry Site was first discovered in the 1940s by his father and grandfather, though I have heard others say it was known to locals for over a century. Initial digs were made in the late 1950s, '60s, and '70s. In high school Shirley was hired to work on some of the digs.

"I figured if they were going to pay me for what I like to do anyway, why not?"

From the cove a steep trail leads up to the top of the hill and the quarry, but neither Fred nor Shirley, who tires easily, seemed up to making the climb. Still, it was fascinating to hear him interpret the area from his own perspective and history. He knows every rock and tree, and what has happened on or near each one of them. He would point out a rock and say, casually, "That's where five men drowned," or indicate the place where he shot his first moose, or "a sweet spot" to put in his boat during a storm, or the tickle he once took a forty-foot schooner through.

Fred enjoys making biblical references, and I was not surprised to learn that he once considered entering the ministry. He gazed up at the Bloody Bay Hills and quoted from a psalm, "I will lift up my eyes unto these hills, from whence my help is come." Once, spotting a hare on one of the small islands, I asked him if there had always been rabbits on these islands. "Ever since Noah let go of the dove, my son."

Shirley told stories of growing up here in the 1950s and '60s. "In the summer, all of us kids in the village would be out in the woods with Dad and Uncle Cleaves and the other men hauling timber out with a tractor. They never got cross with us, I don't know why. And when the last load was hauled out, all of us kids would pile on the wagon so that the men, who had worked all summer, had to walk out of the woods behind us. Geez, and them having worked all day long. I didn't think anything of it then, but now I wonder, why didn't they say, 'You kids got in here on your own and you can get out the same way!' But they didn't, and we rode home in style like we were royalty."

Shirley not only admires but envies her father's deep knowledge of this place. "I wish I could have a memory transplant from Dad, he knows so much. He's always noting things, storing them away for future reference. He'll spot a white pine, which are rare here now, and note it for a table he'll build next winter; or one day he'll say, of a spot, 'Saw a batch of mussels there about two years ago; they ought to be about ready now.'"

That evening I encountered one of the recently arrived visitors on the road, a bearded man by the name of Clar Machem, standing beside his car, which had died in the road. He introduced himself as the husband of Joan Oldford, Cleaves' daughter. Both are professors at Memorial University of Newfoundland in St. John's, but Joan grew up in Burnside. He was waiting for his father-in-law to show up to help him start his car. They are here for a few weeks of "sanctuary" and go out to a cabin they have built at Bloomer's Cove.

Clar told me he will be on sabbatical next year and hopes to go to Amsterdam. He has a sister in Paris, whom he plans to visit. He really *loves* Paris. "Europe, you know, has a lot of *leenage* we don't have here. The US and Canada, you know, we don't have that much history. Oh, we have a few things. But Europe, you know, you can stand in Notre-Dame and say, 'Napoleon stood here,' or 'Joan of Arc was burned here'—now that's leenage!"

But I thought of Fred earlier that afternoon, cruising these waters and saying, "Five men drowned together here," or "That's where my father first found these Beothuk points in '48," or "That's a sweet spot to put in in a sea breeze, my son." I felt I had been taken on a tour of Venice by one of the old Renaissance doges.

The following day I went to see Henry Oldford, one of the church deacons who assist the minister at St. Alban's, including collecting the offering, ringing the bell, and posting the hymn numbers. I went to ask if I might practice on the pump organ when the church wasn't in use—which is ordinarily all but two hours a week. Henry, who lives in a house down near the ferry, replied, "Of course, my son," and then added, without skipping a beat, "And you can play for us Sundays when we needs you." And that was how I became a part-time organist at St. Alban's during my first summer there.

St. Alban's is not a particularly old church; none of the standing ones in Newfoundland are. The cornerstone for St. Alban's was laid in 1934, and the plans for it, according to Fred, were "scaled down" by his father, Esau Oldford, who also supervised the building of the church, though he could neither read nor write. Though the exterior is now sheathed in asphalt shingles and vinyl siding, it is quite a handsome church, of graceful proportions outside and far more elaborately appointed inside than one might have expected from one built during the middle of the Depression, which hit Newfoundland particularly hard as both the fish stocks and the stock market crashed. When I asked Fred where the money to build it came from, he answered indirectly:

"Oh, I read the other day of how a church was built for threepence," which reminded me of Thoreau's comment that, "if necessary, I can live on board nails." I took it to mean that money wasn't important in such a venture. Most of the lumber and labor were provided by the local men, all of whom were skilled carpenters, "except," Fred admitted, "for the steeple. We had some men from Grand Falls in to do that in the summer at twenty-five cents an hour."

Later that day I decided to get the power turned on and arranged for an electrician from Eastport to come over next week.

I met with Henry Oldford at the church today to go over the order for my first service as organist tomorrow. His wife, Ena, had scribbled down some hymns for me to choose from. Henry gave me three small slips of paper to write down my selections for the rector, "the people's warden," and myself.

The pump organ is actually a harmonium, made in Harbour Grace in 1925, and was purchased about thirty years ago. Among his other duties Henry is the bell ringer, though his doctor says he shouldn't go up and down stairs. Still, he took me up two flights of steep wooden stairs into the belfry to see the church bell. On the first landing was a simple wooden chair where the bell ringer sat, placed beneath a hemp rope that hung down through a hole in the floor above.

The belfry itself was festooned with cobwebs and its curling, spotted, yellow, sticky strips of flypaper were dotted with the ancient corpses of flies. The belfry has slatted shutters that open inward on all four sides, giving commanding views of the village and the surrounding countryside. The bell, impressive and handsome, is about thirty inches high and was made in 1958 in London by Mears, "the same company," Henry proudly informed me, "that made your Liberty Bell."

"She's a good one, though he sounds a little sharp, eh?" says Henry, tapping the bell with his fingers and using the common Newfoundland mixture of genders referring to inanimate objects. "We could fix that, though, by putting a little strip of sole leather there where the clapper strikes."

I noticed a number of mark-and-slash figures on the floorboard beneath the bell, in a configuration I had never seen before. Henry chuckled and explained that they were used for funerals, when the bell tolls the deceased's age in years. The ringing for funerals is done up in the belfry, he said, rather than in the bell-rope room down below, so that the ringer can control the number of peals accurately. "Must be why most of us ringers wear two hearing aids."

The marks, he said, were an old form of tallying fish, which were counted in quintals, pronounced "cantals"—wooden barrels containing 112 pounds of fish—as they were loaded or unloaded on the dock. This made a quick and easy method of recording the quintals.

"Some of them lived a pretty good time, eh?" said Henry. "See, here's one—five, ten, twenty, thirty, forty, fifty, sixty, seventy, eighty, eighty-five, eighty-seven—eighty-seven years. Yes, a long time." The pealing for that one alone, I thought, must have taken a few decibels off someone's eardrums. Even in death, it seems, cod informed the lives of these people, tolling their years in fish-language.

On Sunday morning I made my debut at the 9:45 a.m. service. I counted forty-one people at the service, a noticeable increase from my first time there, which I attributed in part to curiosity about this organist from away. Apparently it went fairly well, since I received compliments all around afterwards. Con Oldford, the youngest of the four Oldford brothers, asked me if I was going to stay around. "I'll get ya some wood if ya stay—if yer handy with a chain saw." A woman who seemed to be part of the Oldford contingent came up to me and said, "I could have sat there all day, my son." After the service I went back with the Oldfords and the rector, Marilyn Morse, to Fred's house for coffee and blackberry pudding Shirley had made.

Fred's wife, Betty, is originally from Fogo Island, a settlement off the northeast coast with a dozen or so small villages.

"Did Fred tell you how it took him six days to get to Fogo for our wedding by coastal steamer?" asked Betty. "There were many stops, loading and unloading of wood and supplies, bad weather. The steamer in those days stopped at Flat Island. It got to Fogo the night before the wedding. We spent our wedding night in Father's house and left for Burnside the next day."

While Fred and Betty talked, Shirley sat against a large wall-size mural of a New England woods in autumn, embroidering a hooked rug depicting an old-fashioned schooner. Though she has a doctorate in geology and is about forty, she has a kind of little girl manner around her parents. When she says, "It's so quiet here in winter," her mother gently contradicts her: "No it's not, dear, not when all of them Ski-Doos get going."

Afterwards, Fred insisted on driving me back to the house, though it was only a three-minute walk. On the way he pointed out the handsome white two-and-a-half-story "long-roofed" (steep-peaked) house at the corner. "There's the house I was born in," which now belonged to Con, since when his parents died, Fred and Cleaves had already built their own houses and Con was still at home. No primogeniture here, it seems.

Later that week I had the Mosses—Jim, Jessie, and John—to supper. They seemed quite at ease in this house, where they had spent so much time with Mark and Fraser. Jim took his "regular" seat against the window. They were obviously pleased to be in the house again, yet sad they weren't with Mark and Fraser. They said this without embarrassment or apology to me, for they obviously intended no comparison. I served them chicken paprikash with spaetzles and Caesar salad. When I said that the chicken was my grandmother's recipe, Jim asked, with genuine concern, "Is she gone, b'y?"

Jessie mentioned again that she was from Fair Island and was a cook aboard one of the Labrador boats for some two years in her late teens. She said it was one of the few ways a woman in her day got to travel. It was common to have women as cooks on family boats, and many, like Jessie, met their husbands on a boat down on the Labrador—an effective strategy, perhaps, if an unintentional one, for preventing inbreeding in the isolated outports.

I had heard that John was quite renowned as a singer in his youth on Flat Island, and after dinner he regaled us with some of the old Newfoundland songs he had learned as a young man on the Labrador schooners and the sealing ships. Most were narrative ballads, nautical in theme, many about shipwrecks. It is an old Newfoundland tradition to commemorate every wreck with its own song, one that continues today and has been extended to plane wrecks as well. One ballad he sang, called "A Crowd of Bo' Sharemen," I eventually deciphered as a narrative about a wage dispute among a fishing crew who were to receive shares, or portions, of the boat's profits. As is common in Celtic folk singing, the last lines of each of these songs were *said*, not sung, with a final emphasis.

"Now," said John, "I'll sing ye the Hindian song," and launched into a long ballad about a young man who left his love to join the "Western Rangers" and "fight in a foreign land." I interrupted him at one point to ask him if this was a Newfoundland song, and he said, "No, b'y, I don't know whar it's from." But when he got to a stanza that mentioned "the Plains of Abraham," I realized that it was a ballad about the French and Indian Wars in Québec in the 1760s, possibly brought over intact from England a couple of hundred years ago and transmitted orally among the outports. When I told John and the others what the song seemed to be about, they expressed little interest, for they knew nothing about it.

This was not the first nor the last example of elements in Newfoundland culture I encountered that were borrowed or appropriated from other sources. Many early Newfoundland settlers came from the West Country of England, where Guy Fawkes Night was called "Bonfire Night." The fact that the tradition of lighting fires here on November 5 without any knowledge of its origin reminded me of the "hidden" or Marrano Jews of New Mexico and other places in the Southwest where Jewish traditions were carried for generations though the celebrants no longer knew their origin or significance.

When they got up to leave, Jim grabbed my shoulder in his bony hand and said, "You done good for us, Bob, you done good. Now I want yous to know, you stop by anytime—anytime, hear? You'd be as welcome as the flowers of May"—and pleased with the phrase, he repeated it, "Yes, b'y, as welcome as the flowers of May—you understand me?"

There are, of course, few flowers in May in Newfoundland—not nearly as many as there are in England.

It was another perfectly calm and clear sunset, with an empty, drained sky and the water like shook silk. Jim said, gesturing to the sun in the west, "She's movin' every day now, b'y, she's movin'."

Repeatedly I have been struck by the lack of irony in Newfoundlanders, not in their stories, where there is often plenty of it, but in their attitudes toward themselves and their own lives.

Newfoundland is a place where people still put pink plastic flamingos on their lawns because they think they look nice.

There is a rich lore of "Newfie" jokes across the island that, unlike those of most other ethnic groups, are told against themselves.

In the next town over from Burnside there is a store called the "Traytown Animal Display and Take-Out Shop."

There is a girls' softball team in St. John's called the Forest Gumps.

Walking down to the tickle bridge the other day, I met David Rockwood—Fred's grandson—and three of his buddies there, casting lines and riding bikes over the unnailed boards that clattered like a marimba. This morning David and one of his friends were out in the bay running his grandfather's outboard upwind to Gus Oldford's wharf, then sailing downwind using an old, stained cotton gaff-rigged sail on a hand-carved mast. Over and over they motored up and sailed downwind, pointing, standing in the bow, hunkering down in the stern, intent on themselves, the boat, the wind.

This bids to be my last night in the house without electricity. Frank Squires came over from Eastport this afternoon and drove two more steel ground rods at an acute angle between the leaves of shale. "You'll have power tomorrow for sure, b'y." Part of me regrets having to turn it on, but it has become too dark now in the evenings to read and to be alone without light.

Electricity didn't reach Burnside until 1962. Howard Moss and Ron Crocker, men in their forties now, remember hauling water into the house and reading by kerosene lamp. Fred told me he lived here for thirty years without ever seeing a light on at night, even after electricity was brought in. When they finally put a streetlight by the church, he found he couldn't sleep at night.

I, too, shall miss the quiet and the soft light of this house once the power comes, but the momentum has shifted. *She's movin' every day now, b'y, she's movin'* . . .

Bert Burden, my next-door neighbor, is eighty-six today. I encountered him returning from my circuit walk this morning out in his front yard in his usual garb—red cap, plaid flannel shirt, dark blue cotton pants, and rubber boots—scything the grass around the front of his woodshed.

"Got to do it, or the snow'll lodge on it." If he doesn't, he says, snow catches in the grass and piles up against the shed door as high up as his shoulders.

He invited me to "come up in the evening for a grog." I arrived about 8 p.m., bringing with me a book of Mark's family pictures I had found in the house. I thought they might like to see them since, like Jim and Jessie Moss, Bert and Laura were quite close to my absent hosts. We had nips of whiskey with Canada Dry and pieces of gumdrop cake Laura put out.

His full name is Kenneth Bertram Burden. He has one sister, Adelaide, who is ninety-seven and lives in a nursing home in Saugus, Massachusetts. Bert, like most men on the northeast coast, sailed to the Labrador many times, as well as down to St. John's for supplies, but he has never been on the west coast, or even to Sandy Cove, five miles by road, on the other side of the Eastport Peninsula. He and Laura have no children, and Bert is the last Burden in Burnside.

During the Depression the fishing got "very bad" and Bert went away for work. Like others I have spoken to who "went away" at some point, Bert offers no details of this time. It seems to have been to them like a period in limbo, unreal. When he got laid off there, he came back and put out trawls, or longlines, catching just enough fish to live on.

I asked Bert about the name, Squid Tickle. Was the place really called that?

"Y's b'y, but you see, there's two tickles. Under the bridge there, that's where we gots squid. Then, further down east, by 'Ant's 'Arbour, that's Island Tickle." When I mentioned that some people had told me that it was never actually known as Squid Tickle, he flared up. "Dose des don't know what dey're talking about!"

All the time he talked, Laura, frail and thin, sat silently in her apron holding Mark's book on her lap. She could barely lift it, but looked through it carefully for a long time, turning the pages reverently, pausing over pictures of Mark as a boy, and then fingering its closed cover lovingly. Later Shirley told me that Laura never took much part in the life of the community, being naturally shy and lacking children.

"I wish she had," Shirley said, "because then Bert might have been less reclusive. Take the fire protection fee, which is twenty-four dollars a year. Most people pay it in one check at the beginning of the year, or perhaps half every six months. But Bert religiously comes up to our house every month to pay his two dollars, which annoys my mom because she has to make out a separate receipt each time; but I think he does it in order to visit and catch up on everyone's news. When Mom first came to Burnside from Fogo, she boarded at Bert and Laura's and always said it was the best boarding place for food she was ever at."

I went to the 11 a.m. service at St. Alban's this morning.

After the service I was invited to dinner at Fred's house. Newfoundlanders do not stand on ceremony, and although it took me no more than five minutes to go home, shed my tie and jacket, and return, they were already at table saying grace.

"Come in, b'y, come in," said Fred in his hearty voice, "and help yourself to some fresh vegetables." There were platefuls of cabbage, peas, carrots, squash, new potatoes, and parsnip—most of them picked from Fred's garden, all boiled to a near puree and served with generous portions of fatty salt beef and ham bone with garlic bread, water to drink, and gumdrop cake and tea for dessert.

"Did you ever hear 'the Newfoundlander's Depression Grace'?"

Fred asked. He then recited the following, which struck me as a sort of slippery backhanded complaint worthy of an ingratiating Jewish kvetch:

> *Dear Lord, we're t'ankful fer what we have,*
> *If dere were more we wouldn't be glad;*
> *But since dere is no more to be had,*
> *Dear Lord, we're t'ankful fer what we have.*

Fred, who once thought of becoming a minister, had given several lay sermons in the past. He illustrated his philosophy of preaching with the following example:

"The Bible says Elijah walked forty days in the wilderness. Now, if he only walked three miles a day, then he walked from here to St. John's. Now that made 'em sit up and take notice!"

He believed that to write a good sermon, you have to "read Scripture as if you were seeing it for the first time—find something in it no one has noticed before, and use it to hook 'em in."

"Now I've got a riddle for you," said Fred. "Goes like this: 'I washed in a water never rained nor flowed, dried my face in a napkin never spun nor sewed.'"

It gave me satisfaction to answer him—"dew" and "grass"—but I was even more pleased to discover that the very old English form of the riddle has survived here. Riddles themselves, in fact, are an ancient form of verbal competition, and Fred's manner reminded me of many of the verbal pugilists I knew growing up in West Virginia.

Shirley, as usual, sat in Fred's shadow, confirming, embroidering, and occasionally gently correcting a detail in one of his stories as she hooked a likeness of her father's last sailboat, *Daydream*, onto a small rug. After dinner Fred, who suffered a mild stroke a few years ago and has heart problems, got up and without ceremony lay down on the chesterfield he had built by the picture window, turning his face to the wall.

Because of his larger vitality, Fred, whose back heaved rhythmically in a digestive dream against the wall, expresses more visibly than most of the villagers the deep sense of frustration that characterizes these outports today in the wake of the cod moratorium. Hobbled and weakened by illness, he is like some great, restless steed, snorting and puffing stories and pronouncements, prowling the town all day and evening in his car, stopping for an hour to talk with the staff at the Heritage Foundation building, or at the Oldford family homestead near the wharf, uninhabited for years, to supervise the restoration work being carried out by his younger brother Con, or serving on the Regional Liaison Committee for Terra Nova National Park, or the Lions Club board, or the Municipal Committee for the Development of Progress on the Eastport Peninsula, or assisting each Sunday as the rector's warden, delivering the Scripture readings in his booming, gale-piercing voice and West Country accent, as if he were delivering the shipping news—in other words, being everywhere except, perhaps, where he most wants to be.

Tonight, August 22, at 10:45 p.m., I rejoined the North American power grid. Boiled water in the electric teakettle.

The wind blew hard all afternoon, began to die at dusk, and by midnight a light steady rain fell in a delicious seethe on the gently lapping water, a sound completely different from that which rain makes on land, reminding me of sand blowing against the side of an old dune shack. I woke up in the middle of the night to hear a lone loon give a plaintive call, slowly and repeatedly, out in the bay. It was a perfect night, in which one's body seems to extend out over the landscape, letting slip all human emotions, so that one is both receiving and bestowing oneself at the same time.

It is hard to appreciate how isolated from knowledge of the outside world most of these outports were until after Confederation in 1949.

Ron Crocker told me a story about the rescue of the crews of two American ships that had been torpedoed off the southwest coast during World War II, and the care given the survivors by the outport people. They warmed them with heated bricks and scrubbed them down (apparently they had been covered with oil during the rescue). When a US helicopter arrived to retrieve the crews, one of the women tending two of the survivors apologized: "I've washed and washed them, but I can't get them clean," to which the officer replied, "Don't you worry none, ma'am, that's the way they come."

Yesterday, Jessie let me read the letter and birthday card she had received from Fraser, sent from Ireland. Then the talk passed to all those who were not here, either dead or distant. At one point Jim grabbed me by both shoulders and said, with deep seriousness, "Now I'm gonna tell you somethin', b'y, and it's not gonna hurt you. So spread your anchors and then put the devil claw* in it: It's a bad thing to make friends, 'cause when y'do they goes away and y' misses them. Now, if you hadn't come, then I never would have known ya and I wouldn't miss ya when you go—eg-*zact*-ly!"

About 8 p.m. I left the Mosses and walked up to see Fred, whose seventy-third birthday was yesterday, for a post-celebratory drink of blueberry wine. I have been struck by the difference in the nature of the two households. At the Mosses', one senses a kind of informal, irrepressible democracy, in which, if anything, Jim's daughter, Julia, seems to assume the mantle of authority and the parents seem more like her children. The Oldfords' is unquestionably a patriarchal household, with Fred as the old lion, an Anthony Quinn-like figure, a still-virile physical ruin of a man to whom relatives and friends come to pay homage, drink their rum, and listen to the old man tell stories, while Shirley sits in the

---

* devil claw: an extra, special anchor designed to hold a boat on the ice—in the *Dictionary of Newfoundland English*, "a grapnel to anchor a vessel to ice." Its two tines are bent in the same direction at right angles to the shank.

rocker, like a medieval princess working on a tapestry, as she hooks her father's schooner onto the burlap screen, or goes about getting more glasses of blueberry wine for the guests.

Fred growls, "Shirley, is that fan still working? Get that screen out of the way, I can hardly breathe in here!" I find myself resenting his manner toward her, as if she were a housemaid instead of a PhD geologist who had worked for a major oil company and probably pulled down in one year more than Fred made in his entire working life.

But this is not fair to Fred, nor to Shirley, who not only does not seem to resent her position but has a deep affection for her family and for this small town. She also has a sharp and subtle intelligence behind her deferential manner. An avid reader, she has little patience for pretense in writers who write about Newfoundland. When I mentioned a new "anti-tourist" guide written by a Memorial University English professor, she commented, "What I resent about mainlanders, or even those who go away to be educated and come back, is their *condescension*. This man is all too eager to express his hard-nosed affection for Newfoundland by displaying all of its warts, as if to show his superiority."

Fred, by contrast, reminds me somewhat of a country squire out of Fielding, combining a love of learning with a strong Rabelaisian streak. As the evening and the wine wore on, he indulged his penchant for earthy, bawdy stories.

"Did you hear of the man who cut off a cow's udder, put the four tits down his pants, then when a group of women come along the road, he pulled one tit out of his fly and cut it off with a knife and the woman fainted dead away. He did it again and a second woman fainted. 'Well, that's enough of that,' he said, opened his pants and found out there were still *three* cow tits in there!"

On one of my morning rounds I met Bert in his red cap, forking more grass that he has scythed away, this time from the single apple tree he has growing in his yard, a small, gnarled tree with an abundant crop of reddening apples shining in the morning sun.

"Hi, stranger," he said, using the greeting I get from anyone I haven't called on in a few days.

Bert calls his apple tree "Phoenix" because it has resprouted twice after fires—an unexpected instance of familiarity with Greek mythology. The first was the fire that destroyed most of Burnside in 1912. Some fishermen from Flat Island, he said, were up in the hills to the west "drying sticks"—the branches one uses to dry fish on—when one of the men set the kettle on a fire to boil and a dry birch branch overhead caught fire. The burning embers blew three miles over the water and landed at the very west end of town, where it proceeded to burn down almost every house between there and the ferry landing—including the house Bert was born in.

"The wind," he said, "was like a living storm. One woman, who lived where Gus Oldford's house is now, went back in and got a bed and got on the schooner at the end of the wharf, but the fo'c'sle caught on fire until she put it out. A couple of horses and cows died, but no one got burnt. That were the twenty-eighth day of May-month, 1912. I was not quite three and don't remember much, but I remembers walking up over the hill by Crocker's store, holding my mother's hand and looking down on that scene all black where our house used to be, and I started to cry."

Bert is very proud of his apple tree, which he goes to great lengths to protect from "vandals." He told me about some teenage boys from the neighboring village of St. Chad's who had gotten into his yard the other day. He chased them out, telling them, "Get the hell outta here and go home, if ye's got home to go to—or I'll call the Mounties!"

He made it sound like serious larceny or maliciousness, but Henry Oldford told me that apple stealing was a kind of local ritual, a coming-of-age-dare-you-counting-coup sort of thing that has been going on from generation to generation, and one, he suggested with a smile and a tone of indulgence, that even he, Henry, might have participated in as a boy.

But when I coyly suggested to Bert that of course *he* never did anything like that as a boy, he indignantly replied, "No, b'y, I didn't—and if I had any time after me schoolin'—and I didn't have very much of that—I didn't get out 'cause there were chores to do, makin' nets for fish or cuttin' junks."

I walked with him over to his woodshed, where he had rigged on one side a kind of hammock of poles and wire on which he was drying fish. He told me he had gotten some fifty pounds of split cod from a man in Salvage and was drying them, soaked in brine and lightly salted, skin side up.

"Most people does it face up, but then the pickle stays in it—where if you put them like this, face down, the pickle drains out."

He had covered the bed of fish with alder branches to keep them from "burning" in the sun. A nest of flies was buzzing voraciously on the undersides like a swarm of miniature sharks. Drying time depends on the weather, but Bert says three to four days of weather like this would do.

I made a fish chowder last night. As the chowder simmered and light poured down in shafts over the hills, I went outside and picked another quart of blueberries between the house and the road. I take only the biggest ones, the size of small marbles, growing in bunches of four, six, eight, like grapes. Picking desultorily and fussily, I filled the can in about forty-five minutes. They are so abundant now that it seems somehow sacrilegious not to pick them, not to kneel down in the soft, prickly prostrate boughs of creeping juniper and wrap one's fingers softly around each bunch of berries, taking only those that fall off the stems of their own volition.

After dinner, I walked up to the church to practice a section of Bach's B Minor Mass for next Sunday's introit, likely the first time that music will have been heard here. I stayed about an hour and then, with Bach and Mozart still ringing in my ears, I walked the long way home, circling down by the ferry slip and up around the shore to the tickle bridge, surprised by a great surge of affection for this town and its people that I still know so little about, for the soft lights of the houses shining on the black water, for all the wooden boats rocking gently in their moorings like tethered horses, for the small boy who passes me and greets me on the dark road with no fear and open friendliness in his voice, for all the still-unspoiled, unselfconscious beauty of this place—so that, for a moment, I have a fantasy, see myself as a permanent part of this place, living and growing old here, one of its list of characters: the eccentric scribbler and esoteric organist, maker of paper airplanes and flier of kites, picking my berries, scything my grass, setting my traps, hauling my wood . . .

I have learned a little more of local history lately. Literacy did not come to most of the outports until fairly late, so that old written records are few. Many of the oldest outports, settled in the seventeenth century, did not even incorporate until the 1970s. Even today most local history remains oral and does not go back much before living memory. For the same reason, history has an immediacy here that it loses once it gets put down in print. When Fred tells me about "the Magic Arm disaster," which occurred over forty years ago, he tells it as if it had happened yesterday. By the same token, if I ask him about the specific year that something happened, his response tends to be vague, and even irritated, as if the question were irrelevant. It is as if time compresses and most of the past exists on a single plane here—the Past—rather than in a historical sequence. One could see how that might happen in a place where so little changes from year to year, or seems to.

In Jim and Jessie's house there is a striking photo on the mantel—a tattered and taped black-and-white print—of Jim and his parents on Flat Island. It was taken when Jim was five, and shows a small, unhappy-looking boy in a dark jacket and pants with a burr cut standing between two adults, holding a hand of each. The boy looks scared and sullen and suspicious and seems to be trying to hide in his mother's long, dark skirts. The father is dressed in a dark suit, white shirt, dark tie, and high shoes. Behind them is their house, a plain clapboard structure.

It is hard to judge his parents' ages in the photo. They could be anywhere from thirty to fifty. They have that spare, hardened look of their Appalachian counterparts, their faces lean, hands and wrists worn to the bone. The father's face has sunken eyes and cheeks, a black wispy beard, a pale complexion, and a blank stare, as if sea and wind, fog and ice, had washed all human expression from his eyes, so that he looked out on the photographer and the world with the impersonal watchfulness of a plow horse.

The mother, at first, has the same aspect: high, hollow cheeks, pinched face, thin lips, leathery, lined skin. Her hair, partly undone, is blowing astray in the constant wind. But there is a spark in her eyes that looks off and away to the side, as if something just out of sight held her interest, and possibly her hope.

"There's one thing I can tell you about my mother, m' b'y," says Jim, "and every man and woman on Flat Island will tell you the same. She could sing like a canary. Yes, b'y, she could *sing*."

I walked home about ten thirty under a clearing sky, following the dusty highway of the Milky Way overhead more than the dusty road beneath my feet.

The stars! The stars! They press down on me from the night like the skin of a speckled trout. I found a map of "the Newfoundland Sky in Summer" in the house and stepped outside. It was like being an eight-year-old again, when I was first taken to the Hayden Planetarium at the American Museum of Natural History in New York City and thousands of stars suddenly blazed out of that black dome like miniature white suns. Now they are all there again, as if painted on the inside of a dome, constellations and stars I had never recognized before: Boötes, the Square of Pegasus, Perseus. The twinkling white/red light of Arcturus, like a pale and distant moon, makes a distant patch on the water that stretches from the Bloody Bay Hills to my bedroom window.

I talked to Howard Moss today outside the post office. He is "resting up" for a second crab season, which is scheduled to begin next Tuesday night. He plans to go out on a small longliner from Salvage with three other men. Each boat has a quota of eighteen thousand pounds for the season, which he says they could get in three fine days. I asked if there was any chance I might go out with them, and he said, with derisive fatalism, "I doubt it—I doubt it, my son." It seems that the federal Department of Fisheries and Oceans (DFO) requires the captain of any boat to get a permit for anyone they take out with them, a permit specific to that boat. Technically, if Howard's father helps him load lobster pots onto his motor launch at the wharf, he could be fined. In fact, some older men in Salvage were cited for just that this spring and were told that the next time they would receive $150 fines.

Howard shook his head and said, "Foolishness." But you can see it is much worse than that. It is the deliberate, if ignorant, tearing apart of the very fabric of cooperation, community, and family that has been the core of the bay-outport culture for hundreds of years. The government, having screwed up royally by failing to regulate fishing sufficiently before, is now in fear of itself, destroying the fabric of the communities with blunt, blind overregulation.

Now it is September and Burnside is gearing up for the last weekend of the summer. The ferry wharf has been unusually busy, with cars and boat trailers parked everywhere, and everyone going out to their cabins for the weekend. Within the week most of the summer people will have left and the village will contract to its winter dimensions.

On Saturday I stopped at Ron's store and found it closed at seven. He has already gone to fall hours, didn't even wait for the holiday weekend to be over. But he was there and opened up for me, greeting me with his usual barrage of free-flow stories.

Ron, his parents, and Essie are all from Flat Island as well. Ron left when he was two and a half years old, then lived in Toronto with his family for thirty years. They moved back here eight years ago because they "didn't like the air" in the city. Most of the time he seems to be acting the role of some Shakespearean character, the Jolly Innkeeper or the Educated Rustic, perhaps, with a Falstaffian mixture of humor and pragmatism.

We talked about Canada's new two-dollar coin, which will come out next year. The one-dollar coin, bearing the image of a loon on its reverse, is popularly known as a "loonie." One suggestion I heard on the CBC was to call the two-dollar coin a "toonie." Thus, if you got three dollars in change, you could be said to have received a "loonie-toonie." Ron, pointing out that the new coin will feature a polar bear and that the Inuit word for polar bear is "nanook," suggested calling it a "nookie."

When he closed up, we walked outside together into the evening. As we separated, his parting advice was, "Whatsoever happens, my son, laugh at it," but as I watched him heading haltingly toward the barn, wrapped in a heavy dark blue jacket, he seemed caught in an unguarded moment of isolation, shorn of his usual sardonic and ebullient repartee. He threw me a perfunctory wave over his shoulder like that of an actor after the show is over, going home to his aloneness.

I was picking blueberries late this afternoon when the predicted rain suddenly arrived in large, cold, pelting drops. Twenty minutes later now, it appears to have stopped. The wind has suddenly calmed, shifting to the west-northwest, and the water is quilted with shifting surface patterns.

At 8 p.m. a few more sprinkles fell. Even when the sky is dark and heavy with rain, it seems as if there are always slats, reticules, and crenellations of light breaking through here and there, making it seem that the pall of dark clouds is only so much stage scenery, tattered and ripped in places, the true blue sky showing through—the effect of which is to break the weight of so much gloom, to keep the spirit alert and hopeful.

I think that what I shall miss most here is this very open sky, how it is always in motion, never stagnant, ever changing, a solace to the soul.

Yesterday morning I went over to Bert's to borrow his caulking gun.

"Come to get the punt, did ye?" and so of course I said yes. His "punt" is a twelve-foot wooden round-bottomed skiff he built with a small stern keel and a solidly decked floor. The boat has ten-foot oars, slim and feathered, almost like sculling oars, which are used with one person in the forward set of locks, so that when I sat on the forward thwart I was very near the bow. I expected to be unbalanced and awkward with the long oars but was surprised to find that they moved smoothly and quietly in the oarlocks, and the boat glided gracefully through the water.

Unlike Fred's lightweight fiberglass rowboat, Bert's punt was heavy enough to remain balanced in the water, as if the placement of my weight didn't affect it. When I turned the point of Squid Island and headed over to Primer's, I rowed into a moderate headwind that would have defeated me in Fred's boat. But I found that not only did I make comfortable progress, but also that the boat has such inertia and cutting power that I could ship the oars for twenty seconds or more without losing direction or momentum into the wind.

When I got home, I found Cleaves standing outside the door. It was the first time he had ever shown up at my house unannounced. I asked him in and offered him some of the Barbancourt Port-au-Prince rum I had brought with me.

Though Cleaves also went to the Labrador as a young man, he said that he and Fred only fished a few summers before starting up the lumber mill in the 1950s. Like most of the older fishermen, he has seen both fish stocks and fish prices rise and fall many times in the past, which gives him some perspective on the current crisis. He remembers times as a boy (this would be the mid-1920s) when there were no fish at all in Bonavista Bay. Men would come back from a summer on the Labrador with only fifty to sixty quintals of fish. They got only $2.50 a quintal "for shore fish—hard as a board—you could hold her out by the tail like this and he wouldn't bend."

Other times they got $14 a quintal and flour was only $2 a barrel. "Ah, b'y, them was flush times. There used to be flakes everywhere around here—twelve, fourteen feet high where it was built out over the water."

Like most of the inshore fishermen, he supports outlawing draggers on the spawning grounds (which he compared to "shooting pregnant women"), getting rid of the gill nets, and mandating smaller meshes at the ends of the trap nets. But the price of fish today, he believes, is inflated, government-subsidized, "for the amount of meat on them," particularly flatfish, which he regards with some disdain.

Cleaves has one of the ruddiest complexions of any man I've ever met. He could be one of Hardy's reddlemen. He had just come from his chiropractor in Clarenville, where he was "corseted" and had "steeves"—i.e., barrel staves—put on his leg. It was uncomfortable but he told the doctor, "If you don't hurt me, you won't cure me."

He is more specific about dates than most of the men here, noting that "we got roads here in 1951, two years after Confederation. Before that the road to Eastport was a one-lane wagon track you needed a four-wheel pickup to negotiate."

Shirley had told me she knew they had electricity in 1963 because her earliest memory of watching television was seeing Kennedy's assassination when she was nine. "I didn't know who Kennedy was, but I was sent around town to deliver the news."

Sometime during the night I woke to the sound of fierce wind and rain blowing in through the crack in my bedroom window. When I got up to check the rest of the house, I found that one of the kitchen casement windows had been leveraged open by the wind, uncranking the handle several turns, and rain was pouring in. I closed it and pinned the latch with a nail. When I tried the front door on the southeast side of the house, it felt as if someone, some Wind-Man, was pulling to keep it shut on the other side.

When I woke up this morning, it was still blowing unabated from the northwest, about sixty knots, with higher gusts. The waters of the cove, now the deep steel grey of the open ocean, are plunging and galloping directly at the house. The waves are full of frothy, muddy claws. The rocks are completely covered, and the waves are washing over Gus Oldford's wharf to the west. The house shudders on its pilings, but the large lump of grey shale, like the back of a whale, stands on the shore between me and the fury.

In the evening, I played organ at the church for the second time. Buoyed up by the success of my debut a few weeks earlier, I decided to pick out my own hymns this time, being careful to stay with the old favorites. I began pumping out "Ancient of Days," but after the first few lines I realized with sudden panic that absolutely no one was singing along, that though it was a hymn familiar to me, it was strange to them. There was nothing to do but press bravely on. After the service Henry Oldford came up and put his hand on my shoulder, saying kindly, "We'll give you a list of fifty or sixty to choose from next time."

It continued to blow hard from the northwest all the next day, with intermittent showers and bright-washed sun. About 10 a.m. Laura called me. She didn't identify herself, just asked if I could see Bert on his wharf from my house. I couldn't, so I walked over, and found him in his work shed. She worries about him so, like a mother with a child—the only one she's got.

He knows Laura worries about him, but, with a wide, nearly toothless grin, said, "I always shows up!"

Yesterday and today we have had beautiful fall weather—high, crisp skies, air with the clear complexity of a fine white wine and the pleasure of a draught of mountain water as you suck in a gulp. The scattered red maples in the woods sport red flags now, little bonfires of scarlet afloat on seas of green.

I have finally met Derrick Bowring, the old man with his dog that I have watched all summer out on his sailboat, *Imogene*, in the bay. I was passing his house on the hill that overlooks the harbour as he was raking up crab apples from the ground beneath an ancient tree just inside his front picket fence. He was using a curious tool composed of a long wooden handle with a short, flat, leaf-shaped blade at the end, perpendicular to the handle, like a very short scythe or a sand wedge—used for cutting apples off the boughs.

Derrick Bowring is an unmistakable figure of countrified gentry among the village locals. He is a scion of the Bowring family of St. John's, once one of the most powerful of the Water Street merchants that outfitted virtually all of the fishing and sealing fleets in Newfoundland. His father went back to England to fight in the Great War and married an English girl. Derrick was born there, and stayed till he was five or six, when the family moved to Staten Island, where his father attended to the family business. He went to a public school in England and didn't really come to live in St. John's until he was a young man.

His manner was not at all aloof, and in fact he was eager to talk, seemingly appreciative of company. At eighty, he still has that boyish quality, the self-effacing, unassertive, mildly ironic, hesitant, but quite well-informed manner of the old English-educated class. I got the sense that his background and manner tend to create a distance between him and the locals that is perhaps greater than he would like.

He talked about going out on the Bowring Brothers sealing ships in the 1930s as an "inspector." He always went alone, he said, since no "outsiders" were allowed on sealers after another ship had been chartered by an American filmmaker, Varrick Frissell, who wanted to make a movie about going onto the ice. Frissell had brought dynamite aboard to create spectacular ice-explosion shots, and had managed to blow up the ship and acquire the dubious distinction of causing the largest loss of life to a film production crew in cinematic history. (He told this and other disaster anecdotes with a kind of ironic, jocular tolerance for human foibles, as if they were all mischievous schoolboy pranks.)

One of the ships he went out on was the Bowring sealer *Charlotte*. "All the ships then were coal-fired. Coal was stored everywhere, you see, below bunks, in lockers, everywhere—because, unlike oil drums, as the coal was used up, the space became available for seal pelts. They carried enough coal to go to Australia—six thousand miles—and that's how far they went each season."

All of the captains, he said, preferred Welsh coal, which was relatively clean-burning, as opposed to coal from Nova Scotia, which was soft and smoky. This, he said, was not out of any concern for the environment ("They couldn't have cared less about that. Why, they wouldn't have known what the word *meant*!"), but because the hard coal, burning clean, didn't announce their location to other ships when they found a herd of seals. He told a story about a captain who went up to White Bay, a place sealers didn't like to go into because if the wind shifted and packed the ice in around you, you might be stuck there all winter. The captain found the thickest piece of the pack ice he could, put the ship's bow into it, and started up the engine, creating a huge plume of black smoke. The other captains saw it and said, "Well, he's stuck there now," and went off, leaving the captain to the rich herd of harp seals he had found there.

"So much for cooperation," I said.

"Well, all the Bowring ships were *supposed* to cooperate, and when I went along, the *Charlotte* cooperated more than most."

He said it was "the desire of every bayman to secure a berth to the ice," though he agreed with John Moss that they usually didn't make much money from it. The sealing merchants, in outport lore and in books like Cassie Brown's *Death on the Ice*, are commonly represented as the villains in Newfoundland's history, sending men out onto the ice in blizzards to die, forcing them to risk their lives for a few dollars while the fat cats back on Water Street got fatter. "And, of course," said Mr. Bowring, "there always *were* a few villains—on both sides." But, he maintained, "for the boat crew it was a kind of holiday, a lark for them, a respite from the drudgery and monotony of winter life in the outports, something different and a way of proving yourself." (The tenor of John Moss's reminiscences about his sealing days seemed to confirm this.)

The worst problem they had was with the stowaways: "There would always be four or five on a ship. While the ships were still in St. John's Harbour, they'd get aboard any way they could, climbing up the hawsers at night, coming aboard in trunks, hiding in the strangest places.

We'd have to rummage the ship from stem to stern for them, like rats. The thing to do was to cast off and just hover in the harbour for a while to see if you could trick them out, but you'd always miss a few." He told this as if the stowaways were likable vermin, and with a tolerant admiration for their tenacity and wiliness.

"The problem, though, was that they weren't assigned to anyone's *watch*—and, of course, you couldn't lock them up or put them ashore, so you'd just assign them to a watch and hope they were able."

He described how, at the crack of dawn, two hundred men would be over the side of the ship, disappearing over the white horizon in no time. He didn't see how they would ever all be found again, but the master watches always knew in what direction each man had gone, and over a hundred and fifty years of sealing in Newfoundland, far fewer men had been lost on the ice than had drowned on the Grand Banks or the Labrador coast.

I was surprised to hear him decry the credit system that for generations held so many outport families in debtors' thrall for most of their lives. He agreed that it was organized so as to drive the average fisherman deeper and deeper into debt, but he maintained that the merchants didn't really like it either, since they had no guarantee of being paid back and were taking risks at both ends. "If the credit tabs were paid, it was in fish, not cash. Then the merchants had the fish and had to sell it, and markets were always uncertain."

Several times efforts were made among the merchants to move to a cash basis, but in the end they concluded, "No, no, fish is the currency here. If you don't give credit, the men can't fish, and if they don't fish, you don't have anything."

He said that ties with England remained strong after Newfoundland obtained "responsible government," or independence, from England in 1855, at least among the ruling merchant class. Even in the 1930s, he said, the regular St. John's-to-Bristol steamer was referred to as the "home boat," carrying merchants and their families back to England to visit relatives and family seats.

"Confederation changed all that."

He seemed to have genuine sympathy for the local fishermen and admired Howard Moss as a professional with "get-up." He agreed with Howard and most inshore fishermen that what destroyed the fisheries were draggers and monofilament gill netting.

"Gill nets now lie on the bottom, hundreds of miles of it, still killing fish. It never disappears." (I had an image of ghostly, morbid, gruesome catches, never hauled, never gutted and cleaned, never salted and made, rotting slowly into fish-ooze on the ocean bottom.) "Newfoundlanders would never eat a fish caught in a gill net," he said, "because it was drowned."

Finer-quality fish were caught in traps and on trawls, a more labor-intensive method than dragging. Limiting the fishery to trapping and longlining would, he maintained, not only preserve the fish stocks and raise prices, but also provide that most-needed commodity—employment.

"But it's not so easy to get the ear of the government out here. It's the big fish companies that have their ear, and what they need is to get out from under the debt they went into with their big new plants and factory ships when the fisheries closed three years ago. I don't believe there will be any fishery again until the sea is crawling with fish."

I asked him about his apples and he confirmed Henry Oldford's view of apple stealing as a harmless local tradition.

"Oh, the real danger is that the boys might injure the tree while stripping it. The boys know to come and ask me if they might steal some, and then I stand in the doorway, directing them as to which ones to take." This struck me as a denatured form of apple stealing similar to the evolution of "trick-or-treating" at home, where the "tricking" has largely become merely a part of the verbal formula.

He is quite proud of his English flower garden, a large bed of annuals he has planted on the slope behind his house leading down to the sea, placed so that he can see it from the large window in back. It is quite lovely, divided by a grassy path of bedrock and shaded from the afternoon sun by a drooping birch. There are tiny blue gems of lobelia, hollyhock-like mallows, four or five varieties of brightly painted *Endicia*, large velvet-blue, flop-petaled pansies, and several other species.

I enjoyed talking with him and he seemed to feel the same. He is obviously lonely for company now that his wife is gone, but his class seems to set him apart here. He loves the land for what it is, but is skeptical of any sentimental notions about the noble, oppressed baymen, the evil merchants, the terrible lives of sealers. ("They had great fun, told wonderful stories.") He spoke contemptuously of the fad for "Newfoundland ponies," which have recently been purchased by well-to-do people on the Avalon Peninsula.

"Newfoundland ponies! Nobody called them *that*! We called them Torbay nags. They were the workhorses."

I wished I had a picture, a portrait of him standing there in that late summer light, his fine white hands clasping his cutting pole, his white head and red cheeks in the dappled shade of his apple tree, framed by the brilliant white clapboards of his house and the clear blue cerulean sky.

My ink bottle is about one-third down, most of it since I arrived in Burnside. I calculate that this black fluid has uncoiled itself over the past two months into some six thousand lines, or roughly a kilometer of script—and several times that distance if all the script were straightened out. One could thus say that I have written myself from Burnside to the neighboring village of St. Chad's since coming here—not very far when you think about it.

This morning, up in the cemetery, I found Cleaves painfully going down on his arthritic knees to record dates on a small pad: those of his parents and others. He said he just wanted them to put in a book in his house so he would have them if he wanted.

At one point, side by side, were the graves of two women, Annie and Mable Oldford, both of whom died young in the 1940s. They were the wives of Willis, oldest of the four Oldford brothers, who had left for Toronto in 1945. "He couldn't take it," said Cleaves. "He's never been back, though his son has."

I had Shirley and her Scottish terrier Jock over for supper last night. I made moose sauerbraten and fettuccine preceded by snow crab and fresh corn. Shirley began talking of Fraser, how everyone liked her, though some of the women looked askance at her because she didn't take the traditional role of women here. She went out into the woods with Mark to haul wood, was always wearing pants, etc.

Shirley has been doing a lot of genealogy work on her family over the summer, studying the old Salvage parish records in the provincial archives. Salvage, before it was organized as a parish in 1840, was called King's Cove. She found one ancestor, Mary Trim, who was there in 1786, and was originally an Oldford. Shirley says that three-quarters of her family branches were descended from Oldfords, that the Eastport and Bonavista Peninsulas are the only places in the world where the name is found. The reason, she said, was that many of the early settlers jumped ship, leaving all family behind, and often invented new names to avoid being found out when the British came looking. So when new families formed here there was a strong family loyalty, not only because family was so important to survival, but because many of the men had lost their original ones.

She said that because the men on the northeast coast were usually away on the Labrador most of the summer and often into fall, there developed a strong matriarchal society. When there was an important decision to be made in the town, the menfolk would consult the women elders. She remembers elements of this tradition even from when she was growing up. When she was a young woman and wanted to visit Scotland, she had to go and get approval from her great-aunt Mary, who was actually her great-grandmother. "Well," said Mary, "I've always thought you was a strange girl, and now I'm sure of it."

Later I met Fred on the road in his car, trolling. He had been to Gander and had to go back again for an 8:30 a.m. appointment on Wednesday for a stress test. He said that he thought just getting there was a stress test, and that the doctor ought to say, "Well, Fred, you've showed up. Congratulations, you passed. You can go home now."

Ten p.m. My last night in Burnside. Jim and Jessie had me over for a farewell dinner, a Jiggs' dinner with chicken, and blueberry cake with hot custard topping. Jessie gave me a pair of "thrums," tightly knit socks she had darned for me, shyly and hesitantly going upstairs to get them.

Uncle John and Christine were there, too. I gave John some chewing tobacco, and he thanked me with great emotion, as if I had handed him a lifetime wish: "Bless you, my son—may you live to be a hundred."

As the women were cleaning up, Jim, John, and I went into the living room. I sat on the sofa and Jim sat in a chair directly across from me. Without preliminaries, he began to tell me everything about myself that I had mentioned over the summer, regularly jabbing me in the chest, in that way he has, with a bony finger for emphasis.

When he finished, he said, "So, my son, did I get it right?"

"Yes, you did," I replied. "Perfect. But why did you do that?"

"Well, I didn't want to forget you when you're gone."

"But I'll be back."

"No—no you won't."

"What makes you say that?"

"Well, why would anyone want to come back to a place like this?"

Oh, Jim.

The next morning, I nailed the board back against the inside of the front door, pinned the curtains shut, turned off the main power switch, climbed down through the pantry hatch, and filled up the entry to the crawl space again with firewood. Then I drove out of Burnside.

SUMMER 1996

NOT ONLY DID I RETURN TO BURNSIDE THE FOLLOWING SUMmer, but for fifteen summers after that. The second summer I flew up, arriving at Gander airport on a clear, nearly windless night. Fred and Shirley, who had driven up to visit Betty at Gander hospital, picked me up and drove back to Burnside, dropping me off a little before midnight at Jim and Jessie's, where I spent the night.

The Mosses welcomed me with shy gladness, Jessie in her fuzzy pink robe and slippers letting me hug her, Jim repeatedly poking my breastbone with his long, bony fingers as he talked *at* me, as if to make sure that I was real, and really here.

They sat me down to tea with biscuits, homemade bread, and gumdrop cake, and pumped me for particulars about my life since I had last seen them. Then they energetically relayed a litany of heart attacks, diabetes, cancer, and other ailments that had afflicted Burnsiders and their relatives since I'd left last fall.

Jim said Uncle John has been diagnosed with bowel cancer and has "wasted away to almost nothing, doesn't get around much, only comes over once a week now." At Christmas, said Jim, he "sang a few songs.

Now, if you were here then, you'd have said he was enjoying himself. But if Mark were here, he'd know he wasn't the same."

They are so sweet—I love the way they talk simultaneously, like two parakeets, with Jim the dominant voice and Jessie providing a sort of ongoing nasal obbligato.

Everything is so much easier this time, coming into a known place, with known people, being a known person myself with a real, if slight, history here. Flying into Gander was like walking through a door, compared to the refugee crossing I had made last summer, which had left me drained, on edge, unable to be really here for the first several weeks. It is as if Burnside now inhabits a permanent part of my brain.

I slept soundly, waking a little after seven. After breakfast Jim sent me off with a hammer and crowbar to open up Mark and Fraser's house.

The house opened up easily this time, since I had left a tunnel through the woodpile in the crawl space to the trapdoor in the kitchen floor. Everything was as I left it, as if Burnside and this house were a book I had been reading and put down on its open face several months ago and just now had picked up again.

Near the house I saw a flock of Bohemian waxwings in an aspen grove. They were all fluffed up in the topmost branches of the bare trees, uttering a kind of mass metallic twittering filled with crackling electricity, like starling flocks, and, like starlings, they seemed to exhibit a kind of continuous, nervous energy, flitting from branch to branch, breaking apart into smaller groups that flew off and then collapsed back into a single mass. I stood directly beneath them, dodging a slow rain of droppings. Their willingness to allow me such close proximity confirmed their reputation for sociability and imperturbability. Listening to the constant crackle and twitter, and the rain-like fall of bird shit onto the frozen ground, I thought of their Latin tag, *Bombycilla garrulus*, which translates loosely as "chattering bomb-tail."

The next morning I had the stove going for about a half hour when Bert stopped by. He said he'd seen "black smoke coming up out of Mark's chimney" and thought he'd step in to check on me. He was diffident in his usual manner but smiled to see me. His news was characteristically gloomy. His right knee had "gone out," so that he's been "crippled up." When I asked about Laura, he said, "Oh, not too good, b'y, not too good. Some days she gets up, some days she doesn't."

I told him I'd come up later this afternoon to get the key to the shed and some tools to open it.

A little later Fred also stopped in to check up on me: "I figured a fella like you could wander off in the woods and never be seen again in this world, or you could drop dead and smell up the house for several days afore anyone would find ya."

Thanks a lot, Fred. Mark and Fraser would be pleased to know that you're concerned for their house's odors.

When I returned the hammer to Jim, I went next door to visit John. He recognized my voice and called me to come upstairs. He was lying down on his bed, fully dressed. To me he looked about the same, but he obviously has trouble getting up. His son Howard tells me that he is not in pain—yet—and still has his appetite, so that Jim's "wasting away" description of him seems premature, in anticipation rather than the actuality.

I drew up a chair and sat next to him. When I told him that I had played his "singing tapes" as part of a program I gave last winter on Cape Cod, he was delighted to hear about his "celebrity."

"Was there a lot of people there, b'y?"

"Over a hundred."

"Oh, yes."

"Some of them wondered if it would be possible to bring you down to the States to sing for them—you know, like Rufus Guinchard or Émile Benoît have."

He looked down, embarrassed but smiling, and surprised me by saying, "Oh, I moight like that."

Talking about his illness, he shifted back and forth from fatalism to optimism to bathos:

"Now, I'll tell you something, Bob—you can't do nothin' about sickness, can you? You just can't do nothin' about it."

"Well, sometimes you can."

"Yes, that's right—sometimes you can. When I went down to the slip to see Mark and Fraser off, I told them, 'I don't knows that you'll ever see me again.'"

He told me with enthusiasm about the recent CAT scan he had done in Grand Falls, demonstrating how it moved up and down over his body: "*Vroom, vroom!* Bob b'y, I'll tell you, that machine can see everything—everything!—just like de Lord."

He is scheduled to go back down to St. John's Thursday afternoon for another exam, followed by possible chemo or even surgery—he doesn't know. He struggled to sit up when I moved to go, and shook my hand firmly, saying, "God bless you, Bob," several times, as if he wouldn't see me again, then said, "If I should go, when you see Mark, tell him to remember the times we had, singing the old songs."

I stopped next door and found Christine Moss at her kitchen table making cigarettes with a little machine that stuffed tobacco into pre-rolled paper with filters. She had made a whole bowl of them.

"It's much cheaper," she explained, "though I don't know why I do it. I don't even smoke! So how long you be here this time?" (Most of the people here greet my return in a perfunctory manner, as if I had only been gone a matter of days.)

She told me that Howard was on his wharf. I found him there with his younger son, Chris, who is fifteen, building new lobster traps and repairing the old ones. Though the lobster season runs through July, he doesn't know what his schedule will be because of his father's condition.

"Well, what is you up to, b'y?" asked Howard.

People here don't instinctively shake hands when you greet them after an absence—a verbal greeting is the preferred gesture—like Minnesotans that way.

He is obviously worried about John, though he expresses his concern primarily in terms of logistics.

"Last time we took him to St. John's, we saw the doctor for maybe fifteen minutes, then drove back the same day. It's a hard trip for John, where he can't stretch out—four hours each way." This time they'll go down on Thursday and get a room overnight for Friday's appointment. "I don't know what we'll do if Dad needs daily radiation. I can't be going back and forth all the time, and Christine needs to be here to run the post office."

This summer Michael, Howard's older son, will finish up at the academy in Gander.

"There's nothing for him here, so he's thinking of going out to Alberta next week to try his chances in the oil fields there." This must strike deeply at Howard, but he says it with flat, resigned acceptance: "A young fella, he stays here now, he doesn't know what he'll do. Now, for *me*, it's okay—I knows what I'll do. I'll fish is what I'll do—I've got *my* license—but I'd never get him one. Even if the fish come back, he'll never get one."

Or might not want to, I thought.

The following Friday John was admitted to St. John's hospital for five to six weeks of radiation treatment.

On my way back to the house I stopped at Bert's to borrow some wrenches to open up the shed. He was having afternoon tea and Laura invited me to join them. It was a classic ritual of their day: Bert sat at one end of the table while Laura set out tea, cake, biscuits, cookies, and blueberry jam. There was no place set for her, and after she served me, she sat off to one side in a ladder-back chair beside the stove, her knees together, hands folded on her lap, like a servant or a small girl, while Bert and I talked. Or rather, Bert held forth and I prompted him. He had on a thick, grey-patterned zippered sweater. His face looked softer than I remembered, rosy-cheeked, with his shock of silver-white hair falling over his forehead in a way that belied his stern countenance. In his relaxed and animated countenance and clear, Paul Newman-blue eyes, I saw for the first time a shade of the boyish handsomeness that must have attracted Laura, just as I saw the somewhat nervous girlishness in her, the kind of fragile, submissive adoration he knew he wanted.

We talked about politics, the weather, wood hauling, fishing. From time to time Laura would get up, as if she had just thought of something, and with quick, birdlike movements perform some small chore—refilling the kettle, removing the plates, putting out more biscuits, cleaning the counter—with a kind of business to which she had become accustomed after over half a century of taking care first of Bert and his domineering mother, and then of Bert alone, in this childless house, never gaining the identity and power of a mother, a true wife who establishes her own sphere of power in the house, but remaining always a servant in her own home.

Except that in those tasks she exerted a practiced assertiveness, even an aggressiveness: pushing away Bert's gesticulating arm to clear a plate, moving swiftly and peremptorily around him as if he were merely a piece of furniture, or at most a central icon in a daily ritual. He never glanced at or directed any comment to her. Yet she was the one who had first noticed the open curtains at my house, the smoke from my chimney, and told Bert I was back. She sees far beyond the circumscribed confines of their house, from which she rarely roams.

"It was nice to see a light on in Mark's house again," she said, and showed me a card she had just received from Fraser. Her birthday is Saturday.

A reference to today's provincial election got Bert going on politicians, their ignorance of fish and their lack of concern for the fishermen (a universal sentiment here, though with different interpretations of what "concern" is). Specifically, he feels that the government doesn't understand the nature of the current cod crash or its cause.

He remembers other times when the fish "disappeared," especially in the late 1920s and 1930s, when schooners on the Labrador brought back as few as eight quintals (less than half a ton) of salted cod for the season. Bert's ship made three trips that first summer and caught a thousand quintals, beating a boat out of Salvage known as "the Gobbler" because it always got at least a thousand quintals, but which this time only got six hundred.

Besides his characteristic pride in outperforming others and beating the odds, he implied that even in the bad times, the secret was in knowing how and where to fish—that anyone could catch fish in good times. The measure of a man was what he did when the fish "disappeared," though they always came back.

One evening Jim showed me a photo of an old windmill that a man on Flat Island had made to saw wood with. "The stronger it'd blow, the faster it'd saw," he said several times, as if to be certain I'd understood and was impressed.

"Oh, we had everything on Flat Island, my son."

"Did you have cars?"

"No, no, me son. Motorboats, they was our cars. Get in our motors and go."

"You didn't have any electricity, did you?"

"No, no electricity."

"So you didn't have radios."

"Oh yes, me son, we did. Batt'ry ones, y'know? We had Delcos. And one fella ran he's on a little wind generator. Oh yes, we had everything on Flat Island in its prime, fifty years ago."

Jim was born in December 1923. He said his younger daughter

Audrey was the last child born on the island: "She were three weeks old when we left—that were in 1958."

As I walked home from J & J's a little before eleven, I saw that the living room light was still on in the Burdens' house. I could see Bert, in his T-shirt, sitting in the middle of the room in one of the dining chairs, under the single lightbulb hanging from the ceiling. Laura was standing over him with what seemed to be a Q-tip and was carefully swabbing some solution or cream over the skin of Bert's face. I stepped close to the window, drawn by curiosity about this process, and also by the strong sense of marital intimacy through that shadeless, curtainless front window as she moved about him, from one side to the other, with the professional air of a barber, someone performing a ritual done countless times, carefully swabbing around his eyes, his eyelids, his ears, under his nose, around his lips, all the sensitive and intimate crevices and surfaces of his face.

Was she cleaning his skin? Applying a salve or some other medicine to areas of benign skin cancer? It didn't matter, really. The scene conveyed a deep sense of physical intimacy that seems the essence of the long- and well-married (and which has nothing necessarily to do with marital bliss, or even contentment). It is an impersonal intimacy, dependent not on mutual compatibility, but on time and familiarity, like the smooth contours of water wearing over stone.

I could even hear, through the single-paned glass, the murmur of their voices, no doubt also of a ritualistic, repetitive nature. They appeared on a far more equal plane than when I visited them, suggesting that the dominant-submissive roles they play when I am in their house are just that—roles, played for the benefit of the public.

The next day I drove Fred in his car to visit Betty in Gander hospital. Unexpectedly, he talked most of the way up about Shirley. For the first time I heard him express real recognition, admiration, and affection for how she was always a first-rate student, earned a medal for excellence in mathematics at MUN, got her master's and doctorate in Calgary, and was recruited by ABCO, the petroleum company she worked for as a seismic geologist for twenty years.

"She went all the way through on scholarship, never cost me a cent."

She got sick with what they think was chronic fatigue syndrome while working and retired. She and her husband had a house in the valley there, but they had to sell and move out because of her increasing allergies to insecticides and other toxic chemicals. They moved into a trailer on a ranch and her husband ran a tour bus for eight years. "Then that give out," said Fred.

"Three winters ago she come back by herself for a rest. I don't know what happened. She didn't say nothin'. Come spring I asks her what her plans are and she says, 'I ain't ever goin' back.' She'd already had a legal separation done but hadn't told us. She's been a blessing for us, though. After Mom went in hospital, someone asked her what she'd do if my heart acted up again and I had to go in, too, and she said she'd 'tell 'em to put in a third bed and I'd just move in with them.'"

On Saturday Henry Oldford stopped by with the church schedule and to remind me of my promise last summer to play the services if I came back. We walked up to the church together and went inside, where Henry gave me a list of hymns and tune numbers. "Me and the missus picked these out for yis, just so's yid have 'em. Pick any three you like and just let me know by tomorrow morning."

Before the evening service, I walked up the set of narrow stairs to the small room below the belfry, where I met Sid Hunter, a tall, lanky, elderly, sharp-faced man in a dark suit. Henry has had to give up the bell ringing because of his knee operation and Sid has taken over for him. He pulled the rope down in a long arc each time for the bell's double clap, as if he were a sailor hauling in a sheet. Beside him was the wooden chair Henry used to sit in when he rang the bell. I looked at the chair, and at the rope that answered Sid's downward pulls with its own powerful upward jerks, and it occurred to me that it was a good arrangement for someone ambivalent about suicide.

The bell clanged and stomped mightily with each pull. "You don't want to have a hangover when you're doing this, b'y," said Sid. I noticed that Sid also wore a hearing aid and wondered if their stints as bell ringers were partially responsible for this, plus the fact that none of the men in town wear earplugs or earmuffs while chain-sawing wood. Is there, in fact, a Great and Ancient Fraternity of Quasimodo-like Bell Ringers spread across Newfoundland, something like the hearing-impaired middle-aged ex-rock band members of my own generation?

The readings from Scripture were of Adam and Eve's Temptation, and of Christ's in the wilderness. Marilyn's sermon made me aware again of the power of exclusivity and the absolute unambiguity of the core Christian doctrine of original sin, expressed as "repentance, confession, and belief." Even in this age of acknowledged multiple faiths, Christianity claims uniqueness and preeminence by insisting that no other religion ("Not even our parent religion, Judaism," said Marilyn) so strongly recognizes the need for forgiveness—so that in a sense it does possess a relative superiority. But for what, I wonder, do these elderly Squid Ticklers feel the need for forgiveness? I have the sense that the men feel it abstractly, if at all, and the women more personally, as if they have failed someone profoundly, perhaps themselves.

I have been reading Erich Auerbach's magisterial *Mimesis: The Representation of Reality in Western Literature*, a book that had sat on my shelf for many years. I brought it with me this summer not just because I felt I could read it here without distraction, but because it seemed an appropriate companion under the circumstances, since I was myself looking for a new way (or perhaps an old way) to represent my own reality in words, given that the old way, however successful as writing, had failed me in understanding my own life. At any rate, I knew from the outset that being in Newfoundland would tell me as much about where I came from as about this new-found land. What I did not know was that *Mimesis* would end up telling me as much about Burnside as it would about literature.

Auerbach says that the body is Homeric, the mind biblical. The former expresses presentness, revelation, specificity; the latter obscurity, hidden depths, background. Squid Tickle is Homeric, however much some may quote Scripture. Even Fred is more interested, say, in the dimensions of the porch of Solomon's temple than in the mystery of God's will. Cleaves is the ultimate Homeric figure here, a man who lives in present specificity, expressed in such remarks as, "The man who invented the chain saw *did* something." Young Darren Lane, who rebuilt Bert's wharf, is the type of Achilles. It is difficult to imagine rewriting the Scriptures in a Homeric style: Christ as epic hero. But then, *The Iliad* never changed history.

Yesterday I stopped at Bert and Laura's to drop off some brownies I had made. Laura was washing Bert's hair in the sink. (One never knows what intimate domestic scenes one is liable to walk in on here, but knocking is a practice still not observed in Burnside.) She seemed immediately in control of the household.

"Come on in. I'll be through here in a minute."

She had Bert come and sit in the living room while she dried his silvery hair with a blow dryer Fraser had left for her, though she never uses it on herself. Bert seemed particularly passive under the electronic gun, except to complain, as a small boy might, that he was done.

"I'll tell you when yer done," said Laura. "Don't move your feet now, or I's'll trip over 'em." She seemed to revel in, and even show off for me, her momentary authority, turning to me with a modest grin: "I'm in charge now!"

When she finished drying and brushing him—"Now yer done, Bert"—he struggled up out of the chair and went to sit meekly, as she had done the other day at tea, in the chair next to the stove, though perhaps in both cases it was mostly to keep warm.

When I got up to go, saying I had water to bring in, he repeated that universal Newfoundland mantra of visiting: "Plenty o' time, b'y, plenty o' time."

Plenty of time. It certainly has an obvious truth here now, but the phrase, it would seem, goes back to a time when there was always work to be done. One likes to think it is a sign that human intercourse— chewing the fat, sharing stories, discussing prospects and neighbors— always had a certain precedence for these people, and that, like the dream of every Orthodox Jewish man to be in a position to spend all of his time studying the Torah with others in the temple and *discussing* it, the dream of Newfoundlanders is to have time to talk and visit to their heart's content, and now this generation seems, quite unexpectedly, to have found themselves there.

At five thirty I had just settled down for tea and a read when Howard walked in bringing a loaf of fresh-baked raisin bread from Christine. He began talking about Flat Island, about what a hard time "they"— his father's generation—had had.

"I don't t'ink we would've survived it now, b'y." Howard had not only been born on Flat Island but gone to school there, leaving with his family in 1958 when he was seven. He remembers the winters, heating up bricks to take to bed with him. (Stoves were put out at night, there was such a fear of fires.) In the morning, the first one downstairs had to break the ice on the water barrel on the porch to wash up with. The island had long been stripped of trees, so in the winter the men had to go across the ice to the mainland hills or other islands to cut wood, sometimes setting up camp for a week or more. He offered to take me out there, "though I gets bored to death there now. You might like it, though. You might want to stay for a week. There's not much out there now but new cabins, a few ruins, and, of course, three or four cemeteries—now, *that's* interesting!"

He said that before Confederation 80 percent of Flat Islanders died before they were twenty. "I guess of malnutrition, or TB, or what they called TB then—might have been meningitis or cancer."

Howard harboured the bayman's disgust over the *Newfoundland* disaster, which is as universally impressed on the minds of all Newfoundlanders as the *Titanic* is for Americans, the difference being that the *Newfoundland* is remembered as a morality play about greed rather than pride, with the ship's captain, Abram Kean, as the heartless villain of the piece.

"He turned his son's crew back out on the ice without so much as offerin' them a cup o' tea, and a blizzard comin'. Uncle John Morgan, from Flat Island, he was on the *Newfoundland*. He said that when they found the frozen men, they piled 'em up on the deck, a layer of bodies, then a layer of ice, then another layer of bodies—imagine!"

Later on Jim augmented Howard's remarks about life on Flat Island. He said they did most of their wood cutting on "Woolson's" (Wilson's) Island, a big island in the bay. They would camp there in the fall, five or six of them under a canvas sheet with two built walls and a "cut oil cask" for a stove in the fall. They cut for maybe a week at a time over a three-week period, then returned when the snows came. Since they had no horses or dogs on Flat Island, they hauled the logs themselves by using rope "man harnesses" (Jessie and the other women would make shoulder pads for the men) and loaded them onto the boats. If the bay was frozen over, they would haul them all the way over the ice by hand—"Some hard work, y's b'y."

Jim spent his summers fishing on the Labrador in seventy-to-eighty-ton schooners with cod traps. I gathered that the local inshore cod was not fished at all, except by boys and men too young or too old to go to the Labrador. They usually went in June and returned in August or September. The fish were heavily salted down, with "Labrador salt" in the hold. When they returned, the fish were unloaded and "made"—pickled with heavy salt and dried on wooden flakes, turned and taken in each night—on the shore in the harbour, work that was done by both men and women, as well as young children. The "made" fish were then taken to St. John's to be sold to the merchants.

"Ye didn't make any money at it, b'y—no, no now—maybe a hundred dollars, that's all—nothin' at all."

Jessie remembers making the fish, how cold the water was in the fall, yet like Jim she repeatedly maintained "there was no times like it," as if they were the best times of her life, when life and work and community were all integrated. There was a sense of completion, of the Greek ideal of the full exercise of one's powers, on a soil not hospitable to soul-centered religions—to the point where even Jim felt the need to temper their remarks by saying, "But it was hard, b'y, y's, some hard."

Jim confirmed Howard's stories of the fear of fires at night, even repeating verbatim his comment that "if there was still a spark in the stove at night, why, you'd take a drop of water and—*pfft!*" When it was really cold, you'd roll the water barrel in off the porch and put it by the stove to thaw out. He attributed the heavy death toll among young people to "the work bein' too hard—they just got wore out."

They got very little from outside the island besides fishing supplies, rum, tea, sugar, flour, and certain tools: guns, cartridges, compasses, watches, and hygrometers—to measure the humidity—for pickling fish.

"There was no doctor—if you got sick, well, you lived with it, or you didn't."

The fishing gave out on the Labrador in the 1950s, and that spelled the doom of the Flat Island community. Jim's daughter Audrey was actually born in the hospital in Gander—"a week in Gander, a week in St. Chad's, and a week on Flat Island"—and then they left. He and John bought the land where they put their houses, "haulin' them up the slip by hand, twenty or thirty men"—and from then on Jim was an inshore fisherman, but with no sons to carry on.

On Saturday afternoon I went to the church to practice for the Sunday services. As I passed Cleaves' house I found him in his yard, repairing an old sawhorse. Nearby was his wood saw, a home-built contraption with a sixteen-inch circular blade and a Briggs & Stratton motor "from the sawmill days," mounted on a wooden crib with four bays that would hold a length of log as it arced up to meet the blade, cutting off a piece and allowing the log to be fed forward for the next cut.

He worked in the shadow of a large tepee of logs sixteen to twenty feet long, stacked vertically to form a wooden cone some twelve feet wide at the base. This method of stacking wood, he told me, not only allows the logs to dry faster, but makes them easier to cut up. He demonstrated this by pulling one of the long logs off the tepee so that it landed on a single sawhorse. He then cut the log in two and carried each length to the wood saw.

I stopped at Bert's to pick up a wood saw he was sharpening for me. He was working with some barbed "warr" he had bought earlier, but said it was "no good" because the spurs would slide. He was painstakingly removing each individual spur and threading a perpendicular piece of wire between them to keep them from sliding. He intends—"when I gets the time, if I ever gets the time"—to string the wire on posts behind the existing fence separating his property from the old cemetery to provide a second wall, or line of defense, as it were, to keep trespassers out of his berries. He told me he had "found one fellow" inside the fence last summer with whom he had the following interchange:

"A wall is supposed to keep you out."

"Well, a wall won't keep me out."

"It'll keep you out of everything but jail. Now get the hell out!"

"Well," said Bert, "I haven't seen him again, but there are others."

He can barely hide the relish with which he surveys doom all around him as he goes on, laying new longers on his wharf, weaving wire on the new fence, cleaving birch junks, scything the tall grasses that threaten to swamp his house . . .

With the sun declining over his shoulder, Bert told me a long story about how one year he ended up with "parts of three moose." He seemed mostly interested in the intricacies of the math involved in dividing up the animals: *Now, boys and girls, if Bert receives two-thirds of a moose from Eldon and one-half a moose from Lloyd and one-third a moose from Noel, how many times does he eat moose stew all winter?*

Shirley invited me to lunch the next day. She served us stewed beef and fresh homemade bread with a pâté or head cheese made from moose brains. After supper Fred switched on the TV news and moved to the settee for his after-dinner nap.

Before he lay down, Fred opined that he could never read anything long. "I'm a short story man." When I quoted Shakespeare on brevity being the soul of wit, he said, dismissively, "I never had no use for Shakespeare." Then, more thoughtfully, "I think it was the times he wrote in I didn't like."

Fred has a great appreciation for a story told well or a well-turned phrase. When I told him Jim's quip about the man who was so lazy he got his mother to chew his food, he rose to the challenge and rejoined with, "He was so slow he couldn't stop quick," which showed a sophistication with words that Jim would appreciate but never think of. It was an example of a kind of rhetorical put-down competition that is part of a more general tradition of storytelling here.

I have noticed that Fred's (and others') stories tend to be timeless—that is, they seem set in an unspecified time, like Bible stories, and unlike Homeric storytelling, short on details of place or appearance. If

I ask him when exactly something took place, he seems uninterested, pretends not to know, or is even slightly irritated.

After Fred nodded off, Shirley told me some more about Burnside's history, of which she is the informal chronicler. The Oldfords, she said, originally came from Bonavista to Salvage around 1820. Burnside, she said, was first settled in the 1880s by Fred's great-grandfather John Oldford and his three brothers. They built houses in and around the family "field" where Cleaves' house is now. Her uncle Con suffers from "hairy cell leukemia," one of only six known cases in Newfoundland—two others of which are his cousins. In fact, it's known in Newfoundland as "Oldford's disease." When Con was being diagnosed, the doctor told him it was a rare disease.

"It can't be that uncommon, Doc," said Con. "Two of my cousins have it."

She then showed me a photograph of her great-grandmother Charlotte Ann Oldford taken circa 1928 with her daughter and granddaughter. It is a remarkable picture. The three women are posed against a clapboarded wall, a bicycle leaning behind them. Charlotte, then in her fifties, looks like an old woman in her seventies, with a long prairie-style dress and hair pulled back in a tight bun. Her daughter Sarah, wearing wire-rimmed glasses and a long flapper-style dress, looks quite modern and is holding her infant daughter in her arms.

There is a solidity about the group, all of them facing the camera as if reaffirming not just their familial but their matriarchal identity. But Charlotte Ann, for all her lined, leathery face and thin lips, has kind eyes and a gentle smile. She also has remarkably strong features—high cheekbones, long straight nose, high forehead—and there is talk that there was some Indigenous blood in the Oldford line—not likely Beothuk, given the almost utter lack of contact between them and white settlers, but Mi'kmaq, who arrived in the early 1800s—that is, over two centuries *after* the first European settlers arrived.

Shirley has a great admiration for the strength of the old Oldford women. She spoke of her grandmother Minnie, Esau's wife, whose first son, Willis, was born on March 8, 1912, two months before the fire:

"They escaped the house by getting aboard a schooner on Gus Oldford's wharf and then they stood in the water, dipping their aprons in the sea and throwing them up over their heads and over their children's heads. Imagine, with a two-month-old! Most women today couldn't get you a cup of coffee!"

It's hard, she said, to pin down things like founding dates of communities and first settlers, and not just because of a general lack of written records or cemeteries. "Life here was more nomadic. Before they settled permanently, they might spend summers in Salvage or Flat Island fishing, and winters up here because it was closer to the woods. Some even wintered as far up as Magic Arm. The first child was born here because it was winter and that's where they were living." She said that when the men started going to the Labrador in the 1880s, it wasn't so important to be near the harbour or the local fishing grounds, so they built houses here, where the land was flat and they had some soil, though the "soil" here seems to be composed almost entirely of minute flakes of shale.

When I mentioned the apparent casualness with which her father and his contemporaries treated dates, Fred rolled over briefly to pontificate, sphinx-like, "All bedtime stories begin with 'Once upon a time,'" then rolled back to the wall. He seems to sleep with half his brain—like whales.

As I was leaving, Fred threw me one final hook: "You know, Genesis says that Adam was the first man. Then tell me, how did the Indians get to Newfoundland?"—I knew he wasn't waiting for me to answer—"Well, the Bible says that God created man, but it didn't say Adam was the *only* man he created. For all we know, there might have always been people here."

Newfoundland, then, as a kind of alternative Eden. For Fred, all theology is local.

The wind died by midafternoon. The light became not only intense but still, intensely still, as if light had stopped moving and inhabited the things it landed on: faces, clothes, the sides of houses, gravestones, ranks of trees, the way birds alight in branches, or on water, and fold into the stillness there. It was as if light had texture, pushing against the things it touched.

As I walked through the old cemetery late in the day, objects appeared drenched, weighed down with their own colors, so that once the light went out and darkness came, they might rise up, weightless, into the sky, or rebound, as the land does after long eons of burial under glacial masses that retreat and melt away. I kept waiting for a change—at six, six thirty, seven o'clock—but none came. The light simply *reclined* toward the west, lengthening, becoming less dense and heavy until, at sunset, it finally rested, dematerialized, on the calm waves of the bay, like a long, luminous sigh.

After dinner the sky had a clear wintry look, a clarity and fixedness I had not seen here before. The stars were like cut grey diamonds. Venus hung high, like a distant lighthouse in the sky. Orion, upright, stood in the west, his feet firmly planted on the horizon.

I walked up the road to the Hiscock House. Parked in front of the driveway was a green station wagon, dark and silent. I did not recognize it, but I let it go and walked past it up the hill. The big house was dark but bathed in moonlight. Its window frames and cornices cast highlighted shadows against the bleached facade. The little town slept below me. I could make out the silhouette of the church steeple against the eastern ridge and clearly see the crevices of the hills to the west. What an illusion of an isolated, complete, imagined world the scene presents! Like the world of the Breton courtly romances described by Auerbach, it seems a place out of any historical-political context, made up, existing solely for adventure and the opportunity to test one's mettle. Only the fair maiden is lacking.

I walked back down the hill, and when I got to the dark car, just to be certain there was no dead, stiff body inside it, I pulled out my Maglite and focused its beam on the car windows. They were occluded with condensed breath from inside. When I shone the light into the rear seat, I saw, as if underwater, two twisting and rocking bodies, like dolphins: a bit of orange shirt, blue sweater, green pants, no skin. It was like watching a front-loading washer, but soundless and unaware, like something seen in a dream. I put out my light and set off toward home, walking not quickly, listening for the disturbed start of an engine that never came, and thinking, *Here is, if not Burnside, at least* in *Burnside, the next generation carrying on.*

One evening, as I had just settled myself next to the reading lamp with a cup of tea, Cleaves knocked at the door and came in, saying, "I didn't know if you was in," as if to justify his knocking. He asked if my phone was working. Seems theirs had been out since they got back from Gander. "All we get is a roaring sound."

He sat down, keeping on his boots and coat but taking off his cap, and when I asked if he would like a drop of rum, he replied, overlapping my last few words, "Don't mind if I do." I put out a glass, water, and my plastic half-liter flask of Captain Morgan, which almost tipped over. He snatched and steadied it with remarkable swiftness, saying, "Watch out—that's too dear to spill." Then he gave me a mischievous grin and said, "Too dear to *drink*, for that matter!"

This was the most satisfying audience I've had with Cleaves since I've known him. He came relaxed and ready to talk, loosened a bit more by the rum, perhaps. He began by talking about the cod trap berth lotteries they used to have here—"the draw for fish and salmon berths"—much as they have province-wide drawings for moose licenses each year.

In the dying light he pointed out the window to the western point of Squid Island: "We had the finest salmon berths out by the p'int there. We had a net there for years, Fred and me. We could take twenty salmon a day by midmorning, have breakfast, and go in for a day of work at the mill—till we lost our license."

"Why did you lose your license?'

"Oh, b'y—'cause we was part-time fishermen, you see, and they took all that away twenty years ago. There used to be eighteen families on the island. The boys'd go down and set the lobster traps before going to school. Now they've raised a generation of idle youths. Now you tell me—does that make sense?

"I used to jig squid with my son Terry when he was home. It was all jigger and hook then. The squid never came in before August 1. Oh, my son, there used to be a mess of 'em 'd come in here—by the tickle—the place would stink. A man with six or seven kids could keep his whole family busy jiggin' and splittin' and dryin' 'em—we had ten flakes on the stage to clean and split and dry 'em. We could make a thousand dollars a month. Now you can't split a fish without a license. Now tell me—does that make sense?"

I pointed out that, of course, there are no squid anymore.

"That's because the foreign boats got 'em all outside the bay. But the fish now . . ." And with that he launched into a lengthy polemic on the vagaries and periodic disappearances of fish in the past. He remembered the crash of the cod stocks in the early 1930s, which made the Depression particularly hard here and sent legions of men away seeking work. "I recall as a young man how there was no fish here. You'd jig all day and just get enough to get the pot bilin'. When Henry Oldford's uncle'd go down to Salvage to visit, his wife would say, 'Now ask Uncle Jack for a nice scrod to bring back for Sunday dinner.' That's how scarce they were then. But they come back.

"And there's millions of fish in the bays now. They comes in to get the bait—the herring. Come in for the caplin, too, but the caplin's gone now. And you know if the cod was feedin' on the caplin, what else was feedin' on them that's now got to feed on the cod?"

Howard later told me that the salmon fishery, which was "still going strong" in '92, was closed a year after the cod moratorium "to keep 'em all for the rivers and the tourists, you see," which he regards as another example of traditional rights taken away from Newfoundlanders for the outside dollar. I asked him if he fished for salmon in the streams.

"No, boy! Fuck that! The only way I'd get them in the river is if they let me stretch a net across it—and there's a lot of that being done, don't you think." There's still a salmon fishery in Labrador, but he says, "They'll eventually come around to closing that, too, when they get enough tourists in the rivers there."

The following morning, I was having breakfast when Bert stopped by "to see how yous was getting on." As we were talking, the door opened and Darren Lane, the young man from St. Chad's whom Bert has hired to help him rebuild his wharf next summer, stepped in like a friendly whirlwind, dressed in dark overalls with wrenches sticking out of all his pockets. Already he had hauled out seven loads of logs and a load of birch this morning and wanted to know if Bert wanted the birch. Even when standing in the doorway, he appears to be constantly moving, giving off energy, with his big wide grin and shock of hair over his forehead. He transmits high-voltage optimism by his mere presence, and by himself gives you the impression that Newfoundland is a going concern, not a province of passive welfare recipients. Like filings to a magnet, Bert's attention was immediately drawn to him, and I was forgotten.

Later I met Darren at Ron's store, where he bought oranges, Cokes, and chips to "pay" the woman and man who helped him unload Bert's birch junks. He crossed back and forth across the floor in wide strides, joking, his hands chasing down stray bills in various pockets like hounds after rabbits, grabbing candy bars and cigarettes instead of taking change, dropping change on the floor and leaving it there. You can't help but smile when he is around.

At sunset I walked over to J & J's. They were watching the news, which stayed on the whole time I was there. Jim told me that Howard and Christine had just gotten back from visiting Uncle John in the hospital in St. John's.

"When we was on Flat Island, you know, if you had ever said to me, 'My son, someday you'll travel to St. John's in t'ree hours,' you know what I would say?"—poking my chest—"I'd say, 'You can go over the wharf. You can go over the wharf and drown yerself.'" Sometimes, he said, when the wind was wrong, it could take them two weeks to sail back to Flat Island from St. John's.

Jim, too, was in a particularly salty mood, and was intrigued when I told him I once stayed in St. John's in the house of a single woman.

"Well," he said, "I used to have two women in Petty Harbour, and two more in Maddox Cove. That's when I was going down there on the schooner—twice a year, you know—to get outfitted in the spring, and then to sell your fish in the fall."

I asked him if that was before or after he met Jessie. "Oh before, my son, no question before." Jessie gave me a slight smile.

I walked home about seven thirty under clear stars that got clearer as I outwalked the last streetlight, and then Bert's porch light, into the shadow of the night.

I wake the next morning to the sound of Lonz Crocker beginning to saw and split at the pile of wood he cut last winter. He says he is just doing it "to keep busy," since he can't get any logs out of the woods in warm weather.

I sit at the table with a mug of steaming tea and begin to saw and cut my morning loads of words. Like Lonz, I cut some to warm myself and others to sell. Unlike his, mine can serve both purposes. Like him, I cut only close to the road, and mostly in small areas, easy to haul out. Like him, my criteria for a good place to cut is "anywhere I can get my saw and ax into." Like him, I do not understand why some go so much farther than they have to go to cut. It is all Crown land here, for common use. I look around with amazed but subdued delight at the abundance surrounding me. Like him, I will take all but the smallest saplings, and anything that will burn—the staple, serviceable, ubiquitous spruce; the soft, light aspen, fast-burning, that soon rots and crumbles if not used; the hard, long-lasting birch and sycamore, or red maple, rare and prized; even the occasional piece of juniper, or larch, with its sweet, pungent, hot resin nuggets. Like him, I know the larger trees are to be reserved for logs, to build structures with, but sometimes I take them anyway and use them for lesser or more transitory purposes. Like him, I cut fast but waste fuel and have to refill several times throughout a morning. Like him, I sometimes continue to cut long after the blade has become dull. Unlike him, I usually do not cut the sticks into junks in the woods but haul them home in full lengths and leave them to dry before cutting and stacking.

I drove Fred up to Gander in his car again yesterday, leaving him to visit Betty in hospital while I did laundry, bank business, some grocery shopping, and visited the bookstore. They have moved Betty to a quiet room, waiting for a bed for her in St. John's. He goes up every other day with Shirley or Linda, and always greets her with a big hug and kiss. She immediately starts talking, the only person I have met here who can dominate and direct a conversation with Fred. He assumes a deferential, submissive air, and not, I think, just because of her situation. She said she was "proud" when she heard I was driving up with Fred, for his sake.

On the way back, Fred told a number of jokes, many of which were directed toward Catholics, expressing the kind of open religious bias one heard in places like Boston two or three generations ago, e.g.:

"Two nuns got a liquor store owner to sell them a bottle of whiskey, saying it was for Mother Superior, who was constipated. Later the owner saw them drinking on the street.

"'Sisters,' he says, 'I'm surprised at ye! Didn't ye say that was for Mother Superior's constipation?'

"'Ah, Holy Mother of God,' says one of the nuns, 'and isn't it surely—for won't she shit when she sees we coming in like this!'"

Shirley stopped by this afternoon for tea and stayed to supervise me making my first jar of partridgeberry jam. She had taken "a day off" last Wednesday when I drove Fred to Gander. She went to Eastport and had her hair done. It looks nice, and she seems more rested. Her friend Phil Pomeroy was coming from St. John's later that evening.

Shirley is my reality touchstone here, someone with a foot in each world, giving perhaps the most balanced perspective on life in Burnside, combining an unsentimental assessment of the situation with genuine attachment.

She observed, for instance, that Newfoundland has always been a place of change (borne out by the shifting history of settlement here) and that "I guess now we're in for another one." She discounted the importance of the collapse of the cod fishery as a major factor in these changes, saying that most of her educated generation left in the 1970s and 1980s, when the fishing was still going strong. Family heads, of course, always left the island to find winter work, or when the fishing failed, and she suggested that more would have emigrated earlier, but for the difficulty of leaving the island.

Confederation with Canada, she said, made leaving much easier, in terms of both transportation and employment opportunities on the mainland. Many places, like Burnside, never were primarily fishing communities (or stopped being so with the decline of the Labrador fishery in the 1970s). So, from Shirley's perspective, it has been more a combination of general factors—health and welfare benefits brought on by Confederation, better education (in spite of a continuing bias against education among most rural adults), improved roads, and better economic opportunities off-island—that has been responsible for changing Newfoundland's traditional culture.

She doesn't buy the idea that small communities like Burnside will become "ghost towns" in the near future. "Already," she says, "you're seeing the beginning of a new phenomenon: the children who left Newfoundland a generation ago, or at least their outport homes, are approaching retirement age, and many of them are talking about returning to their homes—more often than not their actual, family homes." (She gave me a sardonic smirk when I suggested that she herself was perhaps an involuntary, though not unwilling, pioneer in this movement, and might in time become the "revered elder" of Burnside in the twenty-first century, the way her grandmother Charlotte Ann was.)

She did admit that real values, like community, generational continuity, and deep local knowledge, were being lost and that it was important to try to find new ways to preserve them (which brings up the old conundrum: Can you preserve cultural values consciously without the earnestness of survival that produced them?). She reiterated her belief that the real effect of the cod moratorium was not on the commercial fisheries, but on the daily life of the older people here, such as not being able to go out and jig cod for themselves.

She also mentioned the "Oldford family salmon berth" out by Primer's Island and how "Dad and Uncle Cleaves always planned as how they would have that when they retired, to go out and set nets every day, and then that was taken away from them, too."

At 4:15, as I was coming back from practicing the organ at the church, the air had taken on a hazy quality, and wraps of fog were beginning to blow in from the outer bay, carding themselves through the stiff brushes of spruce. Layers of cloud already lay in the crevices of the Bloody Bay Hills and were beginning to fill the reaches between them. I walked out across the tickle bridge to the island and up onto the point behind Eldon Hapgood's house. From there the hills to the west became increasingly blanketed in fog clouds, dramatically backlit by the declining sun, the water turning golden before them.

I turned to go back, but a sound like tumbling water from the east and a sense of unknown spaces and mystery lured me into the woods. The fog closed in, the landscape shifted before my eyes, and all at once the ground seemed to move under my feet.

All it takes, it seems, is an unexpected turn of light, a change in vision or perspective, and all my recent grounding here dissolves like dreams, my footsteps and foundation turn to mist, and I am left naked and vulnerable as a deshelled hermit crab, incomplete and heartsore.

By the time I got back to the house, the air had partially cleared, leaving the water sharp and distinct while the hills remained completely swathed in batts of cotton, swallowed up as if these terribly ancient, terribly worn and stone-battered hills were only a mirage, an illusion allowed to exist here for several hundred thousand millennia, and now reclaimed by the Myth Maker.

Jim and Jessie stopped by after lunch today. Jim called up first—no identification or hello, just:

"You got company?"

"No."

"We're comin' up."

Jim told me some stories about Christmas on Flat Island, which essentially comprised twelve days of nonstop partying, starting on Christmas Eve. Jessie would leave Jim's clothes out about 4 p.m. and take off for the best party, not waiting for him to get home from fishing. Sometimes he would be too tired to go out, but his friends would come and drag him out of bed. Once, when he was really tired, he hid himself in the barn and covered himself up with straw, but they came by and found him, and dragged him out.

According to Jim, they were all "good people" on Flat Island, sharing what little they had, going to the Labrador, making fish, hauling wood.

"There were no rackets [fights], even with the moonshine. If someone was sick, or hurt, why then we all was. If you had to go to the doctor, they'd haul you into the big skiff with the engine and there'd be someone waitin' onshore to haul you out."

Even the Flat Island merchant—a man by the name of Burke—seems to have been a paradigm of commercial virtue: independent, fair, compassionate.

"If you didn't have enough for your gear for that spring, he'd say, 'Go out and get 'er, b'y. Go out and get 'er.'"

Jim painted a very generous and rosy interpretation of the merchant system, which was essentially designed to keep an outport fisherman in perpetual debt from cradle to grave.

"Now, I'm going to tell you something, my son, and you don't have to believe me. When I was a boy, there was an old fella on Flat Island had a salmon berth—that's what they did, you know, when they got too old to go to Labrador—and we were hauling his net with him one day when he turned to me to say, 'A man by himself is no good to no one'"—here I anticipated some homespun observation on communal cooperation—"'There's only one good place for a man, and that's in bed with a woman.'"

It was only after Jim and Jessie left that I realized they had come because they thought I was lonely.

There were nineteen worshippers at the evening service. The bell ringer, Sid Hunter, sixty-six, told me that he most likely has stomach cancer. Phil came with Shirley to the service. I had wondered about Fred's reaction to Shirley's girlfriend, a tall muscular woman with short dark hair who teaches math in St. John's. When I finally asked Shirley how her dad was dealing with Phil, she smiled and said, "Oh, they're fine. She and Dad bonded over plumbing."

I not only grow more familiar with the words and references here, but I begin to sense, and sometimes fall into, the rhythms and cadence of the talk, not just phrases and sentences, but larger movements, much of which are built, like the sea itself, on repetition—songs we sing together to one another, like whales beneath the ocean, to let others know where we are, and that we know of them.

Cleaves has got his new engine up and going on his wood saw and spent several hours cutting logs on it, lowering the logs from his tepee, sawing each in half, then feeding it through the bay of his saw. The belt ran over the rollers at each end, sliding from side to side and flicking back and forth like a thick black tongue, the teeth of the saw buzzing and whining, taking bites out of the log. Once the belt flopped off and Cleaves replaced it without turning off the engine.

As with most local practices, there was a pragmatic reason for having a tepee to store wood. His father Esau's house was built only a few years after the Great Fire of 1912. When Cleaves was born they didn't have enough money to build a woodshed. Wood couldn't just be cut and left outside, so it was stacked vertically and cut up as needed.

"Oh, wood was a problem in those days, because of the burn, you see. You could go up the tractor road and walk for miles and miles on the barrens. The fire was so hot it burned all the sod off—right down to the rock."

When the snow came, they took sleds pulled by huskies up to Magic Arm and cut wood; then in the spring they'd bring the motorboats up and haul out the wood and cruise it down to the wharf. He said it's only been a short while since they've been able to cut wood close to home. First the birch and aps would come back, and then the spruce. He has seen cycles and appreciates them.

Their mill, down by the wharf, was built up on sticks six to seven feet above the water. "We run it for twenty year, then tore it down, sold off the equipment. All that work, and it all come to nothin'."

But it was good while it was going?

"Oh, it was all right—just a living—nothing more." He does not share Jim's energetic nostalgia. Temperament colors history. Yet he has his own vigorous appreciation of things, more than he himself knows, or perhaps will let himself recognize.

Of all the men here, it is Cleaves who most reminds me of my father, in his quiet, unboastful manner, his unresentful, unbitter resignation or acceptance of life's terms that has allowed him to enjoy what it has offered him, in his patience and persistence, and a kind of perfunctory pessimism that is constantly belied by his industry on behalf of the future, and his twinkling blue eyes and sly smile.

SUMMER 1997

THE FOLLOWING SUMMER I RETURNED TO BURNSIDE WITH MY partner—and eventual wife—Kathy Shorr. It was a thirteen-hour drive from our home on Cape Cod to Burnside, plus a one-hundred-mile ferry crossing from Sydney, Nova Scotia, to the terminal at Port aux Basques at the southwest tip of Newfoundland.

By the time we reached the ferry terminal at North Sydney, it was raining and blowing hard. In the terminal, I stood with my face against one of the windows, watching the great blue and white shape of the *Caribou* turning slowly, smoothly into its mooring through the black heavy rain. A boy of about nine, highly excited, his hands cupped to his face at the next window, said to his mother, "Look at her come in! Look at her, Ma! I'll bet that ship is as big as two hundred—no, two thousand—dories, isn't it, Ma? It would take two thousand dories—two *million*—to equal that ship, right, Ma?"

I had made a reservation for a cabin, but most of the passengers were stretched out, not only on the seats but also on the deck floors and in the halls and between tables in the cafeteria, many with inflatable sleeping bags. An announcement came over the PA advising that for safety reasons passengers were not allowed to sleep on the floors and would they please remain in the seats, one to a person, as this regulation would be enforced. As far as I could see, the request was neither complied with nor enforced, and perhaps not expected to be.

We drove up the west coast on the Trans-Canada Highway, with the rugged and beautiful Long Range Mountains keeping us company to our right. Flat triangular slabs of old yellowed snow were stuffed into the upper crotches of the slopes, from which long, thin, twisting braids of waterfalls cascaded, like streams of mountain urine. At their base lilacs were blooming in profusion.

We arrived in Burnside a little before 5 p.m., and walked into Jim and Jessie's house without knocking as I called out, "Can a man get a cup of tea around here?" We were given supper: cold sliced Spam with bread and margarine, tea, and for dessert, a rhubarb and partridgeberry pudding with Cool Whip. There is still a preference for processed goods in rural Newfoundland households, especially when serving guests. When these became widespread in the 1960s, leaving a pile of tin cans outside one's house was often a deliberate sign of social position.

John Moss came over from next door. He had gone down to St. John's earlier this month, but the doctors decided not to operate and sent him home. Jim says he is "number one, my son, number one," and he did seem surprisingly alert and perky, though his face and skin had a sallow color. He said he still has some diarrhea, but otherwise feels "good," though he "does no work no more."

After dinner we went back to Mark and Fraser's house and started to unpack. About 10 p.m., I stood outside in the dying light and bright half-moon, with only a few nippers buzzing about my eyes, and heard the faint but distinct call of an owl—a series of short, hollow notes with a slight rise in pitch. It was the first boreal owl I had ever heard, one of those sounds that let you know you have moved out of your own region. The boreal owl's scientific name, *Aegolius funereus*, reflects the peculiarly haunting quality of its call.

At 7 a.m. this morning I left with Howard Moss to help him haul his lobster pots. Kathy walked with me down to his stage, where Uncle John was picking dried seaweed off the mesh of the drying nets. I was struck by how, in such small ways, an old and infirm man like John Moss can still participate in his son's fishing. This, I think, must have been one of the original motives for a man wanting sons—not simply to help him, and then support him, but so that he would, as long as he lived, continue to have someone to work with and for.

As we were casting off in Howard's skiff, Christine leaned her head out the window and said, pointedly, "She din't want t'go, deed she? She *c'd* go ef sh' wants t'."

We motored out a couple of miles northeast across the inner bay to Morris Island, a large round island perhaps a mile across, around which Howard had set his remaining pots. The topography of the island is much more dramatic than Burnside's: sheer cliffs of rose-colored shale rise two to three hundred feet high, with tortured columns of layered sea stacks lining up offshore like the frozen, futile longings of the earth itself. There were vast cave-like overhangs where seals might have sheltered in the spring; massive skirts of broad, dark brown kelp tossed and swung around the submerged rocks like the tresses of drowned women dancing in death; and everywhere the light off the water played on the vertical, slanted rock faces, twisting and untwisting interwoven braids of light. There were grassy ledges with tufts of yellow-blossomed succulents sprouting from the cracks. In one place a long, steep, narrow valley of grassed turf ran halfway down from the top of the cliff and ended in a sheer drop one hundred feet above the water. Howard said this was an otter slide—some drop!

We coasted along the rock shores, inlets, and tickles of Morris Island, looking for Howard's small, hand-carved wooden floats with his license—number 091310—painted in black. When he found one, he snarfed the nylon line with a long gaff, then, hauling the pot out of the clear aquamarine waters, he took out the lobster and placed it on the culling deck, where it adopted its defensive stance, arms and claws outspread and upraised, turning slowly in all directions, looking for all the world as if it were some crustacean gladiator that had just killed its opponent and was acknowledging the plaudits of the emperor and the crowd.

After he emptied a pot and tossed out the old bait, Howard pulled a cod head or flounder from the bait bucket, cut the flounder in two with his "filleting" (pronounced with all the consonants and accent on the first syllable: *fill*-et-ting) knife, impaled the bait on a wooden spike in the center of the pot, put a rubber band over the spear tip, and tossed the pot back into the water, where it slowly sank like a treasure chest.

The wooden pots, all made by Howard and his sons, are constructed from spruce limbs cut in the fall and soaked to make them bend. Pieces of slate from the landwash are pressed between the double-slat bottoms for weights. Two orange nylon twine funnels with metal rings—one leading into the first chamber, the other into the second—complete the pot: a simple but efficient device that reflects the Newfoundlander's willingness to adapt modern materials or devices to his traditional pursuits, though Howard continues to prefer the homemade items and local materials when they make economic and labor sense.

Howard said that each pot lasts about eight to ten years, surprisingly long, I thought. He is always making some, as many as fifty to sixty over a winter. "You never know how many ye'll need. One time there was such a sea that after there was no sign of a hundred pots."

It occurred to me that, except for boat motors and the rubber claw bands and nylon line, his method of lobstering has probably not changed significantly in generations. The equipment is all homemade, self-baited, and manually operated. It is the closest thing left to the old cod jigging: a single man in a small boat, out in the bay by himself, hauling in what the sea gives.

Hauling pots was a pleasant and somewhat mindless procedure. I asked the infrequent, idle question, and was content just to be ferried along the base of those monolithic rock cliffs with sea-reflected light shows dancing across their faces, their beetled brows crowned with a green thatch of wind-blasted evergreens. I lost track, after a time, of how many pots we had hauled, or even where we were. Occasionally the spire of St. Alban's would appear through the sloping cliffs, as if framed there. I said to Howard, "This is the kind of day that makes you think you'd like to be a fisherman." He grinned and replied, "Yes, b'y, even when you're not getting any fish."

Earlier that spring a large iceberg had entered the bay and finally grounded in ninety fathoms off Willis Island just north of Morris. While hauling pots, we occasionally caught sight of it between the headlands—a long white slab in the distance.

As we approached from the south, it appeared as a flat-topped, roughly trapezoidal shape, like a battleship or a submarine, arctic white on its upper slopes, with that unearthly, luminescent, neon green coloration just below the waterline. It appeared to be about 175 to 200 yards long, and some 20 yards high. Howard said that when it first came in it was "a hundred times this size, flat as a board, so that you could have landed a small plane on it." It was grounded now, so that it was impossible to tell how much of it lay beneath the water. However, all around us we could see, in the clear green depths, curved ledges and slopes of ghostly white spreading out beneath the boat like sunken coral reefs.

He circled around its eastern end until the back side came into view, a much more sculptured palisade, from whose smooth icy slopes cascades rang, with fantastic carved forms on the ridges, translucently blue. But the bulk of the mass was fluted into rounded blue columns that gave the whole mass the look of a giant ice sculpture of a Portuguese man-o'-war. We pulled back from it near the shore of Willis Island, cut the motor, and had lunch, watching the self-calving, self-immolating iceberg in all its doomed splendor.

After we had hauled or reset all of the pots, we set off for home, taking a straight shot back, turning into and bouncing over the wake of the ferry headed out to St. Brendan's. When we got to the wharf, Jim and John were there to greet us. It was a family scene reenacted for generations here: Jim with his little jig-like shuffle, arms crooked and held out at the elbows like chicken wings, a kind of quick old man's Walter Brennan-like gait instantly recognizable at a distance; John slower, bringing up the rear, his hands at his sides and spread out.

Howard pulled up beside one of two submerged boxes in which he stores the lobsters until a man from Traytown comes to get them. He put in all but two of the largest ones, which he gave to me. "I saved you one apiece—is that all right?"—then added a couple of flounders.

He may have earned fifty dollars and a bucket of bait for his morning's work. Like writing, fishing has unpredictable, mercurial recompenses; perhaps that is one reason why it fascinates me so.

He was out again the next morning in the rain, hauling more pots.

Bert in his yard this morning, scything his grass; Cyril and his son Josh arriving from Gander, unloading a trailer full of bikes and other supplies for a two-week stay; Essie waving to me from the Crockers' store steps; Fred stopping by to smoke a cigarette; young David Rockwood and his friends roaring around in two motorboats this morning ("Saturday morning cartoons, or speedboats?" said Kathy. "You choose"). All is well and bustling as Burnside opens up for the summer.

David Rockwood, like most outport children and adolescents, seems very much at home with adults, though he is only in Burnside in the summers. When we asked him his plans, he said he wanted to go to college, one that offers a three-year course in sports development.

"It teaches you, you know, to do things like design ski slopes and golf courses."

"So what do you plan to do—come back to Newfoundland and design ski slopes?"

"No, I figured I'd like to develop a kayaking tour business here—you know, adventure tours, lessons, that kind of thing."

Shirley later told me that he is going to have to do a lot better in math to get into college (Phil is tutoring him on the weekend), but I was pleased to hear of someone planning their life around their passion for a place. Rather than submitting to some deadening or dead-end job for forty to forty-five years so that he can afford to spend weekends or vacations at the tail end of his life here, David is planning to build a permanent place for his boyhood.

Suddenly the harbour is full of seiners from all over the east coast, come to unload their holds of caplin. Beginning at Cape St. Mary's about two weeks ago, the caplin work their way up the coast, massing offshore in great black clouds and coming ashore—or "rollin' in"—to spawn. The seiners and the whales follow them.* Each bay has its quota, as well as opening and closing times—usually 6 a.m. and 6 p.m. on a given day. Then, as one bay closes, another opens, and the seiners follow them from bay to bay, taking what they can and unloading them each night, sometimes twice a day, at the nearest available wharf.

Each fish plant also has its quota, a system that creates a buyer's market and helps drive down the price—in some places as low as two cents a pound. Fish are graded and priced according to size and the proportion of females with roe, which are more desirable. Most of the catch is bought by the Japanese, who have inspectors at the local plants.

It is also a system that is disadvantageous to the smaller (less than thirty-five feet) boats, or longliners, which use fixed gear and tend to

---

* Last week Shirley and Phil went down to St. Vincent's on the south shore, where they saw ten humpbacks "lunge feeding" on the caplin: hauling themselves up onto the shelf of the beach, then pushing off the shelf, as if pushing away from a restaurant counter, with their enormous tails.

fish in just one or two bays. They are outfished and outmaneuvered by the large seiners. Cyril thinks that this policy is deliberately designed to drive the smaller inshore fishermen out of business.

There seems to be quite a controversy about the caplin fishery here. Some, like Howard, look forward eagerly to a resumption of a caplin season. Others, like Cyril, maintain that it makes no sense to take the base of the marine food chain while stocks are still trying to recover.

Nonetheless, for the past few days the inner bay has been full of large seiners crisscrossing the waters, with names like *Randy Harvester* and *Random Belle.* They line up at the Burnside ferry wharf every evening, where large semi-trailer trucks that follow them up the coast wait with double stacks of large grey plastic fish bins.

Last evening, about 6 p.m., a half dozen of these behemoth trucks came blundering around the harbour road, puffing and wheezing diesel smoke and fumes as they waited down at the wharf. The little harbour, which usually sees only small boat trailers and the St. Brendan's ferry, seemed positively overwhelmed. There was much hauling of black nets and icing of the bins. On some of the smaller boats the caplin were hoisted out of the holds in large dip nets, looking like giant bags of gleaming, living silver coins—then hauled on ropes over the waiting grey plastic bins and released. The larger boats had hydraulic pumps that sucked the fish out of the holds and disgorged them in a continuous rain of fish and water into the bins.

The docking and loading continued well after dark, the wharf and boats lit up with working lights till 1 a.m. the next morning, we were told. At 9:45 we saw a group of eight or ten men, mostly in their late teens and early twenties, swarthy with sun and fish slime, walking back from Ron's store, where they had gone hoping to buy a beer or two, though Ron doesn't extend his hours for anyone.

In another couple of days, according to Cyril, it will all be gone, headed north, into Notre Dame Bay.

On Saturday, after the bean supper at the school, Cyril and Linda took Kathy and me with their daughter Julie and her friend Jemma on a ride through the inner bay—through Magic Arm, up Long Reach, and into Bloody Bay Cove.

We stopped at the Quarry Site and climbed up the wooden steps to the ridge. As the sun emerged from beneath a cloud cover, we sat on millions of flakes lying on the slopes of the quarry.

There is something astounding in the idea of men and women chipping away with small rocks at some large outcrop of rock year after year, for fifty centuries, for over two hundred generations—for what? For what? I can hear Jim's voice in my head: "It'll all be gone, b'y. It'll all fall down."

As we explored the quarry, I thought again how the modern conservation ethic is at odds with true human bonding with the past. We sat on the stones and wondered at the depth of the marks made on the land here. Kathy picked out a few partially worked points and fish-shaped flakes, while Julie and Jemma searched for ones that looked like whales. We were doing, I knew, what we should not be doing, what could no longer be done as this place passed from a site of anonymous, unrecorded history, of mysterious speculation and undirected exploration, into a place of public knowledge and public ownership.

But as if to confound such self-censorship, the debris of the worked mountain spread about us in such profusion as if to ridicule my misgivings that we might, somehow, either contaminate the present or offend the past. What is the past for if not to encounter it on an individual sensory and tactile basis, and so sense its passion of hidden life? Undirected play has always been the source of human achievement and curiosity.

At any rate, I could not, would not have stopped them from picking flakes, for this they would remember—imagination acting freely, randomly, and communally on the land.

"Which one do you think I should take?" asked Jemma, holding up four small stone whales.

The following day, when I was painting the Carpenters' shed trim, I saw a man walking down the road. He walked with a crippled, hobbling gait that reminded me of John Mills' character in *Ryan's Daughter*. When he came back a half hour later, I waved. He limped over and said, "Back from yer trip, are yer?" and I realized he thought I was Mark. Up close he looked even more like the mute Irish character in David Lean's movie. His right hand was crabbed, his mouth hung open with a few yellow teeth guarding its portal at irregular intervals and angles. His jaw seemed wrenched to one side, and his eyes stared off in two directions. He said his name was Ches (Chester) Oldford, and that he was staying up at Gus Oldford's house with his sister and her husband, who now own it. His grandfather, Old Gus, built a house here before the 1912 fire.

Ches is a cheerful, friendly, enthusiastic, and good-hearted soul in a warped body, exhibiting the natural or untutored good manners all of the older Newfoundlanders seem to have toward strangers. He offered me his crabbed hand when he left, but I demurred, seeing that mine was covered with paint, so he reached out, grabbed my waist with his crooked fingers, and shook it, then went hobbling off toward his house.

Later, Bert and Laura filled out some of Ches Oldford's story for me. He has been crippled since childhood ("since before you came here," Bert said to Laura) with "child paralysis." When Old Gus was alive and in the house, Ches used to come down and play cards with Bert and Laura all the time. When he left them, Laura would call Gus's house and say, "He's leaving now, Gus," so that if he fell down on his way and couldn't get up, they'd be looking for him.

Gus Oldford's uncles were Ed, Steve, and John, some of the first settlers from Salvage. Both Old Gus's and the Hiscock House were, of course, built after the fire, which Bert said was started three miles to the west by some Flat Islanders cutting birch and spruce "rinds"—large pieces of bark used to cover their fish flakes at night or during rain.

"A fellow named Samson lit a fire," said Bert, "not expecting it to catch in the wind and travel t'ree mile. She burned every house from the p'int down to the harbour and across the island. The only one that didn't burn was Tom Ralph's, the second house from the end of the island. He stood his ground and the fire went right around him.

"After the fire most people just built a kitchen shed, just enough to get started again; that's what John Oldford did. That part of the house that's on the back—that come first. He only built the rest of it later, to impress people."

The house somehow passed to a family named Smit, then Gus obtained it "because of some money owed him," and he in turn sold it to Will Hiscock, after whom it is now named. Will and his wife Liz were killed twenty years ago in a car accident going down to St. John's on the Trans-Canada Highway.

"It were his own fault," said Bert. "I think his truck was overloaded with fish and other things. He tried to pass one of them transport trucks on a curve and lost control."

Then Laura said, "I think Liz was nervous to drive. One time she drove the car through Minnie Oldford's fence. They come in and sit down for tea and Will says, 'Quite an evening—we gets to go tru a fence, come out alive, and get a cup o' tea in the bargain.' He was tryin' to cheer her up, you see."

Kathy flew home from St. John's on Saturday. On Sunday, a rainy evening, the congregation was even smaller than before, fifteen I counted.

I walked up the dirt road to the church where Sid Hunter began to peal the bell at 6:15. From outside the bell had the iron-like peal of a hammer on an anvil, God forging the faith of these people on this hard rock of a land. I suddenly realized that I was the only one here now who walks to church.

And what is the "faith" that is so talked about in Newfoundland memoirs and histories? In Squid Tickle, at least, it is simple and unostentatious but strong, one that runs quietly through people's daily lives like a sustaining but unobtrusive chord. I have sensed nothing evangelical in anyone here, and certainly no insistent Puritanical or Calvinistic fatalism. Still, there is a pronounced acceptance of death in particular, almost a respect for it, as an expression of God's will. As Jim Moss said when Ralph Humphries died in a car crash last fall: "It were his time to go." Death is not an indication of the Deity's personal displeasure with individuals or communities, not a *judgment*, but a natural fact. It seems understandable and natural among people who, though proud and independent in spirit, have been powerless for so long against the sea, the fish merchants, and the edicts from St. John's politicians—forces natural, economic, and political.

Given the strong, and often strong-willed, character of so many Squid Tickle men and women, they seem curiously passive as a congregation. Marilyn's sermon was, as always, straightforward, unimaginative, and solid. The message was: To be strong in our faith, we must ask questions about it—this for a congregation that sits so quietly, reserved, and meek before ecclesiastical authority. When Marilyn asked them from the lectern whether the rained-out spring flower service in the cemetery should be rescheduled, there was a long embarrassed silence, like that following a teacher's question to an ill-prepared class. Even Fred, sitting in his pew, seemed cowed, like a hangdog, sullen schoolboy.

"Well then," Marilyn finally said, "I'll just come up with one and put it in the newsletter."

The St. Alban's congregation seem to carry within themselves, unspoken, the recognition of how much the function as well as the size of their church has shrunk over the past generation. A plaque in the "porch," or entrance foyer, speaks volumes:

**The youth of St. Alban's served their
God and church through AYPA
[the Anglican Young People's Association]
from 1960 to 1975.**

The population of Squid Tickle peaked in 1961 with 213. In 1991 it was 68. At my own last count, it was 36.

They know there will be no more youth meetings here, no more local weddings, christenings, or confirmations—only funerals. Or if there are, they will be for outsiders: returning children or grandchildren or come from aways trying to borrow or appropriate a sense of history and belonging, that sense of shared and rooted community that seems wedded to necessity and an acceptance of fate.

That night I felt a strong sense of "going out" in this small congregation. We wheezed through four hymns. I played the first two lines as an introduction, then paused and plunged in, hoping for the congregation to follow me, which they did, though with a dragging hesitation that threatened to stop the singing altogether. We sounded something like a herd of whales.

When the service let out it was raining, and dark. No one invited me back to their house for rum and gumdrop cake. I walked home to the now-empty house, feeling sorry for myself, and lay in the dark listening to a CBC radio dramatization of a Margaret Atwood novel.

Sometime during the black night, the wind shifted northwest and the temperature dropped suddenly. I got up at two, peed, secured the windows, and lay back down, listening to the wind blow and whistle endlessly, as I thought of the burnt figures of fishermen in a dark gale like this, reefing sails and cutting anchors, giving themselves over to the mercy of the seas.

These people's lives—in fact the whole history of Newfoundland—is that of ordinariness lived on the edge of terror and sublimity.

The low rock ridges just offshore have the long, dark shadows of late afternoon on their south faces. The golden rockweed of noon has dimmed to the dunnage of a backlit sun. The ripples on the water are soft, deep blue, endlessly moving, ever staying. It is a timeless moment—no boats, no noise on the bay. Two girls, or young women, sit facing one another, backs against the pilings at the end of Gus Oldford's wharf, talking quietly. The hills are sleeping bears, a rumpled pile of coarse animal pelts. There is only the quiet, steady hum of the refrigerator and an occasional chirp, the soft exhalation of the wind through the open window, ruffling the delicate petals of the daisies in my table bouquet. The raspberry blossoms lining the drive are threaded with the slow-motion buzzing of heavy-bodied bumblebees. It is a timeless moment, and I am all too conscious of time at my back. I think you can only fully experience a place when you are alone. You cannot live in the consciousness of two things at once.

Wind stiff this morning from the north-northeast straight across the bay, some whitecaps, hills a mixture of sun and clouds, creating ranges of shadows superimposed on those of rock and trees. The first flames of fireweed blossoms by the side of the road are beginning to climb their stalks and ignite the fields.

Why have I become so attuned and attentive to flowers here? Where does this urge come from to delineate their form and details in pencil sketches, something I have never done before? More than the massive, rocky coastline or the eerily luminous luxury liners of icebergs sailing southward, more than the vast herds of caribou or thousands of moose, the millions of seabirds nesting on rocky crags around its perimeter, more than the endless, untracked interior of fir and spruce and uncounted bogs, more even than the people themselves, growing older with each year, the shrinking towns, the rotting wharves and old fish flakes—more than any or all of these, it is the spring and summer flowers, with their delicate blossoms and fragile supports, their touches of flame and snow across the landscape, that somehow express the essence of life here.

They represent a continuity, as tenuous and yet as deeply rooted as the oral history that still sings and murmurs within the old flat-roofed houses, around oil kitchen stoves and linoleum floors, that has not yet been completely drowned out by the white noise of television and radio.

Today Jim told me his flying saucer story, which he prefaced with his usual disclaimer: "Now, brudder Bob, I'm goin' to tell you a story—you might a heard it before, from me, or Uncle John, or Howard—now, you can believe me or not, but it's a true story, and if it's not true, den yer not in Burnside—ya understand?

"It was on the twelfth of August, in the year that poor Aunt Sadie died—Uncle John's wife, she died of cancer that year, in July, I think. Anyway, it was the evening of the twelfth of August and Uncle John, Howard, and meself were up to Fair and False Bay on the squid-jiggin' ground. It was dark and we was jiggin' and not gettin' much and all of a sudden we seed this light out on the water, no furder away den from here to the tickle, and I t'ought she was a steamer, with lights all on her side, so I grabbed de flashlight, shone it on her, and up she rose"—his bent arms rise up like a skinny grizzly bear—"and Bob—now, this is true, as true as the Lord is in Heaven, if dere is a heaven—she was like this"—and here he gets up and gets two shallow pie pans out of the cupboard and puts one on top of the other—"round, ye see, and about sixty feet wide, with lights all around the sides, and as soon as I showed the light on her she goes all dim like this"—his voice drops to a whisper—"and she rises up over us, no farder den from here to the ceiling corner, and after a while a spotlight comes on us, so bright you could pick up a pin off the bottom of the boat—and she stayed dere all night and she made no more sound than this"—here he picks up the bowl of sugar and holds it soundlessly in the air—"and when dawn comes she rises up like this"—he raises the can of evaporated milk slowly—"and then she's gone."

"And what were you doing all night?"

"Oh, we was jiggin', but I only caught one squid till morning and then I got half a barrel. Reg Lane, he was out on the eastern point of Squid Island and he sees the saucer up by us, and when he gets into his wharf he asks us, 'What was dat, b'y?'"

It's not so much the story Jim tells as the way he tells it: the rhetorical elaborations, the verbal asides, the physical gestures, the appropriation of domestic objects to illustrate it—the born strategies of the native storyteller.

That evening Jim's daughter Julia and her husband Gerry Squires stopped in to visit, and I witnessed a full-fledged performance of Julia's temper. We were all sitting around the kitchen table drinking Golden Wedding whiskey and ginger ale. Even Jessie had a small glass. Julia has Jim's gift for vivid storytelling, but whereas Jim's default manner is celebratory, Julia's is critical. She held forth uninterrupted, first on her and Gerry's plight as managers of the White Sails Cabins in Eastport, dealing with demanding guests, parents who don't control their kids and let them climb up onto the roof of the inn, etc., followed by a long diatribe on how "kids are worse now than they were even ten years ago, and you can't talk to them, they have more rights than the parents do," and so on.

But she hit her stride when she spoke of the ineptitude and inadequacy of the Newfoundland health system. Specifically, she recalled

Jim's gallbladder operation some fifteen years ago (he had shown me the long vertical scar on his abdomen the day before), how the Gander hospital was a "slaughterhouse," how Jim was taken up there in great pain and operated on by a Dr. Lou, who told Julia and Jessie that they'd removed Jim's gallbladder and gallstones and sent him home. A few days later he was in even greater pain, so they took him back up to Gander and Julia got a call the next day saying they were taking him down to St. John's "for observation" but that he'd be back in Gander by 5 p.m. and the nurse would call.

"Of course, he never was and she never did."

When Julia called back, they told her Jim had been admitted to St. John's and she would have to claim his clothes, purse, and watch in twenty-four hours or they would throw them out. "I said that if they did, I'd come up and throw *them* out!"

This situation went on for a while, leaving Jim languishing in limbo somewhere in St. John's until Julia finally learned they went in to operate again and discovered that neither stones nor gallbladder had been taken out. It seems that during the previous operation in Gander they found an infection and cleaned it out but couldn't remove the stones then. Julia was furious and threatened to take Jim's gallstones out and have them put inside Dr. Lou. She was still mad at Jim for not letting her sue the doctor.

"Dad, you could have money now for all the pain you went tru!"

Finally she recounted the time she took Jessie to St. John's because her mother was short of breath. They put her in the ER, where she was questioned by a Chinese doctor:

"Now, I'm not prejudiced. After all we're all God's children, though some are more damaged than others, but there's some languages, you know, that you can understand, and others you can't. Well, I was sitting outside the screen and I could hear the doctor shouting at Jessie: 'You're a smoker!' See, 'cause she was short of breath. Well, I finally couldn't take it no more and I pulled back the screen and I shouted to him, 'Doctor, I'm the smoker, but she's not! She's never smoked in her life! And you're supposed to be a doctor, and you don't even give her a chance to answer before you ask another. Now you ask her nicely and then shut up and let her answer!'"

Sometime later, I had the opportunity to talk with a doctor from St. John's. When Julia's name came up, he said, "Ah yes, that would be Mrs. Squires, the patient advocate from hell."

Given the passivity with which most Newfoundlanders I met seem to react to figures of authority, I found Julia's unbridled advocacy on behalf of her parents and herself admirable and refreshing.

Yesterday afternoon, walking around the curve at the high part of the tickle road, watching the banks of fair weather clouds ranked in the west with the sun slipping down between them, I realized that my days here have begun to mingle and blend together into "Burnside time," that I have already begun to lose track of dates or days of the week or even how long I have been here—a few days or a few years. Time compresses here; events and people and generations meld seamlessly together with the rest. Though individual events can be picked out with remarkable clarity and detail, there is no specific time to hang them on. It has to do both with the cyclicity of life here and with its centripetal/centrifugal setting. Like the year, all things go out from and return to one place.

The wind has been blowing stiffly from the west for two days now. Bloody Bay is full of whitecaps, like a conquering army that never arrives. Now the sky to the west is clouding up and darkening, and there are fine, transparent, dark showers of rain falling in the north, which Jim says will pass us by. A big sky is one in which you can see other people's weather.

At dinner Jim referred to me as a "bedlamer boy," a term I had not heard before. According to the *Dictionary of Newfoundland English*, it refers to a young man, "seventeen or eighteen years old," and is named after the bedlamer, or adolescent harp seal. If this is not identification with one's surroundings, I don't know what is.

"I'll tell ya, brudder Bob—it was a poor life we had there, a hard life, y's b'y." He doesn't even need to say Flat Island now.

I can see that there may come a time when Burnside will be my Flat Island, when every time I take a step my foot lands on a memory. Every year or two another light that has been here for a hundred years goes out—like Bert Burden's or John Moss's, or Sid Hunter's. Some of those lights might go back on when family comes down to stay in summer, or when outsiders like me begin to acquire them—or they may just stand and fall, or burn, as so many have, phoenixes no more.

I just witnessed a small but significant ritual, or at least a diminished contemporary version of it, an event that has been repeated endlessly here for several generations. Harold Hiscock went out this morning about 6:15 in his small boat with his two sons, William and Simon, and Simon's friend Len from St. John's, hook-lining for cod. They came back about 9:30 with five small tomcods and one good fish—eight or nine pounds.

Harold cleaned the fish on the splitting table at the end of the wharf, throwing the guts into the water among the thin, furred stalks of kelp that rise like thin, green-brown plumes of smoke, then lie flat on the surface at low water. Small green-brown crabs with tiny legs crawled out and dragged away the belly-white scarves of fish entrails (like the Morlocks of H. G. Wells' *The Time Machine*, emerging from their underground lairs to claim the white sacrificial bodies of the Eloi), while Will washes off the gutted fish in a salt beef bucket.

When Harold gutted the one large fish, he cut out the heart and called to his cairn terrier, Glasgow, on the other side of the tickle, who trotted with halting eagerness on his short little legs across the bridge and out onto the wharf. The heart, an irregular red lump about the size of a large strawberry, was still beating regularly, with that slightly off-center thrusting motion.

"He likes 'em that way," said Will as he picked up the heart and set it down on the weathered planks for Glasgow, who snatched it up like an unconsidered trifle, and snuffled over to the bloodied, wet table, looking for more.

That evening I was invited to a chicken and macaroni casserole dinner at Cyril and Linda's. Two of their friends were there: Terry Matthews and his wife Jacinthe, a French Canadian from Montréal who is a flight attendant with Air Canada. Terry is Cyril's age and spent summers here as a boy with his grandparents, also Oldfords. Some years ago, he bought the house next to Linda and Cyril, and they spend regular time here in the summer.

Linda said that her brother Paul and Angela had been going together about four months, and that "he's happier than we've ever seen him. She's the second Angela he's had, which makes Dad happy because he doesn't have to worry about calling her the wrong name. She's got my seal of approval—she doesn't get tired and she can *bake bread!* Oh Lord, all those young women today—they're always so tired. They don't have children, so what are they tired about? Well, we're all hoping with this one—I'm tired of meeting new girlfriends!"

For dessert Linda served us homemade blueberry and partridgeberry wine, after which there ensued a lot of good-natured, bawdy joking between the men and women:

"Well," said Terry, who had just finished playing a game of softball in their yard, "I guess us old guys can still get it up—in the air!"

"Yeah," Linda retorted, "but you need a wooden bat to do it with!" and then turned beet red, nonplussed when she realized that her son Josh was getting, and enjoying, all the double entendres.

At one point Linda leaned over to pour me more wine and the bottle hit the glass so hard it started to topple. I reached out and caught it, but my jerking it back caused the wine to splash all over Linda's green short-sleeved top, her face, her bare arms, and my hands. She laughed her deep, throaty laugh, touched my shoulder, and wiped wine from herself and my hands with a napkin.

"That was a moment, eh?" she said, and there was another deep flush on her face—not, I think, from embarrassment at her clumsiness, but because it was a genuine erotic moment and we both knew it. She is one of those earthy, sensual women—and I have met many here—who, secure in their marriage to a quiet but strong man, are able to open themselves to these moments of unanticipated sexual electricity, which, when discharged without shame or innuendo, form one of life's small but incandescent pleasures.

Linda's father Con is the only one of the four Oldford brothers who went to university. He met his wife Audrey in Port aux Basques, teaching high school there. They married and he went back to university for two years with two small kids.

"It wasn't easy," Linda said. "We lived in a basement apartment and didn't have much. We weren't poor—or maybe we *was* but we didn't know it. When Dad brought something unexpected home—ice cream or crayons, that was special. We were as happy as dogs. When he finished at MUN we moved back here and lived in the old house, the one Grandfather Esau built. Dad taught at the Eastport school—math, English, economics, whatever they needed. We didn't have electricity, or indoor water, not even a radio. We used to gather up at Shirley's, and Aunt Betty would read us stories. When she read from Scripture the other night in church, I wanted to tell her how much it reminded me of those nights, of the comfort I still felt."

The summer evenings here are filled now with the shouts, laughter, voices, and quarrels of children and adolescents, all of whom seem to be children here. David Rockwood is fifteen but acts twelve. All ages seem to associate and get along, the older ones taking care of the younger. When you hear a group of them, unseen around the curve of the road, they sound like the ghosts of voices once heard here, now gone—post-historic.

I met such a gaggle of children's voices in the dark last night about 9:15 as I was walking back from Jim and Jessie's, just beyond Harold Hiscock's bungalow. There were five of them: Josh Oldford; a teenage girl with long dark hair; a small boy named Sam, no more than five, wearing a full-length purple raincoat with hood, who proudly said to me, "I remember going here when I was little"; a ten-year-old Simon Hiscock, who kept saying, "I'm only ten years old!"; and a tall, skinny, bespectacled boy of about fifteen with light hair in a ponytail who turned out to be Will Hiscock, the older son of Harold and Susan Cummings, and the grandson of his namesake, Will Hiscock ("I'm Will the Fourth"), who once owned the Hiscock House on the hill, which was where they were heading to spend the night.

Will was, like most Newfoundland adolescents, remarkably at ease with adults. He and his family live in St. John's on Ordnance Street, "right downtown." He told me that after resettlement, his grandfather came from Flat Island and, with 60 percent of the other Flat Islanders, moved to Mount Pearl, outside of St. John's.

"They all ended up on the same street together, but Grandad couldn't stand it there in the city, so they bought the house out here."

After his grandfather and grandmother were killed in a highway accident, there seems to have been a profusion of relatives with an interest in the house. ("I think about twenty-five of us have keys.") His parents, Sue and Harold, seem to be the main caretakers, but his mother wanted a place of their own, so they bought the small bungalow by the tickle. With Josh carrying Sam on his back, they looked like a motley crew of characters out of a children's book from the forties or fifties, unsupervised and out for adventure.

When I later met Will's mother Susan, I told her what an incredible place it was to have for kids to go to: a large, turreted house on a hill at the very end of a dark road beside the sea, where a group of five-to-fifteen-year-olds were set loose by their parents, given the keys and free rein.

"Yes," she replied. "Needed a break from the grown-ups for a night."

I had a real "dinner" with J & J tonight: potatoes, new turnips, carrots, "plan pudding"—all served on a plate covered with gravy—and a plate of roast chicken. John talked about his three winters "swiling," that is, "sealing," in the early 1930s. He was on one of the Bowring boats out of St. John's with a hundred and fifty men—all on shares. One year he made fifty dollars.

They were "on the ice" for two months—from the end of March to the end of May, and when they got back, they turned right around to go out on schooners up to the Labrador to fish all summer. Occasionally, if a ship was stuck in the ice, they would put gunpowder charges on long sticks, lever them under the bow of the ship, and set them off, first on one side, then the other, "wigglin'" the boat along to widen the channel. He recalled one winter when a line of men was hauling a ship out of the ice-covered Narrows in St. John's Harbour by hand—a dangerous business in any case—"and one man, he held onto the line a bit too long, and the bow of the boat hit the ice pan he was on and toppled it, dropping him right in the path of the ship. She went right over him and he was tore to pieces. It were a poor life, y's b'y."

As the sun slips down behind the hills, I watch each day undevelop through these windows. The bright vastness of the day diminishes. I become more aware of sound, of wind and water, and of the flexed, infinitely delicate, infinitely patient forms of mosquitoes on the gridded barrier between us. Now comes the soft sound of the water lapping in the darkness outside and the sweet moaning of the wind wrapping itself like a cloak around the house. These are the real mysteries, the true companions of one's life—reliable, continuing, speaking the oldest language to our oldest ears.

In the morning there is a haze of meditation over the land and sea that keeps me from finishing painting the house trim. I find I want to look at rocks, or perhaps old boats, all day, to study the soft blues and greens that cling to the hills this morning, like the congealed breath of the night, to exhale my stopped-up being into the endlessly moving, endlessly still forms before my eyes, motion and stillness that both keep me here, steady, writing in my chair, and move my very being out onto the moving water and out of sight.

The next time I stopped in for tea at Linda's I noticed a large, oval-framed black-and-white photograph of a young soldier in the wool cap and jacket of the Great War. This was Cyril's grandfather, Private Hubert Oldford, killed in action in France, November 20, 1917, aged twenty-six and a half years. His wife, Clara, died in 1913, in childbirth.

So Cyril's father, himself killed as a young man in WWII, was an orphan at two or three.

"Were you raised by your other grandparents then?" I asked Cyril.

"Yes."

Linda: "He wasn't raised up—he was beat up."

Cyril: "Great-grandfather used to carry a big black Bible under his arm all the time. He was probably the most ungodly person I ever knew." (All this said in the calm, soft, unperturbed voice that is characteristic of him, such a contrast to Linda's energetic, emotion-laden manner. She is, in a sense, his counterpart and outlet.)

Linda: "There was money, you see—because he was killed overseas, and they lived mostly off that. But a lot of kids then, I always say, they wasn't *raised* up, they was *beat* up."

Then from Cyril's porch we saw an ambulance come out of the west road, lights flashing. I was afraid it might be Bert or Laura, but it turned out to be Manny Oldford, an elderly man in one of the houses behind the Mosses'. "Oh," said Cyril, "he's been sick a while—his legs just give out under him."

When I later told Bert I was glad it wasn't him, he grinned and said, "Not yet, b'y—not yet," with that characteristic backward cock of his head. He had spent the day scything grass around his house, where it lay in long swaths, subdued once again by one whom it will one day subdue.

This afternoon Jim was giving me his usual line, "You know, it's good to make friends, but when ye goes, then you wish you'd never taken up wi' the man," etc. But there was a glint of mischief in his eyes when he said, "Now, someday, my son, you'll come back here and it'll all be gone, and you'll stand right 'ere and you'll say, "'Ere was where Jim and Jessie lived, and over there, Christine, and there was the post office stood, I think 'twas there," as if he were on Flat Island wandering around the ruins; and all at once I was seized by a terrible sense of anticipated loss that none of his more sentimental twaddle had ever roused in me.

SUMMER 1999

IT WAS TWO YEARS BEFORE WE RETURNED TO BURNSIDE. IT WAS an easy ferry crossing this time from North Sydney to Port aux Basques, calm and fairly clear. It has, in fact, been an easy trip overall, and we have taken our time crossing the island, not getting tired, taking things as they come.

The first person we met was Henry Oldford, coming from "the new cemetery," where he had just put seed on the family plot.

"Had five deaths in my family since I saw you last," he told us in that matter-of-fact way Newfoundlanders characteristically convey bad news, including a sister in St. John's and Ellis Oldford, who lived next to Cyril. Sid Hunter, who had had stomach cancer when I was here last, also died this past year. Cleaves walks with a cane now, having fallen from a ladder and broken some vertebrae in his back. His tepee of logs, all cut up, is gone and won't be replaced. Lonz Crocker had a heart attack, "or so they tells me," maybe angina, and Fred a cataract operation. Shirley is "all burned out" from being secretary for the Heritage Association and has gone to visit Phil in St. John's for ten days. Her mother, Betty, is back home and doing okay, though she's "full of drugs and has everything wrong with her."

Only Derek Bowring, in his perennially clean and ironed white shirt, and his black pound dog Toup seem robust and hearty.

Both of Howard Moss's sons have left Burnside. Michael and his wife, Patty, have been in Calgary working for a year, and Chris is in school in St. John's studying computer science. But Howard has had a good year fishing. Lobsters have been plentiful, and they've been getting a good price for culls ($1.50 per pound), over twice what they were getting last year.

Howard spoke of his father, John: "I still misses him a lot. He's been gone two years, but I still miss his face. Whenever I came back into the wharf, he was the first person I'd see—waitin' to know how I made out. I'll keep his house up another year, I guess, to see if Michael's going to stay in Calgary. Then I'll probably tear it down. I don't think I can sell it. There's no land to go with it, and if you leave 'em two or three years, they starts to go bad. So I'll probably tear 'er down."

There is a new minister in town: Father Paul Thoms—a young man from Gambo, who replaced Marilyn a year ago and serves the seven churches in the parish of Salvage, which includes Burnside. His reception seems to have been less than enthusiastic. Henry claims he is making changes in the church without consulting the congregation. "Essie Chaytor was very upset that he arranged the sale of the church hall in St. Chad's on his own. When the parishioners complained, he told them, 'You can have cold suppers in the church if you wants them'—so she and her mother don't go anymore."

When I asked Fred how the new minister was, he gave me a slow look and said, "New."

With Bert and Laura having moved into a retirement home in Glovertown last winter, our road feels strangely deserted. There are no longer any year-round residents on it, and none of the summer people have shown up yet. No one is scything Bert's grass, and his phoenix tree's apples will not be picked or counted or stolen.

As with "quaint" local names, one must be careful about customs here, which to an outsider's eye may seem to be examples of crude or lazy practice, but which, to the local inhabitants, have a solid logic behind them. For instance, the other day I asked Cleaves why the planks on so many of the wharves are not nailed down (or only fastened at the ends). "We thinks they last longer that way," he replied—meaning, where their undersurfaces are not nailed to the "sticks" of the frame, they dry out more quickly and so rot more slowly. It was a practice that, in the old days, may have been adopted partly because nails were expensive. He allowed, however, that the "longers" might blow off from time to time in storm winds.

On Sunday evening I went to the 6:30 Communion service, the Reverend Thoms presiding. Gus Oldford's daughter pumped and played the old harmonium, wheezier than ever, as the congregation followed, draggier than ever.

All of the readings and the liturgy were from the revised Anglican *Book of Alternative Services*, but when we got to the end and the Lord's Prayer was said, everyone instinctively ignored the written text and recited the King James Version with the energy of the familiar.

It pleased me that they did so. The liturgies of any religion have established themselves for good reason. They touch deep chords in our nature. Like Chomskyan syntax, they have deep structure, but the voiced expression is specific to geography and helps to tell us where we are.

Though I have long ceased to be a practicing Christian or even a regular churchgoer, nothing in my later life or conscious beliefs—neither Hebrew prayers nor Yeats's poetry nor New Age "hymns to the earth" will ever touch me like the Confession and Absolution, the Comfortable Words, the Ecclesiastic Prayer, the Intercession, the Apostles' Creed or the Lord's Prayer, the Blessing and Dismissal. I still chafe at the "modern" renderings of Scripture, liturgy, and hymns—however politically or historically corrected they may be—and silently cheer whenever this congregation ignores them.

Kathy and I had supper this evening at J & J's: fish and brewis, fresh frozen and caught by Jim in last fall's food fishery, with great slabs of soaked and boiled hardtack, all broken up and mixed together with heaping spoonfuls of rendered pork fat.

Jim told again how it was his brother, Lew Moss, who was one of the two survivors of the *Lloyd Ellsworth* disaster in Magic Arm in May-month of 1933. The other was Mike Troke, who grabbed Lew by the shoulder (Lew says he can feel that hand on his shoulder to this day) and kept him from going under.

Jim said Lew and Mike managed to get the remaining motorboat off the schooner and went to Burnside, where they telegraphed the news to Flat Island (there was only one phone on the island then, in the post office). Louis Samson, skipper of the *Lloyd Ellsworth*, was lost. His brother Abe managed to raise the schooner and took her fishing the next summer, giving the ship's share to Louis's widow. Five Samsons and a Kelly, all from Flat Island, were drowned, an odd fluke of a disaster that only makes sense in the details.

After dinner, the four of us took a walk down Hollett's Tickle, Jim pointing out all the houses that had been moved there from Flat Island and the names of their owners. After nearly every one he'd point and say, "He's dead," or "She's dead." It began to take on a morbid tone, with Jim interjecting his favorite mantra, "She's gone, b'y—all gone." But at some point it unexpectedly turned into a running joke, as we took turns pointing at each house and chanting together—"And *he's* dead!" and "*She's* dead, too!" Even Jessie got into it, and after we started back and passed the new cemetery, I turned to her and said, "You know what you can say about all the people in there," and she chimed in, giggling, "They's all dead, too!"

It was a light moment.

When we got back to their house, Kathy asked Jim what he did after he came to Burnside.

"Well, I'll tell you now, that's da trut'—the fishin' on the Labrador give out—all gone—that last winter on Flat Island dere was only twenty families and we was one of them. And the next year we was gone. And all the schooners was gone, all of them. The year after that I went back to the Labrador with the Fisheries Products [a fish processing company], you know, and then after that I worked in Gander. Worked there fifteen years—building dry wells and bridges and things like that, you know? For five or six years I went up there on Monday morning and came back Friday evenings, yis b'y."

Even though his family saw him every week, Jim was still away much of the year, in a strange new place, and even at that he was luckier than many of the resettled men who had to go to St. John's, or even to the Canadian mainland, to find work when the government-sponsored "Growth Centers" didn't pan out quite as Joey Smallwood, Newfoundland's first premier, thought they would.

Kathy asked Jim what did a man on Flat Island do if he didn't like to fish?

"Oh, we all fished."

"Did you like to fish, Jim?"

"I—I loved it."

"But were there some who didn't?"

"Oh, I suppose there was a scattered few of them that didn't."

"And they left?"

"No, most of them stayed. They didn't have much choice. There was nothin' else to do there but fish."

"Couldn't they have gone into the church?"

"Oh, if you went into the church, they wouldn't have fed you."

"I mean, become a minister."

"Oh yes, but you see, we already had one."

"What if one liked to write poetry?"

"Then he became a singer. Now you take John Kennedy Jr.'s plane what went down the other day. If that had gone down off Flat Island, there's a man would have made up a song about that." Disaster, set to music, is always preserved, and made more bearable in song.

Jim has an unusual innate gentleness and a baffled concern about any manifestation of unfriendliness or hate. "We always had plenty to eat here, my son—not like on the odder side of the world. Now, what you think about that war and everything, in Kosovo and places like that? Why you think people act like that, hurt each other?" He shakes his head in genuine puzzlement.

One has to be very careful about historical claims in Newfoundland. For instance, at the entrance to Salvage there is one of those "portrait-of-the-view" signs (i.e., a painting of the view seen from the sign) with the legend "Welcome to Salvage—One of the Oldest Continuously Settled Communities in Bonavista Bay." True enough, but not as old as the sign might suggest. Records show as many as five to seven families living in Salvage circa 1675, but these are described as "migratory fishing families"—probably meaning men with five to seven different family names, rather than women and children. The first recorded marriages and baptisms in Salvage stem from the 1820s, which may mean that there were no true families here before 1800.

Except for St. John's, Trinity, and a few communities along the south shore, most Newfoundland history appears to be less than two hundred years old—six or seven generations at most, and in most places only three or four. And those elements central to the popular image of "classic" Newfoundland outport life—cod traps, the Giant or Waterloo stoves, parochial schools, proper churches, Orangemen lodges, and moose hunting—only took shape in the late 1800s, and most began to disappear rapidly after Confederation. In fact, Newfoundland's much-touted "four hundred-year-old culture" only existed in a widespread, recognizable form for fifty to seventy-five years, or two or three generations—long enough, apparently, for an enduring myth to evolve.

On one of our daily walks Kathy and I had a long discussion of what it means to live *in* nature the way the outport people did, especially the men. It seems to me that their minds had to sink into their surroundings in a way we find quite difficult to do today—to take satisfaction and stimulation in the deep and detailed texture of one's environment in inarticulate ways, to read meaning without words, or below words, in the color of water, the alignment of rocks, the sound of the rote against the shore, the smell of land in a fog.

I have experienced this only rarely, and perhaps only once intensely. It was during those days and nights on the ocean out of sight of land when I sailed to Newfoundland with Peter Phillips on his racing schooner *Voyager* in 1991. There was a quiet melding of the subtly shifting surroundings, when meaning is everywhere but only surfaces to consciousness when necessary—that is, when some action is required. It is the kind of alert waiting, or passive readiness, that hunters talk about, but it can apply to almost any activity: gardening, mending nets, jigging for cod, cutting wood, etc. Literacy and formal education tend to remove one from this kind of life more by mental conditioning than by ideas. They create the need for a kind of conceptual stimulation and intellectual novelty, a linear, horizontal progress that is at odds with the lateral, cyclical nature of life in an organic setting. It is usually the first generation out of this primal, preliterate life (people like Harold Hiscock or Cyril) that can continue to straddle these two worlds. Even men who work in cities can, if they bonded with this larger, organic world early enough, continue to escape to it, but they are essentially removed from it. It can no longer satisfy them completely. They have embraced the "better" life their parents wanted for them, and however often they may return to the old life and participate in it, in fact or in memory, they are outside of it, more in their minds than their bodies. It is the old story: no gain without loss.

On Saturday evening, we visited with Sue Cummings, Harold Hiscock's wife, who had arrived Friday with her son Simon at their bungalow across the tickle from J & J's. It's a sweet little building with wide white clapboards and blue trim that had served as a post office and also a boardinghouse.

Sue is a woman of perhaps forty-five, ample in body, with long, already greying hair. She used to be a rock singer with Figgy Duff, the seminal folk-rock band in the "Newfoundland Renaissance" of the 1970s, a cultural self-awakening that spawned a flowering of homegrown music, literature, and art. After her stint with the band, she trained in opera in Europe for several years but "got out of that because the music business was too cutthroat."

When she met Harold, she was introduced to his family, who had been part of the Flat Island community that resettled in Mount Pearl, a large contemporary suburb just west of St. John's.

"I'd never met men like that before," she said. "They were all sitting around touching and poking and draping their arms over one another. They were so easy and *intimate* with one another. And, my God, what were they doing but sitting around mending *herring nets*! They weren't using them there—who and what were they doing it for?

"Later, I drove with all of them to Burnside for the first time. There was this caravan of five or six cars going up the Trans-Canada Highway, and at Clarenville, just before the turnoff, you know, there's the Holiday Inn, and Harold's father signals us to pull over and I'm thinking, 'Oh, thank God, he's stopping so we can all go to the WC,' but no, we pulls over onto the graveled shoulder just before the inn, and what do you think they does but build a little fire, right there beside the guardrail!

"Harold's father Will was a short man who could hardly see over the wheel of the car, and he would always be turning it back and forth—he had to have free play in the wheel, you know, like a boat—so that it would *weave* down the highway. He's the one who bought the big house on the point from John Oldford—the one they now call the Hiscock House—to give the family a toehold in Burnside, and was killed with his wife a few years later in an accident on the TCH.

"Anyway, they roasted up some caplin for supper—right there on the highway next to the Holiday Inn, which Harold's father would no more go into than spit in church, and I thought, 'Oh my Lord, I'm among the gypsies. These people are gypsies and don't know it!' And I thought, 'I can't let this get out of my life.'"

So she married Harold, and for a time they sold Figgy Duff records in Europe, "but then Harold asked me if I'd be willing to move to Burnside so he could try to make a living fishing, and I said yes and so we lived in the old house that used to be at the far end of Squid Island and we started the archaeology project just to be able to survive there.

"But if Flat Islanders are 'gypsies' compared to St. John's people, or even to the comparatively stuffy baymen like the Oldfords, then the Mosses are the true gypsies. Somebody switched 'em at birth. They're Irish, I'm sure of it. The Anglicans, you know, don't have any stories or dancing, but the Mosses, they were different. They were the singers and the dancers."

When I later spoke with Linda Oldford, she concurred, saying, "No one dances at a party like Jim and Jessie. They're Cat'licks, you know, or what I calls Celtic Protestants. When they get to the Pearly Gates,

Saint Peter, he'll say, 'You know you should have been RCs, but somebody switched you. You should have been black, but you were white."

Sue talked about how in the outports any child was everyone's child, looked out for by everyone in the village. A woman might give a child a scolding or even a quick hiding for being out on a wharf if he wasn't supposed to be. That person felt she had a *right*, no, an *obligation* to reprimand the child as his mother would have done. It's what made them feel their children were so safe, knowing they were looked after everywhere. It was the thing Sue wanted for her children here. Simon, as a young boy, would sometimes spend the night at another kid's house in Burnside and come home in the morning and she'd say, "And where have you been?" and he'd say, "I spent the night with Wendy—she let me sleep in her bed."

Linda told us of a day with near gale-force winds blowing from the southwest, when her son Josh and David Rockwood paddled to St. Brendan's in kayaks, some eight miles at sea, and took the ferry back. She told me this with a kind of parental pride.

That evening, back at Jim's house, I heard him for the first time brag about his father. He said that both his parents were fine singers. Then he recounted an incident at Harbour Grace early in the century in which two Protestant men were shot by four Catholics. Of course a song was made of it, by the Protestants.

Another time, while cutting wood on the mainland with some people from St. Brendan's, the only Catholic community on Bonavista Bay, Jim's father cooked a meal using salt pork. "It was a Friday, you see, and one of the St. Brendan's men said, 'Only a sonofabitch would eat that on a Friday,' and his father replied, 'Yes, and only a sonofabitch would say such a thing.'" It was the first time I had ever heard Jim use a swear word, and he apologized beforehand for doing so.

SUMMER 2001

RATHER UNEXPECTEDLY, WE NOW OWN A HOUSE IN SQUID Tickle. Unexpectedly because, for one thing, Kathy and I had not talked seriously about buying a house here, and for another, because we had not even planned to be in Newfoundland this summer.

Then, last spring, I was contacted by my friend Bob Richardson, who owns a small schooner in Maine. He told me he was planning to sail from New York up to Newfoundland and then circumnavigate the island, and he asked if I would like to join them. Of course I said yes, but they planned to embark before I could leave the Cape, so I suggested I fly up and meet them in Burnside, which would also give me a chance to show them the town. My daughter Katy, who had been to Newfoundland a couple of times, asked if she could come along, so we bought tickets and flew up to Burnside, intending to stay at Jim and Jessie's for a few days before Bob and his crew arrived in his boat.

Well, the best-laid plans . . .

A few days before we were scheduled to fly to Newfoundland, I got a call from Bob's wife Annie. She said that in crossing the Gulf of Maine they were caught in a fierce storm. Though they managed to get safely to shore, the boat suffered enough damage that she was no longer considered seaworthy, and the trip would have to be canceled. It was disappointing, but since we had already bought our tickets, Katy and I decided to go up anyway and spend some time together in Burnside.

I arrived a few days before her. When I landed in St. John's, the flight attendant's voice came on—a lilting, perky Newfoundland voice: "Oh my dears, I'll try to tell you what's happening. I've never seen this before. They've wheeled out this beautiful staircase, it's like something from a spaceship, so yous'll have to go outside. That means you can't smoke, or they'll arrest you and throw you in jail."

From St. John's I boarded an Air Labrador prop plane and flew to Gander, crossing the wide coastal bays where the quilted, burnished water looked like frozen seas and the silvered ponds scattered across the dark peninsulas were like ice floes on a darkened sea. Cyril and Linda picked me up at the Gander airport and the next day we drove to Burnside.

Burnside's population continues to dwindle. Ron Crocker figures that there are now only thirty-six year-round residents. For the first time since I began coming here, there are several houses for sale, though Cyril says they're now asking "in the twenties and thirties." (The days of cheap waterfront property in Burnside are over!) The only one that intrigues me is the house across the road from Cleaves. It's a traditional two-and-a-half-story, steep-roofed house (the locals call it a "long-roofed house") with a tall white picket fence and a thick stand of trembling aspens, or "aps," in front of it. Cleaves says it was built shortly after the 1912 fire. Although, like every old house here, it needs some work, it's apparently quite livable as it is. The current owner, Sheldon Ralph, who lives in Gander, has occasionally spent some time in it in the summers. Ron says they're asking $15,000 CAN (ca. $10,700 US)—with no building codes and no property tax.

Many of the children and grandchildren are getting too old or too busy to come here in the summer. Christine and Howard's boys, Michael and Christopher, are in Alberta and St. John's. Cyril and Linda's kids, Julie and Josh Oldford, are both working in Gander and only come down on weekends. David Rockwood has finished his two-year program in outdoor recreation and is working in Nova Scotia and BC (British Columbia) this summer. Harold and Sue Hiscock are here, but I haven't seen their sons Will or Simon yet. Cleaves just became a great-grandfather, so maybe it's time for the next generation to start taking over.

I stopped in to see Cleaves and Ettie. They've brought the bed down into the living room because Cleaves can only be comfortable now when lying down. He can still drive, though, and last winter he had a small patch of tarmac put down out on the dirt road in front of his house where he parks his car. He said that when it was wet, he always carried too much sand into his car, but that now he can "scoff" it off on the tar before he gets in.

I haven't seen Char or Mary Oldford yet, so I don't know if I will be playing for the service this Sunday.

Jim provides the musical score for life in Burnside. As I set up in the shade of Christine's house to write, he begins singing "In the Shade of the Old Apple Tree" and "It's Such a Lovely Morning, the Sun Is Shining Bright." He sings almost more than he talks, spontaneous snatches of song like a running commentary on the day, his mood, or a response to something I say to him, as if song, not speech, was his natural language.

Last evening Jim played for me a tape Mark and Fraser made for them for their anniversary. It was full of stories, poems, recollections, and songs of their time here in Burnside. Jim, in his very serious way, told me he wouldn't play it for anyone else, and made me promise I wouldn't tell anyone, not even Mark, that I had heard it. The reason? At one point on the tape Mark says that he and Fraser might have starved or frozen that first winter in Burnside if it hadn't been for Jim and Jessie. Jim is afraid that if others heard about that, they might take it the wrong way.

Katy arrived yesterday, having taken the bus from the St. John's airport to the TCH Glovertown exit, where I picked her up in Cleaves' car. After dinner we walked up to the old school, where the annual St. Alban's tea and sale was taking place. The sale resembles a miniature Filene's Basement sale, with three of the women "guarding" the sale tables until the signal was given and a stampede of (mostly) older women descended on the tables with no pretense of propriety.

One item that caught my eye was what at first appeared to be a pair of white padded chiffon slippers with a fake pearl broach on the top of each slipper. Attached to the slippers was the following couplet:

With no more months to greet,
This month you get to wear these on your feet.

I was puzzled at first, but then Linda leaned into me and told me that the "slippers" were made from a pair of sanitary napkins. It was a gift for menopausal metatarsals, offered, in typical Newfoundland style, in the form of a verbal riddle.

On Friday evening, Carolyn Ralph, who with her husband Frank is the local realtor, showed Katy and me the Ralph house. It's a long-roofed house with a two-story ell on the back, five (small) bedrooms upstairs, a kitchen spread out into three rooms, a full unfinished attic, solid-looking joists and posts, a 100-amp power supply, a gravity-fed well line, three outbuildings full of old stuff, a "two-holer" outhouse, one half acre of land, a thick grove of quaking aspens in front, and a lovely view of the bay across to the Bloody Bay Hills. They are asking $23,000 CAN (twice what Ron had told me), including furniture. Carolyn said, "Make an offer."

The following afternoon Katy, Jessie, and I walked to Linda Oldford's garden party, which is the social event of the season in Burnside. There were at least forty people there, the younger women in party dresses with large floppy hats provided by Linda, the older women sitting around a table under parasols, the old men sitting in the shade on the stoop, the boys and girls sitting in circles on the grass, Linda having arranged everyone into various family portraits.

I asked Cyril how long Linda had been doing this.

"Forever," he said.

Cyril repeated his earlier offer to take us out to Flat Island in his boat, so the next day Linda, Jim and Jessie, Katy, and I boarded his boat and we set off for the storied island. It was a beautiful morning, with warm light and a soft wind from the west, clear and sunny. We passed great, cracked, tilted strata of shale and slate and rounded, firred headlands. beetling eastward like a giant rolling breaker. Bits of whirring black-and-white feathers pumped across the water—guillemots, known here as "sea pigeons." Watching the depth finder on the deck plummet suddenly from six to sixty-five fathoms, I felt suddenly tossed out of the gentle, pastoral, enclosed world of Burnside and into the wide, exposed world of open ocean. One has, if only vicariously, the sense of quotidian adventure and drama that fibered the lives of these island people for a hundred years or more.

Flat Island is actually an archipelago of six islands, with the largest one known simply as Flat Island. The aspect and geology of the bay islands (there are some two hundred named ones in Bonavista Bay) are much more dramatic than the landscape around Burnside. In fact, Flat Island, which is considerably more hilly and rugged than Squid Tickle, likely got its name from its relative flatness compared to most of the other islands around it.

We motored carefully through the tickle between the main island and North Island, where the rhomboidal shape of an old grey unpainted house was canted at a precarious angle over the water, as if leaning into the wind.

We moored at Sandy Cove, where Cyril and Linda have a small cabin. Linda, wearing sneakers and the same white linen dress she wore to her garden party yesterday, spread out a picnic lunch on a blanket on the wharf with chicken, potato salad, tabbouleh, and various homemade desserts.

After lunch, with Cyril leading, we set off on foot across Flat Island, along a grassy track, one of the many roads that crisscrossed the island, once graveled, now grassed, in places built up with stone to cross shallow gullies. We passed a number of root cellars, those curious dome-shaped structures used to store root vegetables, the newer ones constructed of poured concrete, the older ones made of cement blocks, all topped with a thick matting of turf. Shaggy and rough, they might have been the original dwellings of the Viking explorers a thousand years ago, or the entrances to underground barrows of ancient Celtic tribes. Cyril was impressed by the good condition most of them were in, commenting that "Flat Islanders used to say it takes a hundred years before concrete is thoroughly set." One was made of mortared stones and looked as tight as the day it was made. Each one had a metal vent sticking through the roof.

Near the center of the island we came upon a remarkable, incredibly gnarled apple tree, a dense Laocoönian tangle of dead grey wind-woven limbs and branches, with thinner, newer, light brown coils rich in new leaves woven into, around, and through the grey parent trunks.

No more than seven feet tall, its compacted bulk is a nest of contorted trunks and branches, the former all springing from the mother trunk less than two feet off the ground. It looks like a multi-ventricled, multi-auricled heart, wrapped in the arterial trunks with smooth reddish bark and dead, grey veinous branches, all spiraling and curling outward but with a centripetal tendency that is outwardly imposed by the wind and salt rushing over the scraped rocks and up the narrow valleys.

We kept toward the northern shore and came at last to a protected cove that had been the island's main harbour, a place where dozens of small houses once crowded along the rocky shore studded with wharves completely covered in flakes for drying fish, and where in winter thirty or forty schooners once anchored together, fast-locked in winter ice. A place of times, songs, and stories—now all gone. Post-historic.

Jim pointed up the hill from the harbour to the remains of the merchant Bill Samson's house—a large structure with a concrete path leading up to its porch, a rock wall built up behind it to keep water from the sills, and an outline of support pilings indicating a building at least forty inches by twenty-eight feet. Did Bill Samson have a dark-haired, dark-eyed, curly-headed daughter with white skin and a proud, contemptuous look in her eye as she stared down from her second-story bedroom window at the indentured men under her father's rule? It is doubtful such a stereotypical feudal picture bears much resemblance to the reality of society here. When I asked Jim if the merchant had been a decent man, Jim said, "Oh yis, b'y—none better. Bill, he used to say, 'I never had no Flat Islander's name on my books at the end of the year.'"

Even allowing for Jim's always rosy memories of the place and his generous view of people in general, the outports were probably among the most democratic of communities on this continent, with few having enough to lord it over their neighbors. The merchants in the small outports like Flat Island were not the scions of rich Water Street English families who spent the winter in the "home country," but usually local men who had once been fishermen themselves and understood in their bones the common condition of the baymen and their families.

From the harbour we climbed up the hill to the crest of the island, where St. Nicholas, the massive, spired Anglican church, once stood. At one time the sanctuary held up to 450 parishioners. After resettlement, to preempt looting and vandalism, the diocese decided to burn the church down. All that was left was a small concrete vault where the tithing money was stored, with large iron hinges and a hasp, its steel door missing.

Though the Anglican church was on Flat Island, and the smaller

UC (Methodist) church on North Island, the communities were not strictly divided, religiously or socially, by denomination. Jim said there were three or four UC families in Sandy Cove, which was the closest settlement to North Island, and at least two Anglican families on North Island. Coward's Island, the northernmost of the settled Flat Islands, was more mixed. Harold Hiscock's family, for instance, was Anglican, whereas Lonz Crocker's was UC. They would come across by boat or on the ice to their respective churches, but, said Jim, "if the weather was too bad or they were sick, we would goes to each other's churches, y's b'y."

From the harbour we continued west along the main path ("You're on Main Street now!" said Jessie) over two hills, the taller of which Jim said was "Kitty Grove Hill."

"We used to come down that hill in the winter, b'y, when she was covered wid ice. We'd straps our skates onto our rubber boots—screw 'em on, ya know, wid our keys, and skate right down the hill, across the wash and out to the tickle, and no one ever got hurt, b'y."

At one point Jim pointed out a bit of post sticking up from the rock: "Bob? Bob? Now, ye see, Aunt Liz Chaytor lived here. She'd always be settin' out here on her porch in her rockin' chair. You'd have to go right by her on the way home because ye see there's a cliff on the other side." I could see her rocking there yet, apparently a watchful and unfriendly figure.

But in general Jim didn't so much point out the specific sites of the vanished houses or places as indicate the broad layout of memory with wide brushstrokes: "There were houses all over here, Bob. There were gardens everywhere here, all fenced in, to keep the sheep out. There was no grass here then, b'y, all bald because of the sheep.

"Flat Island is smaller now than she was, b'y, ye know what I mean? Dere was flakes everywhere, wharves everywhere, all along the landwash, pushing the island out. All gone, b'y. All gone."

Cyril said that house sites could be recognized from a distance by stands of roses or monkshood where the front yard would have been, and groves of "roughy," or willow, to windward at the rear. The roses are a pink multiflora variety with a strong sweet scent that Cyril says doesn't grow on the mainland. He calls them "Flat Island roses" and thinks they may be an old English variety. He has transplanted some to their yard in Burnside.

We finally arrived at what Jim said was the site of his family's house, not the house he had floated over to Burnside, but the house of his parents—James and Julia (Roberts) Moss—the one he grew up in, along with his brother John and sister Nellie, who died at twenty-one years. It was notable only for its rather elevated position overlooking the harbour. Jim told me he could see the flashing light on Little Dernier Island from his room.

From there we went down to the "Devil's Rocks" at the southwest corner of the main, or upper, island. This is a strange and unworldly spot, not just for the Devil's Rocks themselves, but for the surrounding geology. Here bare stacks of cracked shale stand in a cirque around the rocks, suggesting old, ruined temples. There is a large erratic on the shore to the north of the rocks called Dog's Head, for it appears to have a large snout and an eye formed by a hole eight inches across. Jim was struck by how much the rocks had changed since he knew them fifty years ago. He pointed to a spot at the bottom of one of the large shelves, which now held a pool of salt water, and said that that was a well: "The says[*] are so strong, my son, they've swamped in and broken them all up."

Harebells and tiny delicate white strawflowers grow from tiny cracks just above the tideline. Jim pointed out a shallow sea cave in the wall of rocks to the southeast, just above the reach of all but the highest storm tides, the mouth of which was stuffed with large, rounded rocks rolled up by the waves. He said this was the "Courtin' Rock," though

---

[*] "Says" is the phonetic transcription of the Newfoundland pronunciation of "seas."

any courting that went on there must have been limited, since there seemed to be no place large or comfortable enough to lie down.

The Devil's Rocks themselves are one of the oddest geological formations I have ever seen in Newfoundland, or anywhere else. They encompass an enormous, flat, tilted shelf of rock slanting down into the ocean, dark brown in color, with a texture like that of a cobbled street: large, roughly rectangular protrusions set in semiregular rows, with inch-deep slits between them, so that the whole surface had the texture of a negative cast of a giant griddle. The surface pattern suggested some kind of rapidly cooled igneous or volcanic rock, studded with separate stones fused in unconsolidated material, like puddingstone, yet it appeared to be a solid shelf of metamorphic shale or sandstone. The shelf was dotted with colorful, ragged mats of bright yellow and red-orange lichen. Where the shelf slid into the swash of the tide, there were several small offshore ridges, forming natural warm pools where Jim said boys and girls swam together naked.

Katy, who had worn her swimsuit, went into one of the bathing pools, its crystalline green waters full of small, thin, greyish, nearly transparent minnows, the cracks in the underwater rocks ribboned with strips of salmon-colored algae. At one end of the pool the rising tide flowed through the opening to the sea in rhythmic surges, like some natural Jacuzzi. The sound and motion of the waves over the rocks were hypnotic and soothing. Katy emerged after a time and dried herself on the sun-warmed rocks.

"We came out here all the time in summer," Jim said. "Boys and girls together—there was nothin' else to do." It was as if a boy from San Francisco said, "We went to a rock concert," or an astronaut from NASA said, "We went to the moon—there was nothing else to do."

Between the narrow slits we found dozens of coins—mostly nickels and quarters, apparently hammered with rocks into the slits and bent over. Jim offered this explanation of how the bent coins got into the cracks in the rocks:

"There was this fellow from Flat Island—Pearce Samson was his name—he went away to the States as a young man—many of 'em did—to Long Island, and he made a lot of money. Anyway, he came back for the Flat Island Reunion in 1992 and came out to the Devil's Rocks—and when he found he had some twenty-five-cent pieces in his pocket, he took them out and took a rock and smashed 'em down into the cracks. I don't know why he did it—but dat's what they say."

I managed to wriggle one of the quarters out of its crack. Its scratched and distressed shape bore the likeness of Queen Elizabeth on one side and the date "2000" on the other, eight years after the 1992 Reunion, which contradicted Jim's story. It didn't matter. Pearce Samson started something that needed no more than the idea of it for others to continue it, like throwing coins in a body of water. What prompted him to do such a thing is not known. It might have been a contrary impulse to drive coins into the rocky face of this cashless place, to make his mark on the place he had left "to make good," and which no longer even existed to return to, except in memory.

Not apparent at first, but common when you began to see them, are the so-called "Devil's Footprints": odd, oblong-shaped impressions in the surface of the shelf, fairly uniform in size, looking as if someone had taken a hot iron and branded them into the rock. Curiously, they all were oriented in the same direction, as if they had been swimming in a school, and often were in side-by-side pairs. As such, they had the look of fossils, but fossils bereft of any detail, like a worn limestone grave—as if a school of strange, antediluvian sea creatures had been swimming over this shelf when it was a flat, horizontal part of the seabed, and had somehow been trapped and buried in sediment, which later hardened and formed the unusual surface pattern of the rocks. But they were obviously formed after the hardening of the shelf itself. They cut across both the "cobblestones" and the slits, randomly distributed across its surface. They reminded me of a school of ghost-fish. I could see why they had impressed themselves so strongly on the imaginations of the children playing here.

As the others retraced their way along the shore to Sandy Cove, I wandered over to the western shore and eventually came to a couple of side-by-side cemeteries overlooking the sea. One was a large Anglican cemetery, the other a smaller UC graveyard. I found familiar names in both of them, with Samsons and Ralphs seeming to dominate. Though the headstones spanned at least seventy years, they all seemed remarkably uniform in style and material. All were made of white marble, with many crosses and clasped, praying hands.

In the upper corner of the Anglican yard, I came upon three wooden crosses painted white and lettered in black. They were in good condition, and had obviously been placed here recently, though two had already fallen over. I lifted them up to reinstate them and realized I had come upon Jim's family graves. One was his father's—"James Moss—65 years"—another his mother's—"Julia Moss—71 years"—and a third his sister's—"Nellie Moss—21 years"—with no birth or death dates on any of them, and no relationships indicated. If, as Jim told Kathy, his father died when he was nine, and his mother when he was twenty-eight, that means his father was born in 1865 or 1866 and his mother in 1879 or 1880.

The lack of stone markers seemed to affirm the sense I have had that Jim's family was always relatively poor—though he had once pointed out his name on the list of pew seat assessments in St. Nicholas in 1950: 90 cents. The price of the seats, Jim told me later, ranged from 60 cents to 110 cents, "depending on how much room you took up, you see—the bigger you were, the more you paid."

What struck me most, though, wandering through that sea of marble with three wooden crosses, was the common legend they all bore. On each one, after their names, vital statistics, relationships, even occasional verses, as if binding them all together, even in death, was the declaration:

OF THIS PLACE.

When we got back to Burnside, Harold Hiscock asked me if we had gotten "a historical tour" of Flat Island. I said yes, but it wasn't really that. I didn't learn that much more than I already knew. It was more the experience of having Jim's living connection to the island life confirmed, seeing how well his visual recollections fit with the actual contours and sites of the landscape.

That evening, sequestered in the Mosses' guest bedroom, I found myself composing the lyrics and a melody for a song that seemed to embody the nature of the place where we had been:

THE FLAT ISLAND ROSE
Far out across the deep blue bay
There's a lovely flower that grows
That all who lived there knew by name
Of the fair Flat Island rose.
That rose, it never did grow wild
'Twas brought by the hand of man
But where it first did come here from
To tell you I never can
For the people they are all departed
From the island in the bay
And of all that once did flourish here
These flowers only stay.
I plucked a blossom long ago
To take wherever I goes

To remind me of those lovely days
And my fair Flat Island rose.

Frank Ralph, who with his wife Carolyn has been showing Katy and me the Sheldon Ralph house, is also from Flat Island, or more specifically, North Island. He told me how, when he was eight, he got to school by rowing across the tickle to Sandy Cove, where he kept a bicycle that he then rode over the path to the school.

His family was one of the last to leave the island.

One day he was out jigging with his grandfather in a dory a half mile from shore when his grandfather suffered a heart attack and died. "We was drifting out with the tide and I didn't know if I could row us ashore by meself, so I tied my guernsey onto the oar and waved it and somebody saw it and came out to get us."

How strange it must have been for the last Flat Island children—Howard, Julia, Frank, Harold—all about the same age, the only ones left in a deserted community—having only the shallow memories of an extended family to sustain them.

The next day Sue Cummings came by and, sitting on J & J's bridge, told me more about Harold's somewhat complicated history and life on Flat Island. She showed me a photo of Harold as a baby on Flat Island, all done up in a bonnet and sweater on the bridge in front of his foster father Harold Ralph's house, and behind him at some distance a train of figures, the people of Flat Island, leaving the island with their belongings in brin (burlap) bags, like the refugees from Eastern Europe of sixty years before.

"It's a lonely picture," said Susan, "a baby with the life he was born to leaving him behind. Harold was the youngest of five children, the next-youngest being nineteen. His mother had TB and had to go into the 'san' after he was born. His father went to the States for work, and 'Uncle' Harold and Dot Ralph offered to raise him. She had lost a child. They did a wonderful job raising him, gave him lots of cuddles. They thought his mother would never get out of the san and that they had him for good.

"He left Flat Island with his foster parents and foster brother Bert when he was five. They all lived with other Flat Islanders in the 'replica' houses on Torbay Road in Mount Pearl, just outside St. John's. When I first went to visit Harold's family in Mount Pearl, his grandfather Will was 'astray' with early Alzheimer's. He looked out the windows at the telephone poles and wires and said, 'There are some schooners in today.'"

His mother did recover, but he continued to live with Harold and Dot Ralph in their apartment while his mother and siblings lived upstairs. He remembers his father, Will Hiscock, once coming to "look" at him, but he never felt at home with his blood brothers and sisters, never felt part of his biological family.

Sue met Harold in university, and after they were married, he said he didn't think he could have his life without knowing the Flat Island fishery, and he asked her if she thought she could live in Squid Tickle for a few years so he could learn the inshore and offshore fishery. They were young and independent. They had a small child, Will. They moved into the old house at the end of Squid Island Road and Harold went fishing.

Harold and Dot Ralph also moved back to Burnside and lived on the same road. "On the island side of the tickle," said Sue, "she was called Dora Ralph, and on the other side, where she grew up in what's now the Bowring house, she was Pearl Lane. Oh, my son, it took me a while to figure it out. When I was over there, they didn't know who I was talking about. The place was still full of sheep and horses then.

"Fred had the best horse ever born. His name was Dan. He knew what you were thinking. You'd hold out the harness and he'd walk right into it. Plowing, you wouldn't even have to touch the reins. He'd come to the end of a furrow and turn on his own. You'd never see him during the day, but if I wanted him, I'd just call 'Dan-Dan-Dan-Dan' and he'd show up at the doorstep. He never went out of earshot."

Sue and Jessie talked about the midwife on Flat Island, who "never lost a woman in childbirth." She carried a string in her apron pocket that she knotted for each child born on that island. "I wish I had that string," said Sue. "I'd rather have that string than a pearl necklace."

She talked again of her upbringing, where, in her father's world, an architect's world of business, men kept a distance, a tension, a protective territorial stance toward others. When she first visited Harold's family, she saw men who couldn't help touching one another, where a story was prompted and couldn't begin without touching or poking, where it was kept going and punctuated through physical gestures (as Jim's always were), where there was a *physical* loyalty, where men daily sacrificed for one another, even gave their lives—a culture where keeping physically in touch was a matter of survival.

This morning the wind turned east, that clear, cooling easterly wind off the water that is so rare on the Cape. A twenty-two-foot open crabbing skiff with a crew of three, including a father and son, was reported missing off Bonavista just before dark last night. A sea and air rescue search has been conducted all day, but nothing, not even debris, has been found. One of the search helicopters passed over Jim's deck in the afternoon, making the tragedy more real.

The loss of the crab boat has bred all kinds of stories of similar losses or near escapes. Jim told a story today of a man from Flat Island whose father drowned on the Labrador hauling trap nets. It was presented as an unusual occurrence, and Jim said, "Dere was no reason for a man to drown on the Labrador—day drowns every day here now."

Howard told of "an open crab boat, twenty-nine to thirty feet long, with just a leetle-bitty deck on her, and no radar, no Loran, and not even a lifeboat or even a raft to get in, just a little GPS and a radio, and two of 'em go out, one of 'em steering and the other one sleeping until they gets to the grounds, and they followed the caplin for seven days and seven nights without a wink o' sleep, loading sixteen thousand pounds so that she sat on the water right down to the gunnels.

"When buddy tried to cut the grapnel, she baffled off, see, and a sea come in and swamped her and she went right down and he drowned, he never even got his rubber boots off. De other guy when he come up he was on his back, see, and he just held his breath between the lops and paddled ashore.

"Ye see the trouble is dat y've got to go when dey tells ye to go. If ye got three days t'fish, ya got to go den—if ye got a crab quota for outside, den ye got to go. When dey could go when dey wanted to, dere wasn't nearly so many drowned."

The next day Katy and I went for a sail with Mr. Bowring on the *Imogene*. It was a perfect sailing day: steady, moderate winds out of the east that allowed us to head up into the wind pretty close most of the time. The electric starter on his boat was not functioning, so we had a bit of a job launching her (a thirty-year-old, six-ton boat, forty-five hundred pounds of which are in her keel, so that she's slow in a light wind but can tack up in a gale and never get knocked down), first towing her around with the mooring lines so she was heading away from shore, and then having to catch the wind to starboard, racking up the jib to get full lateral movement. There is, in any breeze, an animated restlessness in hoisting the sails on a boat like this, an awkward flopping and flapping of the nylon sails and sheets, halyards and stays, denying them the wind until we were ready. It felt like a thoroughbred confined to a starting gate. One could almost feel the *desire* of the boat to be launched, and when we finally cast off, backing the jib and pulling in the mainsheet, all slackness and awkwardness resolved instantly into that smooth, silent motion of the sails yielding to and filling with wind.

We headed north toward Pretty Island, passing the incoming St. Brendan's ferry to starboard, then tacked up into the wind toward "Brown's Storehouse," a rocky, bare pair of rocks streaked with the guano of numerous gulls and shags that set up a visual and audible cacophony as we approached and rounded it counterclockwise.

Except for launching and docking, I had the tiller most of the time, recovering the basic sailing skills I had learned when I was twenty, having to jibe only once. Katy spent most of the trip lying on the foredeck, while Mr. Bowring corrected some information about himself for me. He sounds English because he was born in England during the war. His father was stationed there and married an English girl. When he was seven or eight they returned, not to Newfoundland but to the States, where he lived for several years on Staten Island before returning to England for public school and then university. He didn't come to St. John's until he was eighteen.

We got to talking about the English and their penchant for doing things the hard way, how Scott and Amundsen had skied to the South Pole, but that Scott, who had actually trained on skis in Norway, insisted that he and his men walk there without riding on dogsleds and that that did him in—that and not sufficiently marking his food caches. Mr. Bowring said that the boys in British public schools learn that "dying is what the English do well."

One year, his school won a rowing tournament. They were extra pleased because they had never won before, largely because they insisted on using the older, shorter oars with wide paddles as opposed to the new longer, thinner-paddled oars most of the other schools had adopted. The newer oars were still considered "not quite cricket," and so they took even greater pride in winning the tournament in the more classic and purer manner. They never won another race.

When we got back to the wharf, Mr. Bowring took the tiller as Katy and I lowered the jib, and I stood on the foredeck with the gaff to snag the dinghy, if necessary. I needn't have bothered. Mr. Bowring executed a perfect landing. We could have stepped ashore without ever casting a line.

"That's the way it always is," he said in his teddy-bear-gruff manner. "When you do it right, there's never anyone around. When you screw up, they're all staring at you."

That evening there was a "time" that lasted from dinner to well after midnight, shifting from Howard's bridge and house into J & J's kitchen, living room, and deck. Jim taught us some Newfoundland reels, then he and Sue Cummings sang together, a strong contrast in styles: Jim's nasal, droning chant against Sue's cultured, coloratura, heavily vibratoed soprano.

The youngsters stayed on the deck and at one point young Simon took out his fiddle and played tunes while the full moon rose over the tickle behind him, and Jim came out and sang with him.

Around midnight, Howard gave his account of the UFO incident in Magic Arm fifteen years ago. Sensing a new and appreciative audience in Katy, he greatly augmented Jim's version. He and Jim had come up to Magic Arm in the evening, as squid jigging goes better at night. The UFO—silent, saucer-shaped, and with a line of illuminated ports around its rim—appeared overhead and shone a series of lights on them—red, green, and white. Both Jim and Howard saw it, and Reg Lane, jigging further down the shore, also saw a lighted object over them and asked them later what it was. When Howard shone his light on the ship, it backed away swiftly, hovered there a minute or two, and then flashed off and almost instantly disappeared.

"Why didn't you report it?" Katy asked.

"Oh," said Howard, "no one would have believed it. They would have said the Mosses were drinking again. But we weren't drinking, though I sure could have used one!"

The following morning, I saw Howard standing in a corner of his deck with his two bare-chested sons, their arms all wrapped around one another in manly and familial camaraderie. They could have been an Italian or a Russian family.

So, rather surprisingly, and pending a final closing, we now own a house in Burnside. It was built in 1915 or 1916 by two sons of Eli Oldford, Tom and Esau, for their widowed mother, Charlotte Ann (Brown), who appears to have been the grandmother or great-aunt to half of Burnside. In 1955 it was sold to Nathan Ralph of Flat Island and his son Arthur. Arthur died last year, leaving it to his son Sheldon, who is twenty-six and lives in BC.

Sheldon had asked for $23,000 CAN. I countered with $15,000 and we agreed on $17,500 CAN, or a little less than $12,000 US. No sales tax, no property tax, no title search fee, no surveys, no inspectors. In place of a standard title search, two of the older local residents gave oral "witness" to the history of the house's ownership. We could have just exchanged a check and the deed, but it seemed wise to have a lawyer look over the records. The house is on a half-acre lot with three sheds and a grove of large quaking aps. The sheds appear wonderfully full of God-knows-what, including a half dozen handmade long wooden ladders of different lengths, a number of handmade tools, a pair of old screw-on skates, a bundle of hand-carved spikes, a dozen old fishing barrels filled with nets, and several winters' worth of spruce and birch junks.

The house itself is in reasonably good shape. The brick chimney seems clean and solid enough, the roof is missing only a few shingles, and the clapboards and trim are old but have been kept scraped and painted. The house sits on a gentle slope and was originally set on wooden posts. Over the decades its original support system has been augmented, as needed, with concrete blocks, poured-concrete sauna posts, wooden shims, shale boulders, and any other objects that came to hand, resulting in a Rube Goldberg maze of jury-rigged crawl space. Frank Ralph told me that Arthur Ralph (no immediate relation to Frank) was always replacing any posts that seemed to be rotting. There are no visible leaks, and the house, though essentially unlived-in for eight or nine years, does not have a musty smell.

In sum, it would seem to be quite livable in the summer as is. My brother Dave had offered to loan me $8,000 for the project, and Katy wanted to come in on it for $4,000, which for me clinched the deal. Kathy originally expressed doubts about purchasing the house, partly because she felt I had already decided to buy it without her seeing it, putting her "out of the loop," but also because she fears that it will prohibit our traveling elsewhere. After a few days, though, she came around and said, "Go for it," and then, "Can't wait to get to Newfoundland."

It seems right, on many levels: as a way of returning to Burnside without further imposing on anyone there, of at last fulfilling an old dream of mine to have an old house to care for, as a "family place," something substantial I can share with and pass on to Katy, as a place for my imagination to reside, and even as "a place in reserve," should things become too dire politically for us to remain in the States.

The community as a whole seems pleased for us (though Sue Cummings told me that Joan, Cleaves' daughter, "always had her eye on that house, but couldn't get her act together"). Harold Hiscock says it is "a grand house." When we told Ettie, she smiled a big smile and said, with formal courtesy, "We'll be glad to have you as neighbors." And Jim and Jessie, of course, who said, "We'll come up to see you scattered times."

On Friday, August 11, 2001, at 2 p.m., I met Frank Ralph to sign the final purchase and sales agreement. Thirty days later two highjacked planes crashed into Manhattan's World Trade Center towers, which collapsed, killing nearly three thousand people. Two weeks later I got a call from Carolyn Ralph apologizing for not having completed the title transfer on the house. She has been one of the local volunteers providing food and housing for some sixty-six hundred airline passengers and nearly five hundred crew whose planes were detoured to the Gander airport after 9/11.

SUMMER 2002

THE FOLLOWING SUMMER WE ARRIVED IN BURNSIDE LATE IN the afternoon, tired, irritated, and too drained to feel anything about this being the first night in our new house. I got the keys from Ron Crocker, then filled up our water jugs at the community center faucet and put them in the chest freezer. It was too warm to sleep upstairs with the storm windows still on, so we dragged down the double mattress, set up a bed on the living room floor, and collapsed.

On our way to Burnside, we had stopped at the Dominion supermarket in Gander for groceries. There we met Con and Audrey Oldford, who gave us the scorecard of afflictions since we were last here. Con himself is getting quite crippled up with arthritis. Fred, he told us, has glaucoma and is going blind. Cleaves could no longer deal with the drifting snow, so he and Ettie spent the winter in an apartment in Eastport. Jim had what they were afraid was heart failure, but it seems to have been asthma. Laura Burden fell and broke her hip and is in hospital in Gander. Ron Crocker's mom Ida died of cancer this winter, and Gore Bradley died last Thursday. The community continues to fall apart, but people go on much as before.

In the morning it was clear and much cooler. I spent much of the day taking off the storm windows and putting in some screen frames that didn't quite fit, while Kathy cleaned the pantry and stored our food. Jim and Jessie came for tea before noon and we showed them the three sheds, which are uncatalogued museums of the old life lived here, barely diluted with any contemporary items. Jim said I could "get a fortune" for some of the stuff there. "Y's b'y, I'd say you got a bargain."

The house windows—"two-over-two"—have old-fashioned rope pulleys and lead counterweights. Like the storm windows, they seem not to have been opened for decades. There is uncracked paint inside and out where the sashes meet the frames, and most of the windows have stops so that the sashes can only be raised seven or eight inches. When I asked Howard about this, he said that with a houseful of kids and the man away fishing and the woman outside "making" fish, they wanted it that way so the little ones couldn't climb out the windows. Christine pooh-poohed that explanation.

The house is unusual in not having been modernized very much inside, except for some awful floral-patterned wall-to-wall carpeting in the front parlor and the hallway. Most of the flooring is linoleum, or what Newfoundlanders call "floor canvas," from the painted ship's canvas that was originally used as a floor covering. One day, in a burst of energy, Kathy went upstairs and ripped out the linoleum from the front east bedroom floor, revealing nine different layers, including the original painted canvas.

The Ralphs, it seems, never had a phone or a refrigerator, but the kitchen stove has an oven with a thermometer, four burner lids, a griddle, and a copper-lined hot water box. A two-story ell attached to the back of the house contains the kitchen pantry, with two sinks, a bathroom with a short tub, toilet, and sink, and a mudroom with a large chest freezer, an electric range, and a vintage Thor wringer washer that apparently works, though Ettie said that Nate's wife Blanche didn't use it.

"Why not?"

"Well," said Ettie, "she were scared of it. One day Blanche got a sheet all mangled up in the wringers and she was afraid Nate would come home and find her with it. So I came over with a pair of shears and cut it out for her, all into little pieces. She never used that machine again."

At some point the Ralphs apparently installed indoor plumbing to the bathroom and kitchen sink, hooking it up to Cleaves' cistern, but according to Cleaves, they "didn't get much use out of it." There was never any hot water, and eventually they removed the electric pump. After that they used the outhouse, but because the indoor plumbing had been left intact, they could also use the toilet in bad or cold weather by filling up the toilet tank from buckets and flushing it, a practice we would continue.

This house, we soon discovered, has strong ties to the earliest Burnside history. According to Cleaves, his grandfather, Eli Oldford, was the first Oldford from Salvage to settle permanently in what was then Squid Tickle, sometime around the turn of the last century. Eli and his wife, Charlotte Ann, initially lived in a crude dwelling, not much more than a glorified tilt. Cleaves said that his grandmother spread sand on the dirt floor of the tilt and made patterns in them, and cooked over an open fire with an iron pot and fire tongs and hangers.

Eli died when his boys—William, Thomas, Joseph, and Esau—were still young. The original dwelling burned down in 1912 along with the rest of the town, and a few years later the boys built this house for their mother. Joe, the oldest of the brothers, never married and lived here with his mother, who died in 1926. In 1955, after Joe died, his brother Tom sold the house to Nathan Ralph of Sandy Cove, Flat Island.

Thus, through Charlotte Ann, nearly half the town have direct family (Oldford) ties to this house, and there is a cat's cradle of blood and marriage tying it to the Ralphs. Nate and Blanche Ralph had two children, Arthur Stevens and Alma. Alma and her husband Eldon Hapgood live in a house just across the tickle.

Writing of these things seems like writing of another time, another age, and yet it is mostly a history of the 1950s and 1960s, the time when I myself came of age. But it was, in another sense, a very different time, a quieter world whose members have all but died out. It was a time at once more constricted, physically harder, and more dangerous, more subject and vulnerable to wholesale shifts in weather and natural resources, but also more tied to and deeply aware of its local supports.

There have been a lot of Burnside family members arriving over the past few days. Sue, Harold, and Simon Hiscock are here for the Canada Day holiday weekend. Harold's older brother Bill, his wife Carol, his two sisters Grace and Jean, and their husbands Harry Hollett and Wulf Stender have all been staying up at the Hiscock House. Cleaves' daughter Joan and his youngest son Terry with his wife Dawn and two sons are staying across the street in Cleaves' house.

Cleaves offered to let me hook up to his cistern "if you can find someone to do it." Meanwhile, he said we could fill up our jugs, buckets, and solar showers from his outside faucet. In our dug well shed I found a hoop fashioned from birch branches, traditionally used when carrying water buckets to keep them from hitting the carrier's hips. When I tried it, it greatly eased the task of carrying full buckets.

The front of the house has a small stoop and a double-door entrance that leads into a tiny foyer with a screened door opening into the main house. The stoop is just large enough for the two of us to sit on, and already we have established a ritual of having our breakfasts there, giving us, as it were, a front-row seat from which to observe the comings and goings of the village.

Kathy commented that Squid Tickle is "like the Midwest with water." This is true. There is something about the light here that says Ohio, 1942. All the young men are away at war—but where are the young mothers and the children?

A yellow swallowtail flutters in the understory of our aspen grove, which picks up and translates every breeze and fitful gust into a trembling wave of sound similar to that of swash on the shore. These aps have sent out an underground network of runners that have sprouted an advance army of saplings two to three feet high that surround the house. I sharpened one of the scythe blades I found hanging in one of the sheds, attached it to one of the wooden handles, and began cutting. It took down all but the thickest saplings easily, and after a while I got the hang of cutting the grass. Together Kathy and I managed to clear a path from the front fence to the house, which left us both pleasantly exhausted.

In the evening, from the back porch, we can look at the slope of our land, covered with tall grass, fireweed, strawberry plants, creeping juniper, partridgeberry, and blueberry; at the massive stone root cellar, a Neolithic-looking mound that seems to predate everything here; at the lovely, simple lines of the back side of the house with its blue shingled roof and white clapboarded sides; at the shining, fish-flaked waters of Fair and False Bay; and at the backlit outline of the hills across the bay, fading like the end of a play.

Shirley Oldford came by this afternoon. She looks healthy and in good spirits.

"I envy you," she said. "I looked at this house any number of times and thought of buying it, but I didn't have enough energy. I would have needed someone to go in on it with me, to do what needed to be done, but Phil wasn't around then.

"This is a well-built house. Grandfather Esau and his brothers were all good carpenters." Putting her hand on the wooden stair railing, she said, "Look at all the detail. And they did it all with pretty primitive, handmade tools."

Shirley was the first of a flow of visitors to the house by people who had ties to it but had not been inside it for decades, if ever. One afternoon Alma and Eldon Hapgood came by. Alma set her ample body down in the rocker, and Eldon sat on one of the Formica chairs he had recovered. Alma grew up in our house and remembered her brother Arthur saying, "I wish I could get Dad to open up a window." She thinks her father "didn't like the wind. He was afraid of it."

Alma said that her father, Nate Ralph, continued to fish here and did some sealing on Flat Island in the bay, but never went on any of the commercial sealers. Sometime before Nate died, her mother Blanche broke her hip and Alma cared for her the next five years. "Oh, I made many trips up here, my son, and she niver took another step."

When I told them I planned to hook up to Cleaves' water cistern line, Eldon said, "Y's b'y, you needs water—you can gets along without a lot, but you needs that." He offered to show me where the cistern was, take a look at the pump, and see what might be done. We walked up the slope behind our house from the outhouse to the back fence, where thick alder saplings grow now.

"There used to be potatoes grown there," said Eldon, "though I doesn't believe anything has been grown here for twenty years." We went through the break in the fence and across some bare rocks until we came to the cistern. It was a poured-concrete well perhaps five feet in diameter, covered with a sheet of weathered green plywood, with a hatch in the center. I couldn't see how deep it was, but it was nearly full. Eldon said he thought this well was put in about forty years ago, when Cleaves had the trench dug across the street to his house. He told Nate Ralph, "You might as well lay your line in here now—there's plenty of water for both of us."

Eldon figured out how to put the kitchen's hand pump together. It's a four-valve cast-iron toggle pump, constructed something like a heart, with four chambers. Each pump of the handle moves the brass "leather" some ninety degrees, simultaneously filling up and pumping out each side of the chamber, thus getting with each stroke twice as much water as with a conventional hand pump.

Eldon put the pump together and primed it, then said, "OK, b'y, go ahead and pump."

I took the handle, and after two or three pumps, water began to gush—clear, cold, odorless water! We pumped several gallons, just to be sure there was no air in the line. It seems to hold its prime fairly well, and we haven't had to fill it again since.

The next day, after supper, as we were settling into a quiet Sunday evening, Cyril and Linda stopped by. They had been out for a walk, and when they passed our house, she said to Cyril, "Oh, it's been so long since a light's been on here, we have to stop in." (It was nice to feel that with all the lights going out, we are an old light coming back on.)

As with Shirley, this was Linda's great-grandmother's house, "though I never got beyond the kitchen when the Ralphs had it."

I showed them several small items I had found in one of the sheds, including a small mahogany box with a sliding top. Cyril said, "I noticed that box the minute I come in—it wasn't made yesterday." He also identified an old shotgun cartridge loader and a small wood-handled powder dipper and loader with a calibrated and movable inner sleeve.

But the prize was a small, oval, hinged brass box containing a pair of goggles with small copper-nitrate-colored glass lenses with screened side cups. Were these glasses for welding? Or for viewing solar eclipses? Cyril thought they were most likely used as snow glasses when sealing on the ice to prevent snow blindness.

Jim later confirmed that the glasses in the brass box were indeed snow glasses to prevent "snow burn," a cure for which, he told me—"and you might not believes me, or you might so, but I's telling you the truth—is to put wet tea bags over your eyes!"

Over the next several days I made a thorough inventory of the sheds, starting with the largest one, which I named the "fish shed" because it contains at least a dozen wooden barrels full of fish nets. The middle-sized shed I call the "ladder shed," because it contains six handmade ladders of varying lengths from eight to eighteen feet. The smallest shed, which is attached to the ladder shed, is full of split birch and spruce junks, and so is known as the woodshed.

One day I invited Cyril, Harold Hiscock, and Albert Oldford over to help me identify many of the items. In the ladder shed, for instance, we found a twelve-foot spruce oar with a perpendicular grip near the handle end that Cyril identified as "Nate Ralph's sculling oar."

"It'd go through a hole in the stern, there, you can see where it'd chafe in the hole, and you'd scull her like this," he said, working it in a motion like a fish's tail, but with the blade horizontal. "See, you could just go along working the oar with one hand and jigging a line with the other. Nate would come into the harbour, and he'd cut his engine way out there—way outside—and just scull into his wharf, where Crocker's is now. Nobody knowed if it was to save gas or if he was afraid of the rocks."

There was one item, however, that stumped all of us. It was a pine cylinder about four inches thick and fourteen inches long, rounded at each end. Wrapped around the cylinder in two places was a collar of copper screening. Jim, Fred, Cleaves, Harold, and Cyril all offered suggestions as to its purpose, though not very confidently. But when Howard saw the mysterious object, he instantly said, "I'll tell you what that is, b'y—it's *nuthin'*! That's what it is!"

When I told Sue Cummings this story, she said, "He's right, of course. People didn't keep things because they were interesting, but because they were useful. It had no use for Howard and that's why he said it was 'nuthin'.'"

Albert told me that Nate Ralph had "a big old muzzleloader, an enormous thing, must have been eight feet long, and on the stock it had carved in it 'Harbour Grace Affray.' That was the name of a deadly encounter between Irish Catholics and Anglican authorities in Harbour Grace in the 1840s. If she was in that, she's some old."

I couldn't find "affray" in the *DNE*, but when I mentioned it to Jim, he knew immediately what it was and sang a snatch of a tune from the song that had been made about it.

"Now, I'll tell you something, brother Bob, and you know this is true 'cause you met him, John Cheater—you saw him, with your own eyes. He's a hundred and six, the oldest man in Newfoundland. Well, one time Uncle John and my father—Jim, he was, too—went up to Grand Falls to work. They got to the rail station, and there was mostly Irish Catholics there, going to Grand Falls, too, and one of them says, 'Sing us a song, Mither Moss.' So he sings them that song, 'The Arbour Grace Affray.' Now, John Cheater, see, he's quaking in his boots, he's some afraid. And when Dad finished, there wasn't a sound, and then buddy says, 'That's a damn fine song, Mither Moss,' and another says, 'And damn fine sung, too!'"

"Oh, Father was a strong man, a very strong man," said Jim. "And Lew, my brother, he was strong as an ox—not a big man, you know, but had more meat on him than me. One time he and Uncle John was on the wharf in St. John's and they each carried a wheelbarrow with seven-hundred-weight bags of flour the length of the finger wharf and out to the ship."

"Who was the strongest man you ever knew?"

"The strongest man? That's a good question, brother Bob. Let's see now—now, I'll not tell you a story, you know that, don't you? Why would I do that? Now, my son, I guess—I guess I would say that that was—Sidney Hunter. You know, he was the one started the fire that burned down the town. He was strong as an ox. Not big, but short and stout. Now I'll tell you, and it's no lie—he could throw one bag of flour over his shoulder and another over the other, and then pick up a third with one hand and a fourth with the other, and carry them all—near four hundred pounds! He was some strong."

He told me again how they had no dogs on Flat Island, but that the men would go out in the bay and cut wood and haul them to the shore on wood sleds they called "catamarans" with just a rope over their shoulders, "and when we got home there were sores all over our shoulders and down our backs, and even when they healed there was creases there. Jessie made little pillows, you know, pads for the shoulder, but I still got sores. Each man pulled his own slide, and each slide had a pile of turns—oh, ten to twelve feet long—and it wasn't all downhill either, no b'y. Sometimes he's up and down the slopes, and sometimes buddy would help you up and out, and then you'd help him. On the ponds it was hard going, you see, not like you'd think, 'cause you see he'd be all level."

Fred gave a different description of "Uncle Nate's" muzzleloader:

"He had a big old muzzleloader, six feet long, flint and steel fire, we called it—not a very good system. I think he kept it there in the hall under your stairs, and carved in the stock was his father's, or maybe it was his grandfather's, name. Now, there's a story attached to that gun"—in Fred's world, there's a story attached to a paper clip—"In those days, if you got a sealing bert', it cost you two dollars, but if you carried a gun, you got it for nothing. You see, late in the season you'd be shooting old seals and the ships didn't carry any guns. Anyhow, Uncle Nate's grandfather, or *his* grandfather perhaps it was, took it with him one spring on a swiler that got rafted in the ice up in White Bay—got all crushed up, you know—so the crew walked on the ice till another swiler picked them up, and so they operated with a double crew. And then that one got rafted up, too, and so they found a third ship, and now they had a triple crew, and that one went down, too. They was getting a reputation now as a crew without much luck and no other ship'd pick them up, so they walked on the ice with their guns to Twillingate, where

Nate found the magistrate, and he collected all the guns and brought them to the magistrate and said, 'Your Honor, we've walked with these from the Grey Islands and now we've got to walk to our homes on Flat Island to get in the spring planting, and so we'd like to have you have these taken to St. John's, where we could pick them up when we all goes there next May-month.' And that's what he done, and he walked home to Flat Island on the ice, over a hundred miles. Now that's the story they tell. Where did that gun go to? Perhaps the Lanes got it."

One of the more curious objects we found, stuffed up into the loft of the fish shed, was a homemade lattice or gurney of some sort, about five or six feet long, made of rope, cotton straps, string, and padded canvas. After lunch I took the object over to Cleaves. He and Ettie were lying down, but he perked up when he saw what I was carrying.

"That's a dog collar, see. My, my—I think that's Old Sport's collar. Y's b'y, *that's Uncle Joe's dog's harness*. My, my! Sport was a husky, you know, and some strong. I remember him when I was a boy. You could sit on the dog sledge and he'd take you anywhere. That dog has been places you've never been. Old Sport! You see, the padded collar'd go over his head, like this—then these straps went under his belly, see, and the spreader under his tail. Ho, ho—Old Sport! How many times did he shit on the spreader!"

The harness had likely been put in the shed by Joe Oldford after his dog died, and was in remarkably good condition. It was nice to see that it could bring a smile and a laugh to Cleaves' usually solemn face some three-quarters of a century later.

Cleaves then gave me a variant of the post-burn history here. The fire took place on May 27, 1912. The men were in St. John's getting supplies for the Labrador, and when they returned they found nothing but a charred landscape. Only Harold Ralph's house on the island and Brock Bradley's house down by the harbour escaped. There was not even time to build temporary shelters as the men left for the Labrador on June 10 ("and we already had our caplin in the ground"). Families boarded with other families, in Hollett's Tickle or in St. Chad's, until the men came back in the fall. Then they built the tilts or sheds they lived in that winter and that eventually became the kitchen sheds attached to the back of the old houses. The following spring, 1913, they cut lumber in the woods and began building their houses.

"The kitchens, you see, came before, not after, the houses themselves.

"Now, for nails, we used the wire from the flour barrels. That was the only way you got flour then, in barrels, a hundred and ninety-six pounds. We cut the wire around the staves and used them as nails. They was as thick as a ten-penny nail. That's how scarce and expensive things was then."

Cleaves referred to his uncle Joe as "a very smart man, though he never went to school a day in his life." Fred elaborated on this, saying Joe taught himself to read and had a photographic memory. "He could remember dates and calendar days you wouldn't believe. He'd tell you you bought a pony on a Tuesday, July 15, 1924, twenty years before. Now, how'd he be knowing that? One time he brought home *A Short History of England*, took it up to his room and began turning the pages. Before he went to bed he came down to his father and he could tell him everything, all the kings and queens and reigns and dates. I don't know how he did it. I learned more listening to him than I ever did in school.

"One year the census man came down from Grand Falls and asked Uncle Joe if he could read. He says, 'Yes—and I can figure, too.' He could do multiplication and long division, you see.

"'How often did you go to school?'" the census man asked.

"Uncle Joe scratched his head and said, 'Oh, let me see now—about once a year, I reckon, when I goes up for the woman's sale at the chapel.'"

"'B'jeezus!' says the census man. 'We need more fellas like you! I've got some up in Botwood can't tell a bean from a bull's foot!'"

Back at the house now, I sit here on the front stoop, pouring my third cup of tea of the morning from the pot set on an old brown wooden lunch pail, chronicling the life of the small village as I see it, raising my head and my hand to each passing car, whether or not I know them, or can even see who they are. I feel in some strange way connected to Joe Oldford, and not just because I now live where he lived some fifty years ago and sit on the stoop that he surely sat on, waving to the town as it passed by.

"Uncle Joe," as he is referred to even by Joan Oldford and others who only knew him through stories; Uncle Joe, whose brothers were Tom, Esau, and William; Uncle Joe, oldest of the four Oldford brothers of that generation according to Joan, who, because he was the oldest, remained unmarried, living with and caring for his mother, Charlotte Ann, postmistress and matriarch of Squid Tickle, whose own husband, Eli, one of the pioneers who settled Burnside from Salvage, died young (at age fifty); Uncle Joe, who, with his younger brother Tom, built this house for their mother after the Great Fire, using only hand tools; Uncle Joe, who never went to school but nonetheless taught himself to read, somehow found copies of English history and Shakespeare, and could and did recite the names of the monarchs of England and passages from the plays (what was that like, hearing iambic pentameter spoken in an equally antique tongue on shores unmoored from the culture and history of their origins?); Uncle Joe, owner of "Sport" the dog, continued to live as a bachelor in this house after his mother died. After he died, it devolved to his brother Tom, who, living in Grand Falls, in turn sold it to Nate Ralph in the late 1950s, from whose grandson Sheldon we bought it in 2001.

On Saturday evening we took Jim and Jessie to the newly refurbished Beaches Heritage Arts & Heritage Centre in Eastport to hear Fergus O'Byrne and Jim Payne, two of the best musicians in Newfoundland and part of the Newfoundland Renaissance of the early 1970s. The theater was packed when we arrived and the boys gave them their money's worth, and more: a high-energy, professional, polished, audience-savvy performance of songs, dances, stories, jokes, etc.

The audience was mostly local, middle-aged to elderly, with a scattering of young people. They all responded enthusiastically and as one, exhibiting the sense that this was *their* music, *their* people. Even hokey "Newfie" songs like "We'll Rant and We'll Roar" sounded authentic in their hands.

We had supper at J & J's: buffalo wings, dips, canned corn, carrots and peas, cold red jelly with crème fraîche. I heard some more about how Jim met Jessie on the Labrador when she was a cook on her family's schooner. She was eighteen, Jim was twenty-four. Jim's crew came aboard Jessie's boat for a scoff, and Jim said that he indicated Jessie to one of the crew members and said, "There's my wife." That was in 1948. They didn't marry for two years, though Jessie was of age and Jim didn't need to ask her father's permission. Jessie said, "I just didn't want to get married right away." Jim said that for a few years he worked in the salmon canning plant on Flat Island, earning fifty cents an hour, "which was a lot more than I ever made fishing. My son, some years we only made five cents a pound for lobster—five cents!—and now they is getting five dollars and seven-five cents. And fish—fish was worth nothing—two or three cents a pound, that's all. After a trip to the Labrador, you might make five hundred dollars, but that was good. I rarely made that—maybe three hundred dollars—you'd go down into the ship cabin after the fish was unloaded, after the voyage was out, you know, and the paymaster would count out your money. Now, the captain, he'd get half of the take, the ship's share, say it was five hundred dollars, and then you'd get your share, say fifty dollars, and then he'd get a share, too, another fifty, so you see, you'd get fifty dollars, he'd get five hundred and fifty dollars then out of that"—here gesturing strongly, reenacting the talking—"they'd take back the money for gear, for food, for baccy, for flour, molasses, sugar—and there was nothing left."

No wonder they made whatever they could and never threw anything away.

The next day I stopped to see Essie at Ron's store and told her she must come down and see the house before we go, but she said, "Oh, my darling, I don't have no time. As soon as I finishes up at the store here, Ron and I we goes up to the pond every evening—troutin', you knows. And then on the weekend Ron's da goes with us to the cabin. It's a change for him, you know. No, my dear, I don't haves a minute to meself."

"We have a word for that at home, Essie. It's called slavery."

"Oh, you can say that."

SUMMER 2003

THIS AFTERNOON I WAS PICKING BLUEBERRIES IN THE OLD CEMetery when Fred stopped by. I asked him why the old cemetery was located where it was. He said that he had two answers. The first was, "because it's not located somewhere else." (Thanks, Fred.) The second was that "when Grandfather Eli came to Burnside from Salvage in the 1880s, they had a couple of winter houses—tilts, we call them—on the rise where the cemetery is. They had a little girl who died one winter, so they buried her there, and when others died, they just placed them next to her. It just became the burying place. At least that's the story."

Most of Fred's stories are comical in nature, but sometimes they contain an element of the supernatural. For instance, he told me of the time when he was nine or ten and making hay with his uncle Will.

"We had got two pooks made—I guess you'd call them stacks—when the weather cleared and Uncle Will decided we should undo the pooks and spread the hay to dry. He said, 'I wish the devil would take this hay,' and no sooner had he said it than we heard a mighty roar to the south. We turned and saw one of those whirlwinds we had in those days come down the hill and lifted up one of those pooks and carried it up into the air and spread it out in a circle around us a hundred feet wide, neat as you please, and the last we saw of that hay, it was being whirled out across the bay in a golden heap! It didn't touch the other one and Uncle Will didn't say a word."

A gentle warm breeze is blowing through the grove of tall, trembling aps between the house and the road. I've strung a hammock between two of the larger trees, a perfect place to lie down and look up at that lacy canopy of shivering green leaves and blue sky. I still find it hard to believe that I own a house with a water view (albeit a distant one) purchased for less than the price of a used car, and on which I pay no taxes.

Even Kathy now admits we did the right thing to buy this house when we did. There's been a real demand in Burnside for old houses lately. Bert Burden's house recently sold for $70,000 CAN, a price that seems ridiculously high to many people in town, despite the fact that it's a lovely piece of waterfront land that has enough room for another house to be built on it.

There's also been a minor influx of young people into town. One of them is Megan Chiperzak, a young woman in her early twenties who moved here last fall. She bought a small house down at Hollett's Tickle with some sheds that she has turned into cabins, and is now running a "tourist retreat" where, among other things, guests can go on "guided vision quests." For eight hundred dollars, she will supply you with a tent and water and the privilege of living on the edge of a cliff without food for several days, being eaten by gallinippers the size of miniature helicopters, and growing mildew inside your ears.

Fred's grandson, David Rockwood, who always dreamed of returning here, is running a kayaking tour business out of Terra Nova National

Park. He and Megan met this spring—"it was 'love at first sight,'" said David—and now they both plan to stay here year-round.

The weather has turned cold and wet. One afternoon, I decided to walk out the new trail I discovered east of town that follows the rocky shore at least a mile or so along increasingly sheer cliffs. I donned my mackintosh and Cape Ann sou'wester, grabbed a gaff out of the fish shed for a walking stick, and hiked the trail for about a half hour in steady rain until I was completely out of sight of houses.

The wind was east, blowing in my face, but the sou'wester worked perfectly, draining water out over the back of my neck, and the cloak of my mackintosh kept my backpack dry. At one point I came upon a dramatic cut in the shore, with great blocks of shale overhanging a small cove. When I came around it, I saw the last thing I expected to see in that place: an orange nylon tent staked to the edge of the cliff.

Though it was still raining lightly, the ground outside the tent was strewn with an open sleeping bag, a hat, and various pieces of clothing, as if set out there to dry. The tent was completely zipped up except for a small vent near the top, through which I could see a blond-haired woman sitting up, either unaware of or studiously ignoring me. Not wanting to startle her, I stomped around, banging my gaff pole on the rocks, deliberately making noise so that she could inquire who was out there. But there was no response. Then I realized the image I must have presented: a humpbacked old man with a grizzled beard, unshaven and untrimmed for the past two months, wearing an ancient mariner's hat and carrying a wooden pole tipped with a sharp point and a hook. Well, if I had been in her place, I'm not sure I would have called out either. So I left her there, undisturbed, and headed back.

When I later told Megan about my encounter, she said, "Yes, that's one of ours. She's been out there two days. She'll be back tomorrow. By now, without any food, she's probably in a fairly intense state. I suspect she thought you were part of her vision. It'll be interesting to see how she incorporates it." I said I hoped she wouldn't be disappointed and demand her money back.

O Squid Tickle, Squid Tickle! What would Bert Burden make of this!

Another young couple, Diane Hollett and Sean Tiller, who have two young kids, Eli and Josie, just bought Susan Davis's trailer next to Bert Burden's house. They're from "town" (St. John's), but Diane has roots here. (Her mother Grace is Harold Hiscock's sister.) Sean was a piano tuner for years, traveling all around the island, but when they started a family, he decided he had to earn "real money" and is now a pharmacist. They brought a piano with them, the first in Burnside. He only plays by ear, and when I sat down and played a few scales and chords, they both said, "You're in!"

Sue and Harold have also arrived back for the weekend. They told us the story behind the sale of Susan Davis's trailer and Bert Burden's house. It seems that Susan was expecting to get Bert's house: "Everyone in the community thought Bert was going to leave it to her," said Sue, "her being a nurse who had done a lot for them over the years. So she sold her trailer to the Tillers in anticipation of getting Bert's house. But when Bert and Laura moved to the retirement home in Glovertown, he sold his house to the highest bidder and Susan Davis was left with nothing."

As Jim said, Bert's father, Stan Burden, "was a ha-a-a-rd man, and Bert's hard, too." His mother, who lived into her nineties, "used to paint her face up like this"—here he pulled his cheeks back—"and we'd see her out in the carrot patch picking out weeds."

Jim is a kinetic man. He cannot say things without to some degree acting them out physically, with bodily or facial gestures. When he wants to tell you something, he will sit up, lean forward, and hold your wrist or hand, as if physical contact were necessary to convey his meaning. Life flows in and out of him as though through an electric conduit.

Jim's speech, like ancient Greek poetry, has certain ritualistic conventions, or repeated phrases. He must have said to me a dozen times or more, "Now, Bob, I'm going to tell you something, and you can believe me or no. The hardest thing about making friends is when they leave. Now when you leaves, we'll be lost for days."

My role is to reply, "Yes, but it's better to have made friends and miss them than not to have any." To which he will invariably reply with equal energetic assent, "Eg-zactly! You've got that right, my son!"

Jim seems to have the ability not only to hold two contradictory ideas in his mind at the same time, but also not to see them as contradictory, but rather as complementary and mutually valid truths: two halves of life, the light and the dark, like these fair and foul weather days, equally acknowledged and expressed. This seems to be the essence of the Newfoundlanders' view of life, and the source of their mental health.

This is light-switch weather, with fronts and showers, clearings and clouds, calms and sudden gusts, flicking on and off with a disorientating suddenness. I can step out the side porch one moment into a hot sun of 25 degrees Celsius and think at last we will have a solar shower day, go back inside to take off my shirt, only to step outside minutes later into a brisk wind, heavy cloud cover, and 14 degrees, the aps leaves crashing softly like green surf.

The rapid changes give one the sense of living in one of those stop-motion, high-speed weather sequences so common now in films as a cheap way of indicating the passage of time and/or supernatural forces.

Last Saturday we took J & J again to hear Jim Payne and Fergus O'Byrne play to a full house at the Beaches Arts & Heritage Centre in Eastport. It was another professional, three-hour, well-received concert by these two veteran musicians. You know it's a Newfoundland audience because within a measure or two of the first song, half of the feet in the house are beating time on the floor and half of the hands are slapping half of the knees.

Many of the songs they sang were written by Jim Payne, and I was struck again by the element of joy that seems so inherent in them, even, perhaps especially, when that joy is qualified, as it must be to ring true. Their signature song, "Wave Over Wave," for example, has the telling, repeated phrase, "I'm as happy a man *as the sea will allow.*"

In most oral cultures verbal dexterity is regarded as a virtue, and Newfoundland is no exception. One can see displays of this skill in "list songs" like "Ships and Captains," which catalogues all of the wooden-wall sealers and their skippers in the 1920s; or the one that circumnavigates the island with place names, providing a musical map to the coast; or in the tongue-twisting "cumulative songs," such as "The Crooked Crab Tree," which is a variant on the "House That Jack Built" model.

Much of Newfoundland history is recorded in local ballads, and Fergus sang an old one about a clash between Confederation and anti-Confederation forces in a town on the Bonavista Peninsula in the 1860s, in which an anti-Confederation mob pelted one man with "soldiers."

"Now," said Fergus," do any of you know what 'soldiers' are?"

"Yes b'y," spoke up a large man in the audience. "Them's rotten squid!"

After the concert, we were "commanded" by Jessie to come back to their house for some soup she had prepared for us. As we ate, Jim retold the story of the Magic Arm Disaster, adding several details we had not heard:

"The crew had loaded five thousand junks of birch in the skiff when the five men pushed off from shore and started up the make-or-break and down she went, bow first. Three other men stayed onshore, otherwise they moight have been gone, too."

Jim said that his older brother Lew was forever "marked" by the disaster. I assumed he meant in the psychological sense, since Lew was one of only two survivors, though I should have known better. Newfoundlanders hardly ever refer to the inner life of others.

"No," he said, "it was when he come up and Bill Troke, hanging on with one hand to the skiff as it resurfaced, grabbed onto Lew's forearm with such force that he always said, 'I can feels it to this day.' Five men were buried under the load of junks and drowned—five. Lew"—Jim demonstrating this with his long, bony arms—"picked them up out of the water and set them out on the deck of the skiff. They sailed back into the harbour with the men laid out and covered in canvas on deck with the ship's flag at half-mast. One of them had only been married for six months. The night before, Uncle John had a dream of their boat coming in with her flag lowered to half-mast."

David Rockwood is the son Fred never had, and always refers to him as "Pap." He said that when Willis, the ninety-one-year-old and oldest Oldford brother, came for a month's visit last spring, it was his last trip.

"He came to say goodbye to everyone. I thought they'd be reminiscing about old times, but what did they talk about? Tools! And it wasn't even about the tools themselves, which might have been interesting. It was all about who had loaned what tool to who and where they was now.

"'I gave you that saw twenty years ago.'

"'Yes, but I give it to Cleaves.'

"'Y's b'y, but it's been up Con's store the last five years.'

"And on and on and on until it had all come around and they had determined where every last wrench and bit had ended up! My son!"

As Cleaves always says, "Tools is where it's at." I guess Shirley is right: there's carpenter's blood in the veins of every Oldford.

Then David told me about the "goons" from St. Chad's who had come over to Burnside the other day "to get rocks":

"I was outside Megan's house working on an old engine when this car-truck shows up, a big black 1970 Ford that's all canted back like a speedboat planing and the muffler going *clank-clank-clank* over the ruts. It brakes on the hill and settles back on its rear like a dog sitting up. Then this hulking goon steps out and with him is an eight-year-old kid with the thickest set of Coke-bottle glasses you've ever seen. They walks over and stands in front of me. I says, 'How you doin'?' and the goon just nods and then they just stand there looking at me, not saying a thing. I keeps talking, trying to pry a few words out of them 'cause Megan's getting a bit nervous, and finally the goon says, 'Rocks. We come over to get rocks for our yard. They ain't no rocks in St. Chad's.'

"I figure out he means they ain't no *loose* rocks in St. Chad's, just ledge, and that they use them to extend their yards, you know, piling up the rocks on the landwash and then covering it up with peat and sod, increasing their frontage, though God knows why. That trunk was full of rocks. I tells them I've about given up on this engine and the eight-year-old goggle-eyed boy says, 'I bet we could fix that engine up,' and the goon shoots him a look and says, 'No we can't.'

"Well, I figured out what was going on, and later that day I dragged the engine out to the side of the road with the truck and sure enough the next day it was gone. You could see the little yellow exhaust pipe from it sticking out of their trunk, the chassis going *clank-clank-clank* on the road. It's still in there—guess they haven't yet decided if they can fix it, or maybe just how to get it out of that trunk. I'd love to send some of Megan's vision questers over to St. Chad's. I guess they'd get some visions all right."

On Saturday evening Kathy and I went once again to the Beaches Arts & Heritage Centre in Eastport to hear a concert called "Island Voices." It was a fine show, with professional singers from around the island, but it was a special treat for us because it included Sue Cummings and Jim Moss, the first time we ever heard Jim sing in public.

Sue introduced Jim, saying how he had been such "a presence" for them over the years, sitting on his bridge and regaling the neighborhood in song. Onstage, however, he was very formal, and stiff, like a little boy at a recital. Though towering over Sue, he stood there, holding her hand, just like in that photograph of him as a boy on Flat Island holding his mother's hand. He would whisper something in Sue's ear and she would say, "Well, tell them yourself, Jim," and he would say the name of the song, encircle the mike with one hand, and begin in a loud, clear, strong, sliding voice. He sang three songs, one an old love song about springtime in the month of May, the tragic ballad of the *Union* of St. John's, and a third about a crew that mutinies against a drunken skipper.

Most of the singers sang a capella songs that they ended in the traditional folk ballad way, that is, by *speaking* the last several words, finishing on a downward pitch, like a *tump*—a convention, it seemed to me, calculated to bring the singer and his audience out of the artifice of the song and into the real world of the spoken word. A similar function is served by the traditional, and standard, "nonsense endings" of many folktales. Yet Jim Moss, the only unschooled singer among them, ended all of his songs with long, held notes.

Yesterday afternoon Kathy prepared supper—chicken thighs with roasted vegetables and an apple-strawberry-blueberry crumble using the first of our blueberries, some of Ettie's apples, and strawberries from the sister-in-law of a woman clerk at Foodland—which we took over to Cleaves and Ettie, who were quite pleased. Kathy wore her new fringed white crocheted shawl that Shirley had just finished for her, and I put on a clean dark blue cotton shirt I got at "New to You," the Glovertown thrift store, for seventy-five cents.

Cleaves talked about cutting timber in the winter with his brothers on the Terra Nova River before he got married. His father, Esau, took them over to Magic Arm, from where they walked along the shore ice to Alexander Bay, catching the train at Glovertown to Terra Nova. They arrived there at 3 p.m. and immediately set out for Eight Mile Dip, camped overnight, then walked another twenty miles to the winter camp on the river. The three brothers (Willis, after burying his first two wives, had already moved to Toronto) worked all winter and came back with one hundred dollars shared among them, while their father, Esau, who had gotten work building a steeple on the Anglican church in Grand Falls, was paid the princely sum of thirty-eight cents an hour and put one hundred dollars in his bank account.

Cleaves "went away" to work often, both before and after his marriage, living in Gander, St. John's, or Toronto. No wonder a strong matriarchal tradition grew up here.

(Jim said that when the men from Flat Island were away on the Labrador, the women did all the men's work, including, when necessary, rowing a sick person over to the doctor in Salvage and back.)

Cleaves and Ettie had planned to get married in March, because he had to leave for a job in Toronto right after Easter. But the minister refused to marry them during Lent—"there's a lot of foolishness in the church," commented Ettie—so they had to wait until Easter Saturday to get married, and as it turned out Cleaves had to leave *that evening*—right after the wedding dinner. He didn't return until August, when Ettie was, presumably, still a new bride.

He talked about various injuries to his head, including falling into his shop's auto pit one night, or having a frozen block of logs he was chopping at suddenly give way and turn his ax head so the blade split open his skull above his left eye. I told him he had blue eyes that reminded me of my father's. He asked me when my father died, and when I said fourteen years ago, he said, "That must be hard on you, b'y," and I realized I was tearing up, as I had not done for my father for a number of years.

Willis's son Wayne was here this summer, surveying a piece of Bert's land he is buying to build a summer house on. He said the land looks "wild" to him, that "forty years ago this was all gardens, all fenced in and taken care of. The yards were fenced in to keep the animals out. Going down the road, you might meet a herd of sheep, or even a herd of horses."

I look now across the street at a field of waving fuchsia fireweed where, only a half dozen years ago, Cleaves stood beside his tepee peeling off the turns to lay across the wooden bays of his sawhorse. The engine, the saw pulleys, and the saw bays were all but submerged, sunken in the tall forest of flowers, as under dream snow. These artifacts now resemble the family plots in the cemetery, buried in the blossoms of foliage gone wild. So abandonment grows up to original beauty here.

There is a poignancy in listening to Jim talk, as he often does, about the old schooners he knew and sailed on from Flat Island, that is more than simple nostalgia. For him these vessels are a benchmark of memory, a measuring stick for a life that is disappearing ever more rapidly.

"One time, my son, there were forty schooners tied up on Flat Island in the winter. Now all are gone, even the wharves. Dere were fourteen men sailed on her to the Labrador, and now I'm the only one left."

Listening to him, I thought of the men, the veterans of World War II, Jim's age, who used to write in regularly to the "Ask the Globe" column of the *Boston Globe*, inquiring about a ship they had served on in the war. The answers, always given at some length and in a tone of respect, related the tours and battles and honors that were "hers," and then, in a tone of sadness, recorded when she was sunk or, much more frequently, sold, serving in a series of increasingly shabby roles, like an old horse, until, ultimately, inevitably, she was "sold for scrap" to some shipwrecking operation in Thailand or Hoboken.

Like these ships, the Flat Island schooners were the repository of their crews' lives and well-being, not only the place where these men bonded in a communal act of self-survival, but also the means of that survival. These ships contained their youth, their collective strength, their participation in something larger than themselves, and the survival of their communities and their way of life.

I met Henry Oldford in his yard the other evening. He told me the disturbing news that the church committee voted to stop the ringing of the bells—except for weddings, funerals, and other special occasions.

"You see, we're getting up there. There's only four of us left—Eldon, Cleaves, Reg Lane, and myself. Cleaves can't get up the stairs anymore. Fred can ring the bells as well as he can do anything, but he never hardly did it, you see? We tried it without opening the shutters, but it sent all the sound down into the church. So we voted to stop ringing them. We all knows when services are anyways; notices are sent around. So we don't really needs them." (Oh, Henry, reason not the *need*!)

I asked, "If somebody wanted to ring the bells, would they let him?"

"Oh, I don't know—I suppose they would."

So on Sunday evening I rang the bells of St. Alban's. At first I thought I would have to do double duty, as Mary Oldford grabbed me at the school on Saturday and said, "You'll play for me tomorrow, won't ye?" Linda and Joan were both unavailable, so I couldn't see how I could refuse her, though I wasn't sure of the propriety of running up and down the steeple stairs and back and forth across the chancel between ringings to play the prelude. But in the end, they got Dot Rose from Eastport to come over and play, so my duties were much simplified.

I went over to the church about 6:15 and found Henry and Albert

Noel, the lay minister in the small side room that leads into the chancel. I asked Henry why they didn't just cut another hole in the second-story floor and extend the rope to ground level, thus sparing the arthritic knees of the aging bell ringers.

"It's not just the stairs, b'y," he said, rubbing his shoulder. "I've got bad arthritis in me arm as well."

Nonetheless, he climbed up the first flight of stairs with me to where the bell rope hung down beside the single chair whose seat had a strip of carpeting laid across it. A piece of cotton rope two feet long had been spliced onto the old hemp rope so that the bell could be rung from a sitting position.

I climbed the narrow stairs to the belfry, wondering how long it had been since the bell was last rung. The inner wooden, barred shutters were stiff on their hinges, and as I opened them hundreds of dead flies dropped onto the pine floor.

Henry said I needn't open the windows in the belfry, as the bell "wasn't for calling people to church. Everyone here has their printed schedule and knows when services is. If they aren't coming, ringing the bell won't bring them." But I knew that Jim and Jessie and other "backsliders" liked to hear it, and that Cleaves could no longer make it to services.

The bell, cast in 1954, was first heard by Cleaves that winter when he was in the woods, loading turns on his slide:

"It rang in the middle of the day, and I knew she was ringing for a woman in town who had been sick for some time. So the first time it rang was for a funeral, and I thought then that someday that bell will ring for me and for my brothers."

There was a sparse congregation there that evening, similar in number and makeup to the congregations I had first played for seven years ago. The service was scheduled as a Eucharist service, with the retired bishop officiating, but Henry told me that "family troubles" called him away, which was just as well, since Henry said that "evening services aren't a good time for Communion since most of the congregation is tired."

I came down from the belfry, and before I could ask when to begin, Henry took the rope in hand and gave it a powerful pull that immediately started the bell ringing. It sent an umbrella of steely sound down through the plank floor overhead, as if a shell of ringing bronze had descended over the building. With each blow of sound there was a hard *tunk*, like the stomp of a great foot, which, I surmised, was the great bell rocking in its cradle.

Henry handed the rope to me, shouting through the din, "Start at 6:20, ring for five minutes, then wait a minute, then ring again until 6:30." With that he left me to ring the bell, and it did not take long to convince me of my theory that this instrument of summons has been a major cause of deafness among the older men in town who had served as bell ringers, so that some, like Cleaves, can no longer even hear it from their houses. It also has, as I had been warned, a powerful back kick, and I found I needed only to give it a gentle, sliding pull at the end of the rope's descent to keep it pealing. It definitely had a rhythm, a cycle of its own, which I could not have controlled if I had wanted to. The bell essentially rang itself.

I sat on the chair, looking out the small window on the northeast side of the steeple tower, over the harbour and out to the bay islands. Every activity here—ringing the church bell, painting one's house, picking berries on a hillside, sitting in one's outhouse, etc.—provides a stunning view. I felt as if I was in a distinguished line of men who had, at first, stood, then sat, ringing the bell, summoning the community, at first on foot, then by car, to worship God and to pray, first for the king, then for the queen. It was a privilege for which it seemed deafness might not be too high a price to pay.

The five minutes went slowly, so slowly that I thought perhaps my watch had stopped. The great, majestic sound of the bell seemed to flatten time again, to hold us in its grip, unchanging, in its iron will.

Between its peals I could hear the wheezy sound of Dot Rose's prelude coming up from below. She played the old harmonium, which each year loses one or two more keys or a stop, like someone giving CPR to a cardiac patient who responds reluctantly, as if resentful of being resuscitated.

When the congregation began to sing the first hymn, it could not have been called music so much as a communal exercise in sacred noise, but the intent was sincere, ancient, unselfconscious, containing nothing retro, neo-, revived or preserved, but only itself, true to itself and to its history, like a bird calling from a forlorn and diminishing plain.

At 6:24 I released the ropes and skipped up the stairs to the belfry. I decided I would close the shutters in order to intensify the sound on the second ring, as Cleaves told me he liked to have done, so that he could "feel it in my bones." It took me a minute or so to do, and when I came back down the bell was still clanging with no discernible diminishment in frequency or volume. I let it ring another minute or so, and still felt no change. It seemed to have the inertia of Bert's wooden punt long after I had shipped the oars, cleaving its way through the wind and waves that day I had taken her out into the bay.

I finally grabbed the rope and, as if applying a brake, drew it sharply to a halt with a single, truncated *clunk*. I had the feeling that if I had not stopped it, the great bell would have gone on ringing, minute after minute, undiminished, so that Albert Noel, the lay reader, would finally have resigned himself, removed his vestments, and signaled mutely to the small congregation that they were dismissed. Dot Rose would have stopped pumping, pulled the loose leaves of the music book back together, closed the keyboard cover, and turned off the light, and still the bell would keep ringing. Reg Lane and Eldon Hapgood would lock the vestry door and replace the old-fashioned key on the magnetic strip attached to the underside of the podium, then turn out the rest of the lights and exit the sanctuary, leaving its door, as always, open to anyone. And still the bell would ring, as one by one the inhabitants of the tiny village died off, providing an uninterrupted and uncounted tolling for the years of the dead, who fell rapidly now and overlapping, like the last waves of those World War II veterans, into the vault of time, so that finally the bell would ring through an empty church, reverberating throughout a town of empty and dark houses, the bell rope slipping back and forth, up and down through the small hole in the spruce ceiling, as if moving unhurriedly, with controlled passion, toward rapture.

SUMMER 2004

A LINE STORM JUST CAME THROUGH OVER BREAKFAST, ONE OF those sudden, characteristic yet always surprising changes in the weather here in Burnside. As Kathy and I were listening to a CBC interview with P. D. James over a second cup of coffee, I noticed some slanting raindrops outside the front window. Within two minutes it had developed into a full-fledged, deluxe deluge, with hail and thunder, driving almost horizontally from the southwest, and the temperature dropping nearly ten degrees Celsius. Even as we raced around the house, closing windows and bringing in chairs off the back porch, I could see patches of blue to the east, and now the storm has blown out to sea and we are back to our usual, if somewhat cooler, mix of sun and clouds.

We had arrived at our house on Wednesday evening, and within seconds Ettie came out on her porch, waved, and shouted, "Welcome to Burnside!"

She and Cleaves had moved back here from their Eastport apartment in April. Ettie says she thinks this may be their last summer in the Burnside house. She said it's just too much trouble bringing stuff back and forth, but I think she's just lonely.

"No one visits here in the spring, and then, after the summer, you're gone."

Cleaves is more philosophical, and also angrier. "Now when I leaves here and turns the key, I think I might never come back here again! You work and you work and you work trying to make everything just right. I built every window and every door and every stair in this house, trying to make it perfect, you know, and now *I just doesn't care!* I can go out and close the door and think, 'That's it—I might never be coming back!' Isn't that strange?"

"But you're not sorry you did all that work, are you?"

"No—no, I can't say I am," he admitted, with some irritation at not being allowed the full measure of his dismissal.

We had brought over some books for them to take with them. Cleaves had always been an avid reader, but now, he says, "I don't read much anymore, not like I used to. Just my Bible—I read through the Bible twice this winter, from start to finish. But I'm just not interested in *stories* anymore, you know? I've lost interest, for some reason. And when you've lost that, then what's the point?"

They express it differently, but both Cleaves and Ettie are in the process of letting go of their lives here in Burnside, Ettie with some sadness and regret, but also with an emotional segue into new relationships that women seem more easily capable of; Cleaves with a kind of insistent refusal to feel the loss of things, to dismiss life before it dismisses him (and what, after all, is the Bible but a dismissal of this life?).

Even in Cleaves' decrepitude one can still see the spark between him and Ettie. When Kathy kidded him about Ettie finding a new man if he died, he grinned at Ettie and quipped, "I've had the best of you, old girl."

Our house seems to have weathered the winter reasonably well, though the chest freezer has apparently given out, probably from all the starts and stops we imposed on it using it as a fridge the past two summers. It is time to order a proper refrigerator.

Woody Oldford drove by in a pickup full of scrap wood he was hauling to the dump. Woody, a man of about sixty, bought Bert Burden's old house last summer. He has reroofed the building with red shingles and repainted the clapboards yellow, putting more color into this house than I imagine it has ever seen. It looked so bright and cheerful, so welcoming and outgoing, that I did not at first recognize it as Bert's house. Bert and Laura are still surviving, Bert at the Manor in Glovertown, Laura now in the hospital in Gander. As Cleaves said, she's "dying and dying and dying, but keeps going."

I met Bill Hiscock on the road. He has been here since late April lobstering with Reg Lane and working on an addition to his and Carol's cabin, which sits on a rise above the tickle. We have visited them several times, and of all the people we have met here, they seem to be the ones we feel most compatible with.

The oldest male member of the Hiscock clan, Bill worked for Aliant, the Newfoundland phone company, for thirty years, hating most of it. Carol said it nearly did in their marriage. He took early retirement and has been spending more and more time in Burnside, which Carol said has "given us a second chance." We have been spending a lot of time with them, sitting on the deck of their cabin, sipping cosmopolitans and enjoying easy, undirected conversation.

Cyril and Linda arrived yesterday for the weekend. Linda lost her voice for several weeks, but seems to have gotten it back, hugging me and saying, "It sure is nice to be able to sing in church again!" Sue and Harold arrive tomorrow, and who knows how many more to come for the long Canada Day weekend? And still Jim repeats his mantra: "I'll tell you, Bob b'y—the day will come when not a soul will be living in Burnside and St. Chad's, nor Salvage nor Eastport nor Glovertown neither." And in a way he's right—no one he knows, anyway.

After supper we walked over to Jim and Jessie's and found they had company—two sisters from Fair Island. Bracketing them with his long, bony arms as if showing off a prize giant pumpkin, he said, "Brother Bob, you come just at the roight time! Here's two fine women now, Sadie and Vickie. They're both Picketts—you know, that you nails to a fence!"

They are cousins of Jessie's, both now in their mid-sixties. Sadie has a sturdy body, short blond hair, a clear-eyed look, and a sense of boundless energy. When Jessie said that Sadie was a first cousin once removed, Sadie said, "Oh, I don't know about removed. We never did removes." She is, as Jessie kept repeating quietly in her presence, "a case." More like a force of nature. She dominated the conversation as a band dominates a dance floor, or a wind a field. She seemed to be talking to all of us at once, forcing everyone to smile or laugh. She wore a white sleeveless blouse with a starched collar and a black bra, and when she talked she kept leaning toward us with her full breasts and her bright, burning eyes.

She told of a friend of hers on Flat Island whose family was RC:

"Whenever there was a storm, the mother would have all the children get under the kitchen table and then she'd throw a big sheet over it, and when the thunder started, she'd grab some holy water, lift up one edge of the sheet, and sprinkle the water on them, saying each time, 'Fathersonandholyghost, fathersonandholyghost, fathersonandholyghost,' and then if the lightning flashed she'd do it again and say, 'Blessem, blessem, blessem,' until, by Jesus, by the end of the storm the children was all soaked!"

She and Vickie used to visit Jim and Jessie on Flat Island, and she remembers Howard Moss, "who was just a little brat. We thought we was something out on Fair Island 'cause we were a bigger settlement than the others, and we had a post office there, and then, you know, when we lefts and I went to school in St. John's, I looked around and I thought, Jesus, maybe we weren't that sophisticated after all, and I vowed niver to say a single word about Fair Island after that, because, you know, I felt we weren't up to snuff.

"I had a cousin served on an army base in Ontario, and when mail call come he stepped up and said, 'Wellbyenymailfrme?' and the sergeant said, '*What* are you talking about?' and he said, 'Enymailfrmetday?' and they had to find a nurse from here to translate for him, he talked so fast, you know.

"Then one year I went down to New York City. Well, you know now what New York City's like—Jesus, everybody walking around as much at 3 a.m. as at 3 p.m. Anyhow, we wanted to get on the highway out of town and we were there at the ramp, but there was so much traffic we'd ease forward and *zoom!* we'd scoot back, push out again, and *zoom!* pushed back again, over and over, so's I thought we'd never get out, and from that minute I decided I'd never fail to talk about Fair Island— outhouses, ballycatters, whatever, to anyone, because, you see, I realized then what a wonderful life I'd had there."

As they got up to leave, Sadie said, "Now, you might sees me tomorrow again, or you might sees me in another ten years. Tell Howard you seen Sadie—likely he'll remember me. That were fifty-two years ago—oh my Lord!"

Vickie said maybe twenty words during the whole visit.

After they left, Jessie said that Sadie had married "a German gentleman, but she doesn't live with him now. They might still be married. She goes up to see him now and then, but she can't stand living with him. She lives now with a younger man."

I could see that. It would take one to keep up with her. Like a force of nature, she waters a field, or scorches it black, and then moves on.

I cannot tell you the sense of well-being that this place gives me.

More members of the Hiscock clan have been making inroads in the town. Sean Tiller and Diane Hollett, who bought Susan Davis's trailer, have added a large deck onto the back of the trailer and filled in a large part of the bog surrounding it. Sean hopes to build a sauna, and Diane has beds of herbs and vegetables growing. Diane's brother, Ken Hollett, and his wife Sandra Tilley, both lawyers in St. John's, have also recently bought an old house at the end of the island road.

More houses have been sold or built over the last few years than in the entire previous generation, though the transactions still take place primarily within the old families. An exception is the Chiperzaks' house, which was recently sold to Jennifer Stender (Bill Hiscock's sister Jean's daughter), a doctor, and her husband Eric Pike, also a doctor in St. John's. The Chiperzaks apparently could not take the isolation they found in Burnside.

We went over to Carol and Bill Hiscock's last evening for drinks and finger food, including mussels Bill had caught and smoked. Today was his last day with Reg, hauling in lobster traps, which, he said, was fine with him since "my back's been hurting me something fierce." Word is this may be Reg's last season going out.

Linda and Shirley also dropped by. Linda, Burnside's Wife of Bath, said she had been hanging out her new, lacy underwear earlier that day:

"You know, a green bra, orange and yellow panties, little underpants. Anyhoo, I went inside and I hears a knock and wonders who can that be, so I goes to the door and there's a fellow I've never seen before. He mutters something about having bought a motor from Terry Matthews next door, who's not up from Halifax yet; but I could see him eyeing the underthings on the line as he's talking to me, looking at me, glancing at the green and yellow things flapping at his ear. I could hear him thinking, 'My Lord, who is this woman?' I think he thought I was going to jump him. Finally, he backed up into the flower patch and I had to reach out and catch him. He left kind of quick. No, I haven't told Cyril yet—there's some things you don't tell on the phone."

The next evening Ettie, Linda, and Kathy did each other's nails, put on their dresses and lipstick, and went over to the newly opened cybercafe in Eastport for a girls' night out. Ettie loved it. She had a big piece of pink strawberry cake, and when Kathy ordered coffee with steamed milk in it, she said, "I'll have some of that," and then looked around for more.

I stayed with Cleaves, who didn't feel up to going out. I poured him some Leffe beer, to which he responded, "Nothing wrong with that beer, b'y"—and had another.

Cleaves was born in 1915, three years after the Great Fire. He remembers staying with relatives "down the tickle" before their house was rebuilt. "Some folks never did rebuild, and Father never did finish his house inside. It was hard to rebuild, you see, because there was no wood around after the fire. It killed a lot of animals, too. The cows got into the fish flakes, you see, trying to get away from the heat, and it all crashed down on them."

Cleaves is due to go back to Grand Falls for further evaluation to see if they will operate on his urinary tract, but at eighty-nine years old, wearing a pacemaker, with a history of heart attacks, he is probably not a good candidate for surgery.

The women came home about 9 p.m., Ettie all girlish and coy, saying, "We won't tells where we's been—got to keep some secrets."

Kathy told me that when they arrived at the cafe, Ettie looked around and her eyes lit up as if she'd been taken to the Rainbow Room in Rockefeller Plaza, and said, "This is our first night here, but it won't be our last!"

Another evening, as we were about to sit down to supper, Joan Oldford stopped in for a visit. She sat her ample body, draped in a red and black dress, down into the turquoise rocker and stayed for about two and a half hours. She told us that the divorce papers came through for her and Clar Matchim (the man who disdainfully told me nine years ago that Newfoundland had no "leenage").

Joan is in her mid-fifties and is one of those Newfoundlanders of her generation who have "come a long way." Beginning here in a one-room schoolhouse, she eventually received a PhD in education from Ohio State. She was in her cousin Donna (Oldford) Rockwood's class when the Burnside school was K–11. There were five children in her class and perhaps that many on average in the others, some forty or fifty total. The local school population got a bump in the mid-1950s when the Flat Island resettlement children arrived, and then "the men got out some logs and made it a *two*-room school." When she was fifteen, her uncle Con took her to Eastport to finish high school. When she graduated, she became, at seventeen, the last principal of the Burnside school, which closed in 1968.

It sounds as if they essentially taught themselves. There was a single male teacher in the school who tested them from time to time, but "there was a group of textbooks in each grade, and we knew we had to get through them by the end of the year. We were pretty good at math, I guess, but social studies never took. It was never about anything we knew. It had nothing to do with Burnside, or community, or even Newfoundland history. It was all British history, you know, and Henry VIII chopping off his wives' heads—that sort of thing."

The Oldfords seem to have valued education highly and to have been exceptionally literate.

"Dad was always reading, and Grandfather Esau, even though he couldn't read, he loved to listen to Grandmother read in the evening. Great-uncle Joe taught himself to read, you know, all those histories of England. There weren't many books around when I was a girl, though. Every house had a Bible, of course, but if you had any money, and most didn't, it wasn't for books.

"I remember the first time I received a book. One Christmas I was looking through Eaton's catalogue with Mam and she says, 'This year you're going to get a book.' Oh, there were some books in the school library, but we couldn't take them out. There was a twenty-volume set of *The Book of Knowledge* with shiny, slippery pages that we could read after lessons. I think I read every story in them and remember most of them.

"Dad always loved to read western novels, and then later he moved on to information, history. One time I went up to Grand Falls (we never went to St. John's) and I bought him a copy of *Crime and Punishment*. I thought it was a detective story. I couldn't figure out why Dad never read it. I suspect it's still around somewhere.

"I suppose there were a lot of reasons why we loved to read, but I think the church had something to do with it—being Protestant, that is. You'd learn to read just by repeating and following the words in the *Book of Common Prayer* every week, by rote. And then there was the emphasis they put on reading the Bible, and not just reading but *analyzing* it. The Irish Catholics, by contrast, always had the priest as the interpreter, you know, and the service was all in Latin, so even if you memorized it you didn't know what it meant. They discouraged reading. Later I found out that the students at MUN who had gone to the Catholic board schools had ten percent lower scores on reading tests than the Protestants.

"Now, when I went to MUN in St. John's in the early 1970s, I found out that if they knew you were from an outport, they'd be less likely to give you an A, because they thought those from the bays weren't too smart. It's the other side, the dark side of vetting, you know, when a stranger would come to town and you'd try to see if you could discern some family connection with him, and if you did, then you'd let him in, 'cause you knew he was safe.

"It's all about expectations, you see. They had a course then called Oral Communication, which teachers had to take, but what it really was was training to get rid of your outport accent, which they thought was necessary if you were to teach. They still have the course at university, but I think it's changed now.

"Then, when I went to Ohio State, my son, they had no idea where or what Newfoundland was. They thought it had something to do with Greenland, something north. That was about it. So you see, they didn't have any expectations of me. They thought I was as good as anyone else. It was liberating."

She never knew Nate Ralph, but said his son, Arthur Stevens, was a quiet man who would say "wise things." "He would quote from Scripture, or Proverbs, at apt moments. I think that his mother, Blanche, was an oppressed woman. She was afraid to go beyond the gate, like Laura Burden. Only when Nate came home with his wheelbarrow of fish, she'd go down and open the gate for him. She'd stay in the house all the time, except when Nate was gone; then she'd come out and talk to Mam across the fence."

The following Monday Cyril took me in his skiff to get a closer look at the large iceberg that has hung several miles off to the north for the past week or so. It's about thirty feet high and over twice as long, with wide shelves of green ice just below the waterline.

Cyril kept a respectful distance, though he said that in their "irresponsible youth" he and his friends had all jumped aboard the bergs. One day he went with his father on one that contained a large, deep pool of water in a shelf. There was a flock of eider ducks in the pool, and when the two men came close, they all dove.

"I could see them clear as glass swimming underwater," said Cyril. "Dad said, 'If you can't get those ducks, I don't know what's wrong with you.' I waited till they come up and picked off several, and the rest dove again, so I just waited again till they come up again and picked off a few more. Good for me, bad for the ducks."

There were several large bergy bits in the water, and Cyril carefully sidled up to one of these, a chunk of Greenland ice cap several tons in mass. He took out his hatchet and began to chop off a piece when suddenly, as if it were alive, the whole chunk rolled over toward us. He quickly pushed us off, though if there had been a protruding shelf under the water, it would likely have caught and overturned us, as he said a smaller one did up in Tilting last year, drowning two men in a skiff.

Once the bergy bit stabilized, Cyril approached it again more gingerly, and we were able to bring home several large chunks of amazingly clear, highly compressed iceberg ice to sizzle in our scotches that evening.

I felt a wonderful casualness, or relaxation, being out there with Cyril. It is the same feeling I have had at other times this summer, the sense that everything is no longer a potential onetime experience I must absorb and record completely, but rather a part of a continuum, a once and future thing, that lends a quotidian quality to everything, that lets me accept whatever the day offers, or withholds.

In this, it is like being in a good marriage, where a sense of unlimited time and opportunity allows one to let certain chances pass untaken, for there will always be other ones. I suppose this is simply the sense, at last, of belonging here.

One morning Sue Hiscock stopped by wearing her wide-brimmed straw "umbrella hat" and green rubber boots over her bare feet and painted toenails. She brought me a "piece" she had written after Staish Lane's funeral last week and thought I might like. In it she wrote about "how different Burnside feels now since so many of the old people have died or left." She has missed seeing Staish waving from her window. She wrote about missing sounds of the old life, like the *putt-putt*-ing of the old make-or-break engines as Harold and the other men set out for the cod traps at 4 a.m.—"and they felt no need to be quiet about it. I said, 'Just go, just go and be done with it!' Of course, I misses them now.

"And voices. I'll miss Fred's voice, you know—it's so distinctive, so deep and rasping and preemptory. By the way, I've always loved your aps. The people here call them the 'talking trees.' It's one of the gathering places in town. If you set me down blindfolded in front of your house, I'd know exactly where I was to. It never ceases."

I have gradually been gaining some skill in cooking on the woodstove. On Sunday morning I made French toast, coffee, hot milk, and slab bacon on the top, heated the plates in the oven, and kept the teakettle boiling on the back burner to keep moisture in the room. In cool weather like this, it's a treat to cook on a woodstove. Ours is of fairly recent vintage, a Fawcett "Corvette" dated "1950" on the underside of the water reservoir lid.

After breakfast I made my first attempt at woodstove baking. I used a ninety-nine-cent packet of brownie mix from Crocker's store that may very well have been on the shelf for decades. I got the oven temperature up to a steady 350 degrees but made a classic beginner's mistake of setting the pan on the rack nearest the top of the oven, as I would at home, forgetting that in a woodstove like this the heat is flowing *above* the oven, essentially broiling the mix, so they came out looking more like blackies than brownies.

Still, I enjoy cooking on this stove and would like to become more skilled at it. Part of the pleasure is the direct connection with the source of heat, feeding the woodbox with wood that I split and carried, if not cut, myself. But I also like the sense of largesse it gives, the wide black iron top surface with its many concentric lids, the infinite number of heat "settings" it offers, depending on where one places the pot or the pan or the kettle, and the copper water reservoir on the right side that is heating water to wash the dishes with the same heat that is cooking the food to be put on the dishes.

I wrote till about six thirty and then, since Kathy was still napping, went for a walk in the damp, grey, and darkening day. I walked through the thigh-high grass out to Bert's wharf, where, eight years ago, I watched young Darren Lane in astonishment and admiration as he single-handedly repaired and rebuilt Bert's stage in a day. But it was apparently more appearance than substance, for the ballast had given way and the frame has skewed, sagged, and slanted nearly to the water. Bert, after all, had done it on the cheap, which was another example of my friend Penny's saying that "you can't get anything cheap, fast, and good, only two out of three."

I went up into the old cemetery for the first time this summer and found that only a very few family plots are still tended. I came upon Cleaves' parents'—Esau and Minnie Oldford's—graves, and next to them a small marble stone with a lamb carved on it, marking Cleaves' baby sister, who was born at the end of December 1910 and lived one week.

After I returned to our house, Shirley stopped by. She sat rocking slowly and steadily in the blue platform rocker while I made omelets on the woodstove. I told her about finding her grandmother Minnie's grave next to her baby girl. She said that before her grandmother was twenty-five, she had lost two sisters, her firstborn child, and had had her house burn down around her. She lived to be eighty-four and once said to Shirley that she wished she would die then because all of her remaining children and grandchildren were healthy and happy, and that she'd like to die before she had to begin worrying about them again.

At one point she told us of recently meeting a disgruntled woman from Trinity who was unhappy about the takeover of her town by "outsiders." She asked Shirley if "those Americans" were buying up Burnside as well, to which Shirley had replied, "Oh, there's only two of them so far, and they're not so bad." We took it as the ultimate compliment.

As she got up to go, she said, "Can you believe that Mark and Fraser had only met Ron and Lonz before they bought land here and started to build a house? I mean, can you imagine anyone doing that without wanting to meet at least a few other people to see if everyone else in town wasn't like Ron and Lonz!"

On Friday night we went to Howard and Christine's for a lasagna supper. Howard told us that one of Christine's in-laws had recently died at sixty-four: "Poor old slave. He hauled on boats all his life and niver got nothin'. He were all broke down."

"Still," he said, "I niver likes to see land. When I sees land, that's when I'm down. I's only happy on de water. Jesus Christ, I've seen forty-, fifty-, eighty-foot swells on the Banks, but I loves to fight it. I don't know why I does. I've been on the southwest banks trawling for cod and we'd go to set our lines, b'y, and she'd be foaming—no more than two fathoms of water there."

To which Christine added, "I don't like it when he talks about fishing. I finds it boring. It's all he ever talks about."

On Sunday I went to the 6:30 church service. It was a beautiful evening—clear, calm, in the mid-60s Fahrenheit. I walked into the church and found Reg Lane there, posting the hymn numbers, and Linda Oldford, practicing the hymns. Mounting the two flights of narrow stairs to the belfry, I folded back the four sets of inner wooden shutters, with their complex and jury-rigged system of latches, stops, and notched retainers, opening onto a panoramic quadtych of Burnside and the surrounding landscape.

I rang the bell hard and loudly, so that even Cleaves and Ettie might hear it. I rang it to wake the deaf and the dead.

As the service began, I sat in the last pew, intending to leave during the first hymn, but I found myself lingering, feeling more stable, buoyed up by the clear evening light that came through the windows, striking aslant all of the familiar faces scattered across the pews. Father Thoms seems to have come into his own lately and delivered a surprisingly good sermon on the story of Mary and Martha, connecting Martha's opening of her house to Jesus to the Newfoundlander's "native hospitality" and "the need for rest," for simply listening to "the love that permeates the world," a message that perhaps does not easily penetrate the skin of men now forced to be idle, for whom life has always been inseparable from active, physical work.

The hymn singing was as unmusical as ever, with the harmonium's drafty, reedy sound and a seemingly built-in time delay, which only doubled the inherent foot-dragging pace of the congregation: I could pick out Fred's unmistakable grating growl, Char's high tenor, Maxine's reedy alto, creating a sort of blended, gluey miasma of sound trailing behind, but heartfelt and imbued with the resonance of generations overlapping like waves on the landwash.

After the service Kathy and I went over to visit with Cleaves, who is scheduled to have surgery on his urinary tract tomorrow in Grand Falls. He seemed cheerful and to be feeling better.

He told us that there used to be "a beautiful bridge" across the front of our house, "with real latticework that Uncle Joe nailed together himself. But it was rotted when the Ralphs got it, and they took it down and never did replace it, but just put on that scrawny stoop."

We wished him well tomorrow and Kathy kissed him, not knowing if we would see him again in a day, or several weeks, or at all.

Three days later Cleaves came home from the Grand Falls hospital. He seemed to be in fine fettle and delighted in making bawdy remarks about the nurses there: how he "showed my dick to everyone," and that it took three nurses to reinsert the catheter, "two to hold it in and one to look on. I could have sold tickets."

The other day I was discussing class distinctions in Burnside with Scott Hapgood, Eldon and Alma's son. He said that the descendants of the earliest families to arrive subdivided even Squid Tickle, using that term to refer to all the shoreline west of the tickle bridge, and calling everything east of it East Tickle, down to Henry Oldford's, where it became Hollett's Cove.

"Once I said to Uncle Fred, 'There's a boat coming up Squid Tickle,' and he said, 'That's not Squid Tickle, b'y, that's East Tickle.'

"You see, the first settlers got the best growing ground and the best harbours, and so they tended to look down on the others—not in obvious ways, but indirectly."

This confirmed what I had noticed in Fred, a patronizing attitude, especially toward the Flat Islanders who arrived here during resettlement. The other afternoon when J & J were here, Fred blew in, set himself down at the kitchen table, and took over the conversation as he does, his back to the Mosses, talking directly to Kathy and me, ignoring them, despite Jim's efforts to be sociable.

On the other hand, at Jim's eightieth birthday party held last winter at the old school, Fred got up after the dinner and said, "You know, I think happiness is the greatest gift God has given man, and I don't think I ever saw Jim or his brother Jack with a frown on their faces. After they come here from Flat Island, Cleaves and I had six or seven salmon nets out, and we was also running the sawmill. And one morning when we was out on the nets, here comes Uncle Jack and Jim in from lobstering in their skiff and one of them is singing away at the top of his voice and the other is rattling on with another song and they're both singing so loud they can't hear the other, and I turns to Cleaves and I says, 'Now, b'y, if I could be as happy as that, I wouldn't want for anything else!'"

Saturday, July 24. Jim Moss was taken to Gander hospital yesterday afternoon. He had not been well the night before, throwing up, experiencing weakness in his knees, and losing his balance. Jennifer Stender went over to evaluate him and called an ambulance. She said it was not necessarily another stroke, but the "signs are not good."

There was no answer at Jessie's last evening when we phoned her. This morning Kathy reached Christine, who told her that the hospital had sent Jim back home but he apparently suffered another stroke during the night—couldn't walk and his speech was all garbled. Howard and Woody Oldford got him in the car and took him and Jessie back to Gander, where he is now, his speech still muddied and confused.

Tuesday, July 27. Jim's condition continues to worsen. Christine went to see him yesterday and says that his left side is completely paralyzed; he can barely open his eyes and can't close his mouth but can apparently hear and responds by squeezing her hand. His daughter Audrey flies in tomorrow from Calgary.

Wednesday, July 28. The end seems near for Jim, and if I am honest, I hope so. I cannot help but wish him out of his pain and indignity. We had planned to drive up to see him this afternoon, but this morning he slipped into a coma just before his daughter Audrey arrived in Gander from Alberta. She, Howard, and Jessie have been up there all day.

Thursday, July 29. Jim is gone. Christine called us about an hour ago to let us know that he had just passed away. She had been at the hospital all night with Jessie and Audrey and left about eight this morning. She thought he might have "slipped away" while she was still there, but "he held on longer." Howard drove into Gander to bring the women back. The funeral will be Saturday or Sunday, depending on when Audrey's husband Dan can get a flight out of Calgary.

So a vital bit of glee is gone out of this sober town, a rare exuberance that Sue Cummings called the "gypsy Mosses" but which was only fully embodied in Jim. One wouldn't have wanted him to linger longer in this state. It is impossible to think of him, whose whole joy was to sing and interact with others, lying there voiceless, sightless, and motionless. I prefer to think of him as he was, dancing only a week ago Saturday at Gerry Squires' sister's wedding, or carrying five-gallon buckets of water, or painting his shed only two days before his stroke, and then talking and waving cheerily to Alma next door as the ambulance took him off to the hospital in Gander.

Later that day, as we were walking across the tickle bridge, Jessie, Audrey, and Christine were coming out of Jessie's house in dress jackets and skirts, on their way to Eastport to pick out Jim's casket at Squires Funeral Home. I had not seen Jessie since Jim died, and I walked toward her, opening my arms, but she raised her hands as if to ward me off and said in a breathy, flustered voice, "No, b'y, I can't talk to yous now," and scurried past me into Christine's car. Audrey, a handsome woman with straight-cut blond hair, she looked stunned and only nodded blankly when Kathy introduced me. She has essentially had no sleep for four days.

Howard told me that the funeral would be Saturday or Monday, and that Jim would probably be waked at the funeral home rather than at the church, as John had been.

"Y'see, Bob b'y, if they wake him at the church, the church warden has to be there all day and evening, and they's getting old. They got to raise and lower the casket lid for viewing and close it up at night. I waked *my* father when he died, and you have to be careful that no cats get in, because they could tear up the face something awful."

Howard had stayed with Jim most of the time at the hospital. I said it must have been wearing to keep a death watch over a dying family member, but he said he didn't resent the time.

"If they're going, I wants to spend as much time with them as I can. I feel it's my responsibility, you know, even if they *is* in a coma—because you knows he can hear us—hearing's the last thing to go, they says. The doctors all say that."

Christine said that Jim's breath had changed during that last night, and a couple of times he stopped breathing completely for a minute or two, so that they thought he was gone, and even the nurse did. But then with a series of heaves he'd begin again. Late into the night, Jim began breathing very fast and shallow as his lungs filled with fluid.

"He was reaching for it," Howard said. "You know, *reaching*."

Later that day we stopped by the funeral home, a small building next to the Squires Esso Station. There was only one viewing room, in which Jim's body lay in a large solid birch casket with a tufted white silk interior portraying a scene of the Last Supper. He looked, of course, no more like Jim than a wax figure. In this case the dissonance was increased by his unnatural stillness, the lack of glasses, and the fact that, dressed in a grey suit and tie with a formal, sober expression on his motionless face, he looked more like a lawyer than a fisherman. The hands, when we felt them, were unnaturally hard, like the arm of a wing chair. There were a good many viewers, and we soon left.

I couldn't help but wonder what a wake on Flat Island would have been like. Were the ghosts of Jim's old crew members standing around his casket scratching their heads and saying, "You call this a wake? Where's the singing and the dancing? The laughing and the drinking? Where's the stomping and the ranting and the wailing and the roar?"

Friday was warm and dry. That afternoon we went over to see Jessie, Audrey, and Julia, who, having finally gotten some sleep, seemed more themselves. I gave Jessie a long hug, glad I could do that. She said she "has no tears left," but then at one point, apropos of nothing in particular, she began sobbing, and Audrey put her arm around her, saying, "Now, Mom, get ahold of yourself. You know Dad wouldn't want you to go on like that."

The funeral was held at St. Alban's on Saturday afternoon at 2:30 on the warmest day of the summer. I arrived a half hour early and was surprised to see dozens of cars already parked by the church. There must've been at least two hundred and fifty people in that hot church. For once, the sound of the congregation's voices drowned out the organ, determined to go at their own slow pace, regardless of what tempo the thankless organist tried to set. I was surprised at the number of high, nasal, Appalachian women's voices, the sliding and piercing quality of them. For once the sound filled the church as it was meant to be filled, with the voice of an entire community, not just a faithful remnant. It took the loss of one of the best-beloved and least-churchgoing members to do this.

Along with Father Thoms, the Reverend Ralph Moss, Jim's nephew, officiated. He spoke of his "Uncle Jim," acknowledging his friendliness, his singing prowess, his smile, his way of treating everyone with respect—all true. And then, trying to address some of the "spiritual aspects" of Jim's life, the best he could do was to say, "I'd like to think that, however much he loved Jessie and Julia and Audrey and his grandchildren, he looked forward to his life in the world to come. I'd like to think, however much Uncle Jim enjoyed this world, that he never forgot his true home."

He didn't—it was Flat Island. *We had everything there, b'y, everything.*

SUMMER 2005

WE ARRIVED IN BURNSIDE ABOUT 3 P.M., UNPACKED THE CAR, and had tea with Ettie and Cleaves. They seem in good spirits and glad to see us. Our arrival was easier this time, more rested, the house feeling cleaner than before, and our modest improvements reminding us of what we've accomplished.

We went over to Eastport yesterday to see Jessie, who has been living all winter with Julia and Gerry Squires since Jim died last summer. We sat in the hot sun on the bridge of the White Sails Cabins office. It seemed strange to focus alone on Jessie without Jim. She was so much his contrapuntal presence, his gloss, his backup singer—her consonantless scrawl of a voice only fractionally more understandable than Jim's. She has been back to their house but won't have the water turned on until Audrey and Dan come out from Alberta later this month. She said, in a tone slightly resentful, unusual for her, "We got the house all fixed up and then Jim went and died."

The next day we walked over to Lloyd Ralph's house on the island for his annual Fourth of July party. Lloyd worked for Newfoundland Hydro for thirty years and took early retirement. Then, eight years ago, he and his wife, a medical assistant, went to the States and settled in Hutchinson, Kansas, which he seems to like well enough, but the problem is that he also likes to come home often, while his wife apparently would be happy never to see Burnside again. Lloyd, who grew up here, would move back if he could, but, "deciding to make the marriage work," has stayed on in Kansas, coming out to Burnside with his two children for about three weeks each summer.

Lloyd is a rugged, good-looking, quiet man of about sixty, with reddish hair and mustache. He was wearing red-white-and-blue suspenders with little white stars on them, and his lawn furniture was painted with red, white, and blue stripes. His heart is in Newfoundland, but he holds these celebrations, he says, for the sake of his children, who grew up as Americans. All bets are off as to what will happen when all the children leave home. This is Lloyd's second marriage.

For an hour or more people kept crowding into his small kitchen drinking rum, beer, wine, and Canadian Club with ginger ale and Pepsi, as several foil-covered platters remained unopened on the table.

Lloyd announced that food would be served after singing the United States national anthem. He then handed out copies of all four verses of "The Star-Spangled Banner" (I had never seen verses two and three), labeled "United States National Anthem in English Text" (as opposed to what—Spanish? Newfoundlandish?). Then we all went outside, where we sang the first verse (Father Thoms, Kathy, and I forming a strong trio with Lloyd, who played the chords on his guitar) as his son Joey raised the Stars and Stripes to the setting sun and I set off a single rocket that rose high into the still-light sky and exploded with a satisfying report and spray of light. ("Nice touch," said Bill Hiscock.) Standing there leading a group of Newfoundlanders mouthing those unfamiliar, belligerent, war-saturated words, I sang with more patriotic fervor than I have felt in a long time.

Having literally sung for our supper, we all went back inside and dug into the platters of cracked crab legs, salmon cakes, cod cheeks, fish balls, and shrimp. Lloyd said, "If you want a Newfoundlander to sing, you've got to offer him fish." There were at least twenty people in that tiny kitchen, and yet it didn't seem crowded at all, as if all the camaraderie and good feeling lubricated our bodies and expanded the walls.

After supper we stopped by to see Cleaves and Ettie, bringing him a bottle of Bacardi from the States. I asked him how he got his name, Appleton Cleaves, and he told the following story:

"There was a feller from Maine—Cleaves was his surname, Appleton his Christian name—who worked up in the mill in Gander at the turn of the century. He was keeled wit' a two-by-four. Dey don't knows who done it, nor why—maybe he was fooling around wit' de wimmen—or maybe buddy wanted his job—I don't know. Dere was another feller—a historian—and he was researching to write a book about Appleton, Maine, and he came around to ask me if I knew anything about it, but of course I didn't, the dern fool."

"So you were named after Appleton Cleaves?"

"No, b'y, no—dat were just a story. I had an uncle by dat name."

While we were there, Willis Oldford walked in. Now in his ninety-third year, he is the oldest and, in many ways, the liveliest and healthiest of the four Oldford brothers. He flew down from Toronto on Friday and is now staying with his son Wayne, daughter-in-law Nancy, and their two teenage grandsons—Graham and Michael—in Con's house.

Willis is "supervising" Wayne and his boys as they assemble the floor beams on the concrete pillars for the house they are building on a portion of Bert's former land. Wayne has a slow timetable for his house. Last year they got the sauna tubes poured. This summer they plan to get the deck on. At this rate, it may be done for Willis's centennial.

Kathy had met him earlier in the day. "He was sitting in a rocker on the ground watching the boys put on the deck. He got up immediately and says to me, 'So you're the one from Cape Cod, eh? What do you want to be here for in the summer? You got all that sand and water back home'—talking nonstop and never taking his eyes off me. He's got quite the eye for the girls."

He struck me at first as a larger version of Cleaves, more of Fred's stature though leaner, and, like Fred, still a heavy smoker, though openly, since his wife died and he has no one left to reprimand him. Wayne introduced us: "Would you like to meet Papa—Le Grand Papa—the Big Cheese—Le Grand Fromage?"

Without preamble, Willis said, "I buried two wives here, up in the cemetery—both of them in their twenties. One was tuberculosis, the other pneumonia. I left here on July 6, 1948, fifty-seven year ago. I suppose I could have had a lifetime job with an architect in St. John's, but a buddy of mine was going to Toronto and asked me if I'd like to go with him, so I did, and I stayed. Married Wayne's mother. She died two and a half year ago."

His folds of freckled, weathered skin hung down over his oversized old man's nose and ears like loose clothes on a hanger. His eyes are watery blue, but clear. His manner is authoritative and preemptory, like Fred's, but without Fred's bossiness, having no need to assert or bludgeon you with its authority. He is, simply, the Oldest Brother. Harold Hiscock said that after Willis's visit here last summer, both Cleaves and Fred seemed more energetic, spryer, as if they felt, *Hey, we've got more years ahead of us!*

He didn't want to come this summer, "and wouldn't have except for Wayne asking me. I'm alone now and prefer it. Sometimes I go for days without seeing anyone. I don't mind—I'm past my time anyway. There's not really anyone here I know now except for my brothers and their wives."

He was "just an infant in cradle" when the town burned down in 1912.

When I said something about Bert still being up at the home in Glovertown, he said, "Bert's dead."

"What? Bert's dead? When?"

"Months ago."

I was immediately struck by the irony of it, that Laura, consistently frail, always "poorly," "dying since she got here," as Jim said—frail, sickly Laura, who was afraid of everything and everybody and never left the yard; Laura, who had so much love to give and nothing and no one to give it to; Laura, whose mind by now may have drifted completely beyond reach—still lies up in the nursing home in Gander, her body having outlasted Bert's.

Howard stopped by about 4 p.m. He has his rare day off amid weeks of crabbing and caplin fishing. At fifty-five, swarthy, mustached, still wearing sixties-style thick-rimmed black glasses and close-cropped hair just beginning to be peppered with grey, he is probably the strongest man in town—which may not be saying all that much these days.

They were supposed to go out again this weekend to the Banks 90 to 110 miles east of Fermeuse, but the forecast is bad, so he may get the weekend off, too. Nonetheless, he says, "this may be the last year for me, b'y, I tells ya. It's gettin' hard. Last time out I went for days without a minute in me berth. Man, I was beat. It's not worth it, I tells ya. I'm thinking I might chuck it all and go out by myself in my own boat inshore crabbin', ya know. I could rig up the hydraulics for four to five thousand dollars. My quota is eleven thousand pounds—just the same as I get on the big boat. I'd do just as well, and I wouldn't have to take those man-beatin' trips, nor go out on those banks. I've never seen it ca'm out there, ya know. There might not be a breath of wind, and still the sea is always rocking and heaving with three-to-four-foot swells.

"Last week, when we was comin' out of Fermeuse, we'd been seining caplin all day in Conception Bay, not a wink of sleep in forty-eight hours, and I was lookin' forward, ya know, to four to five hours in my bunk when the skipper comes up to me and says, 'Howie, I'm beat. I can't take her no more. Can you take her up through Baccalieu?' You know, off Horse Chops. The skipper, he always comes to me. The others, they don't know nothin' about navigation, ya see. Well, they does, but the skipper, he comes to me and says, 'I'm beat.' 'Well, I'm beat, too,' I says. 'Yes,' he says, 'but can you take her?' 'Well,' I says, 'sure, I can take her,' and so I did and he went down to his berth. Well, I took her through into Trinity Bay, heading towards Catalina, and there was a lot of traffic in the night there, b'y, three or four boats crisscrossing your bow, and after two hours I looked at Cal sitting with me in the cabin no further than you is to me now, and b'y, I swears to God, I couldn't have told you his name to save my life—I didn't recognize him—so I called the skipper up and said, 'I can't do it no more, I'm beat'—and he took over and it was gettin' light by then and I never did go down. We was four days without sleep, and that's not good, you know. We should have stayed in Conception Bay, but the caplin, you know, they drives you—or rather, the trucks do. They're lined up at the wharves, waitin' to load up, like hungry dogs, and if you aren't there to feed them, you up and lost out. I likes it once I gets out there, I do—but man, when I think of going out again, b'y, it hain't worth it. Not like this."

Yesterday Kathy and I spent about two hours working on Wayne's deck with him and Nancy while his father Willis sat in a chair doing his *Weekend at Bernie's* imitation.

On the way back we stopped at Bill and Carol's for a glass of white wine. Carol told us the story of how she was the one who got her nephew Ken Hollett and Sandra together by convincing Sandra to take a hunting course with Ken so that Ken and Sandra could go in as partners on a moose license. After the season ended, they got engaged.

Ken practices law in St. John's and is a natural-born storyteller. He told us one about a man who was trying to explain to the judge that he hadn't been able to restrain his teenage daughter because she was "hearing-impaired."

"How so?" asked the judge.

"Well, Your Honor, I blares and blares at 'er but I don't get no reply!"

That night I went to bed but found myself stark awake, so at midnight I got up, threw on some clothes, and went for a walk with a honeying gibbous moon following me low in the southwest sky. It was a silent, still night, the moon a witness, muting but not gilding the dark landscape. Although there were still some soft lights on in Con's house, where Wayne and his family are staying, and still more over to Gus Oldford's, it only made me more aware of how dark and empty this road has become, even since I first stayed here ten years ago. I began to think of all the year-round lights that have blinked out since then—and that set me to counting the remaining year-round residents. I was disheartened not to be able to get beyond eighteen on this side of the tickle, and another six or eight beyond the ferry wharf.

I walked out onto the Oldfords' wharf, where the surface of the water was dimpled with scattered raindrops. When I shone my light across it, a sudden scattering movement broke the surface. I found I could move the surface with my light, herding the scattering feeders this way and that with insubstantial force. Was it caplin? Or mackerel? Or perhaps squid? The next morning, standing on the bridge with Bill and Carol, we saw a squid come through the tickle—a squid in Squid Tickle!—and I watched our four shadows and the rail we leaned against projected onto the clear channel bottom as the tide direction changed in a matter of ten minutes. Char Oldford walked by and said, "You don't see that everywhere."

We had invited Bill and Carol and Cyril and Linda and Joan to dinner the following evening. Joan is selling her Boston whaler and 30 hp motor for $3,500 and Cleaves insisted she attach the FOR SALE sign to the boat with masking tape because duct tape "costs too much." That led to a whole raft of stories about Cleaves' "frugality."

Cyril said that when Cleaves' neighbor Mike Nurse got rid of his old oil tank a few years ago, it still had about fifteen gallons in it. Rather than watching it be drained and the oil go to someone else, Cleaves tottered up to the Nurses' house with his cane and a bucket and, gallon by gallon, drew the oil and carried it back to funnel into his tank.

The next evening Scott and Emily Hapgood came over to visit in our gazebo tent. Scott is retiring from teaching in Goose Bay next year, and they are debating where to live. Scott would like to spend as much time as he can in their "cabin" behind his parents' house here, but Emily doesn't fancy being a Burnsider year-round. She thinks they might live "somewhere between Gander and Clarenville" and visit here often.

"But tell me, Bob," said Scott, "I'll bet you observed that the relations between husbands and wives here are different than where you're from."

"Why do you say that, Scott?"

"Well—ha—take Granddad Nate, for instance. He was the authority in the house. After work, he'd be sitting in his chair in the front room, have his drop, light his pipe, and Grandma Blanche might be all the way back in the kitchen pantry and he'd say, 'Here you are, old woman. Take the match,' and she'd have to scurry out and take it out of his hand and put it in the stove."

Emily looked at him.

"Yeah," Scott continued, "but still, old Nate was a pretty nice fellow. And I'll tell you something: he had the cleanest stage you ever seen, everything shipshape. He'd scrub down his splittin' table every evening, and still be scrubbin' it when all the others had left. Then, of course, he'd come home and traipse across Blanche's clean kitchen floor in his fish boots!"

Later we dropped in at Val and Joel Fish's new house at Hollett's Tickle. Val is a Hiscock on her mother Grace's side. Joel is a burn specialist at a hospital in Toronto. They are here for a month. They have four very bright kids ranging in age from fifteen to six. Val converted to Judaism when she married Joel, and we quipped that, with Kathy and me, we were getting close to a coed minyan in Burnside.

Char Oldford told me the story of his uncle George, who lived in a house on the island, just past Howard Moss. Apparently he was getting older and the house was too much for him to care for alone, so he decided to sell it, and did so, furniture and all. He didn't mention it, however, to his sister, Char's mother, who was ninety-two, and Char found out about it from a friend.

"Well, where's he going to live?" asked Char.

"Why, he says he's going to live with you."

"Well, b'y, he's welcome, sure, though we don't have a spare bedroom."

So Char called his son Wayne, who was away at school, and said, "Wayne, your great-uncle George is coming to live with us, but he is going to have to share your room."

"That's fine with me, Dad, whatever you wants to do."

"So I put up a rod and strung a curtain down the middle of the room, put in a single berth, and give George the double bed. He lived with us for five years.

"Mary said, 'He ate everything I cooked for him, never complained. He was no trouble at all.'"

We spent our last day in Newfoundland at Bill and Carol's house in St. John's, then drove to Argentia to catch the ferry to Nova Scotia. Bill's chronic back pain has gotten worse over the summer. He joked that it was probably a good thing Reg Lane was retiring from lobstering after this year, so he wouldn't need Bill's help. When we left for home on Tuesday, Bill and Carol insisted on "escorting" us out of St. John's, where they waved and blew their horn as we got on the TCH, feeling fortunate to have made two such new friends.

September 20. We got word from Carol Hiscock Monday that Bill's persistent back problems have been diagnosed as cancer of the spine, a metastatic cancer, which means it spread from somewhere else. He collapsed yesterday morning with a fractured vertebra and has been taken to hospital. Bill's niece, Jennifer, told Carol that the aggressive chemotherapy Bill will begin on Friday will, even if it works, not "cure" but only "prolong" him.

Bill died a few months later at fifty-seven, which these days seems like the prime of life. He was one of those vital, life-affirming people, with a deep, hearty, comforting laugh, a welcoming manner, and an easy friendliness. He had been married to Carol for thirty-eight years.

His loss blindsided us for reasons we did not fully understand at the time. In retrospect, he and Carol represented the first experience we had had of forming a close friendship here with people of our generation, and thus offered us the possibility of creating a life here even after the disappearance of the old people.

SUMMER 2006

WE HAD SET OFF FROM CAPE COD ON FRIDAY MORNING, JUNE 23, with our Dodge Caravan loaded to the gills with my old bedroom set from my mother's house. This, I think, will give me a deep sense of familiarity when dealing with an unfamiliar house.

Linda Oldford came down from Gander to their house in Burnside for "sanctuary" and shared a haddock dinner with us Friday night. She told us that she hoped to live to a ripe old age in Burnside, and that "if I lose my mind, I hope I'll still retain my fashion sense. I'll still be taking my morning walks, and people will say, 'There goes Linda—she had a mind once, but she still knows how to dress.'"

Linda told us that she had never had a room to herself in all her life. She moved with her family to Burnside when she was ten and always shared a room with her sister. When she graduated high school, she went to Gander for trade school and shared a room with Christine Moss. Then she married Cyril, so she actually looks forward to the time in Burnside when she and Cyril are working opposite schedules. He kids her, saying, "You just looks forward to the nights, don't you?" and she replies, "You got that scalled!"

She has her choice of rooms these days. Con recently made over his house to Linda, so that, together with their Gander house, Cyril's family house in Burnside, and the cabins on Flat Island and in Bloomer's Harbour, she and Cyril together now own five houses.

The building boom in Burnside continues apace. "Willis's Wayne" Oldford is coming down from Toronto again this summer with his two teenage sons to work on his new house. Meanwhile, Sean Tiller and Diane Hollett are expanding their small cabin into a two-story, three-bedroom house with a covered side porch and a large shed. It is still under construction, so they and their two kids, Eli and Josie, are staying up at the Hiscock House with Diane's parents, Grace and Harry Hollett.

On Friday Kathy and I spent the afternoon at Carol Hiscock's cottage, sprucing it up so it wouldn't look too abandoned when she arrived on Saturday. We bought some lobsters from Howard and cooked them with corn and salad. With Reg Lane retired and Mac Babstock, Char Oldford's son-in-law, not going out this spring, Howard is now the only active commercial fisherman left in Burnside.

The transformation of this place from a viable, if aging, year-round outport into a summer community is becoming more apparent. One sign is that Ron has shortened his store hours, so that he now closes at five every day. As Kathy observed, his business has depended in large part on people like Jim and Jessie who didn't drive and ordered all their groceries from him. Now there are almost none of those left. Few of the summer people buy at Ron's, and it's a question how long he will hold on.

Still, it is good to be here and watch the town fill up over the weekend with various Hiscocks, Oldfords, Vivians, Ralphs, Lanes, Holletts, and others of the "old lines." There is a bustle and energy of families arriving, taking up the old family residences or old houses they have newly acquired and are renovating.

Sitting on our front stoop in the slanting, glowing light of evening, I can see across the road into Cleaves' yard, where Terry, Cleaves and Ettie's youngest son, is sitting on a bench under the apple trees with his arms around his two kids, Joey and Bethany, their bicycle helmets still on their heads, just sitting there, unmoving, for a long time. The wonderful thing is that this is such an ordinary, unexceptional sight here.

I have bought a boat, a Rodney-design fourteen-foot wooden skiff with a flat stern, built by Everett Saunders of Eastport. She's a narrow-planked, edge-nailed vessel made of local spruce and fir with juniper (larch) ribs (easy to bend), four thwarts, and a small stuff box in the bow.

Everett was born on Coward's Island—the same as Bill and Harold Hiscock—and came to Eastport in the mid-fifties. He went to school here and taught for a while in the area. He has a wharf and a small store in Burnside just in front of the museum.

Everett is a friendly, soft-spoken, easygoing man of about sixty, with glasses and a slightly bulbous nose. He told me he builds one boat per year from a mold and lines the inside with fiberglass to prevent rot and give it a good seal.

The boat was in his yard on the highway in Eastport, and I knew at once that it was exactly what I was looking for: a solid, stable boat, locally built, not too big, that would take a small motor and could also be rowed. He said it would also take a sail and a "dagger board"—a kind of removable centerboard fastened to the side of the boat. There was also a hole in the stern for a sculling oar. He charges $100 a foot for his boats, so for this one he was asking $1,400.

I already knew it was a done deal but he offered to take it over to Burnside and let me try it out with a 6 hp Johnson he keeps at his wharf. We did so, and he took Kathy and me out for a spin, and then I went out on my own just to get the feel of it. A 6 hp motor seems quite adequate for its size, and it rode quite steady on the water. It needs one more coat of paint, but Everett said he would do that for me at the end of the summer. We moored the boat at Carol's wharf, using a killick[*] he had made as a mooring anchor.

We went to a Canada Day party at Lloyd Ralph's house yesterday that was attended by most of the year-rounders. Alma Hapgood, the elder Wife of Burnside, greeted me from the rocker with her usual salutation: "How's yer pecker, Bob?" Fred, using a cane now, says he can't get around anymore unless someone takes him. "I had to give up my license." What will he do now without the ability to trawl the streets of Burnside for listeners?

When I told Char, by far the most cheerful member of the Oldford clan, about buying a boat from Everett, he took Kathy and me aside and, putting an arm around each of us, told the following story:

"There was this old sailor living down in Goobies and had a young daughter, a lively and pretty maid. A feller from Hillview came down and courted her and eventually went to her father, who is hard of hearing, to ask for her hand.

"'I'd like to marry your daughter, sir,' he said.

"'Well,' said the father, 'her squirrel hole's pretty worn out but you can have her if you wants.'

"You see, he thought he wanted to buy his *punt*."

Jennifer, Jean Stender's daughter, has been trying to start up a track and field program for young people in Eastport. She put up signs, but except for her own kids, and Val's and Diane's, nobody showed up. She

---

[*] According to the *DNE*, a killick is "an anchor made up of an elongated stone encased in pliable sticks bound at the top and fixed in two curved cross-pieces, used in mooring nets and small boats."

seemed disappointed and a bit hurt. I suggested that perhaps the kids here weren't used to the idea of structured summer activities, that perhaps there just weren't that many of them around looking for something to do. She allowed that might be so.

So instead, she and Eric have tethered a canoe at their cove to a hundred-foot line so that their kids in life jackets can "have fun without us worrying about them being carried off." I thought of how the boys and girls of a generation or two ago went clambering across the ice floes in winter, unsupervised and unworried about.

Yesterday was one of those patented Burnside September-in-July days: cool crisp air, about 20 degrees Celsius, and a dry breeze from the northwest. In the afternoon Kathy and I went for a row around Squid Island in my new boat. I rowed through the tickle and up into the wind, around the point, then into the shelter of the back tickle between Squid and Primer's Islands. I gave the oars to Kathy, and she rowed downwind along the back side where the clear waters were filled with moon jellies and the darker, bloodier, deeper forms of lion's manes.

We slept in the screened tent for the first time this summer, beaten into a sound sleep by the thrashing of the wind through the ventilator flaps. In the morning, we woke to the clear clarion calls of the whitethroats and the whinnies of loons on the hidden inland ponds. A flatbed truck bounced down the road with a load of lumber and staging for Wayne Oldford's new house, while nearby the sounds of hammers came from where Wayne Martin is building a new house for Shirley and Phil in front of Fred and Betty's.

About eleven thirty Cleaves swung by in his car. I had asked him earlier if I might use one of the grapnel rebar anchors on the Oldfords' wharf to moor my boat. In his usual way, he had demurred: "I don't know, b'y. I'd have to see 'en, I don't knows who owns 'en. Dere's one belongs to de speedboat, and Fred owns one, and I does, and Con, but I don't knows which is which unless I sees 'en."

He honked his horn peremptorily and said, "Get in t'other side." So we drove down to the wharf in his bright purple Neon, and he eased it down the slope into the sand just before the wharf. I got out and brought four of the grapnels, two light and two heavy, off the wharf, with Cleaves warning me, "Don't walk on the starboard side, the beams are gone there." I deposited them on the ramp in front of the store for his inspection.

"You could use that one," he said, pointing to one that had lost two of its six claws on one side.

"But wouldn't it slide over the rocks on that side?"

"Not if you ties it up right."

"How is that?"

"See, you ties the rope on the claw end first and then up through the ring at the top of the shaft."

I must have looked doubtful because he said, pointing to the other light anchor, "Well, I suppose you *could* use that one"—pause—"I suppose you could use whichever one you wants."

I said I would take the second one and put the others back on the wharf. Again Cleaves warned me, "Be careful, that beam's gone, and I don't know who's going to fix it."

I said I would carry the anchor back, but he said, "No, no. Get in. You can baby her on the way back. You can baby her so she won't cry."

So I slipped into the passenger seat, holding the anchor gingerly. Cleaves put the car in reverse and gunned it backwards, sliding sideways into the soft sand and off the road halfway into the grass. He tried to go forward, but his left front wheel only kicked up sand and gravel. It was clear the bottom of his car was hung up on the berm of the sand. I found an old rusty shovel in his store, dug out the wheel, and pushed from the back as he tried again, but no luck.

"I guess you're going to have to walk and get Shirley and Fred to pull us out."

So, leaving Cleaves in the car, I walked up to Fred's house. They had just finished dinner. I said to Shirley, "Would you like to come and help me rescue your uncle Cleaves?"

She looked alarmed for a moment, then asked, "Where is he?"

I explained, and she smiled, "Some people think New York City is the busiest place to live . . ." picking up a folding chair and coming with me to my van.

As we left, Fred came limping to the door, shouting, "What happened?" Shirley yelled back an explanation, and Fred shouted, "You want the rope in my car?"

"No—Bob's just going to give him a push forward with his van."

But it was clear to me, looking at the flimsy plastic front of my car, that I was not going to push it. As we drove around the corner to the wharf, I saw Calbert Ralph in his shed, working on some piece of machinery. Cal has the largest collection of vehicles in Burnside, including a large tow truck with long rubber flaps across the back, two quads, and a white painted school bus he bought a few years ago "just to take into the woods." He has a house up in Twillingate but spends a few weeks every summer in Burnside. He hauls heavy freight, like RVs, in big trucks all over Canada and the US for a living. I thought, however, he might be able to push Cleaves out with one of his quads.

I left Shirley in the car and walked up to Cal's shed. He and I had waved casually to one another over the seasons, as one does here, but had never really spoken. He is a large man with a huge beer belly overlapping shorts, a boyish face, and reddish curly hair. Down the center of the shirtless chest ran a wide white scar at least ten inches long where they had split his breastbone open after a heart attack.

I explained the situation, and he said he'd be down in a couple of minutes. We drove down to the wharf and Shirley set up the folding chair beside the car.

"What's that for?" asked Cleaves.

"That's for you to set in, Uncle Cleaves."

"Don't need that. I'm comfortable where I's to."

So we waited for Cal, who arrived in one of his quads, swerved down in front of and facing Cleaves' car, and unhooked a small winch from the front of his vehicle. He managed to get it around the front left wheel strut and pulled backwards with the quad, but he got no purchase in that soft sand. Then he tried mauling a board under the driver's wheel, raising it two inches above the road, but it only spun futilely. It was clear it was solidly stuck.

There followed a discussion of options, with Cleaves insisting we could put a jack under the right side, lift her up and push her out, Shirley explaining that there was no access to the one place you can put a jack on these cars, Cal explaining that everything is plastic now and you've got nothing to hitch onto proper, and me reassuring Cleaves that if we had to call the Canadian Automobile Association for a tow, it wouldn't cost him a cent.

While I was explaining this, Shirley and Cal were having a confab. I told Cleaves I was going to see what they were looking for. Cal said that if Cleaves didn't have to go anywhere, calling for a tow truck might be the best bet. He thought maybe he could pull the car out with his big truck, but "not with him behind the wheel. I'm afraid he'll gun her forward and push us both into the drink."

"Well, I don't think he's going to move," said Shirley.

"I'll find a way to tell him," I said.

"You're a wonderful man," said Shirley.

I went out, and Cleaves said, "What's happening now?"

"Well, I think we may have to get a tow truck. Cal's got one more idea, but he'll only try it on one condition."

"What's that?"

"He wants me behind the wheel."

"What for?"

"I don't know, but that's what he said."

By this time Shirley and Cal had emerged from the shed and Shirley was cajoling him. "Come on, Uncle Cleaves, just come out and set in the chair."

He fussed and demurred, and I said, "Come on, Cleaves, let's get this over."

So he agreed, grumbling and complaining, helped out of the car by Shirley and me, leaving his armada of wooden canes and his walker in the car.

"I still don't see why we can't just get a few of the fellows and haul 'er out like we used to."

"And where are we going to find them, Uncle Cleaves? Wayne and the boys have gone over to the pond for a swim. Joel Fish has a bad back—remember he was all crippled up last summer? Albert and his boys have gone home."

"Well, what about Martin and his crew up at your house?"

"Oh no you don't, Uncle Cleaves. Martin hurt his back last summer, and I'm not going to have him do it again and put me behind another three or four weeks. Besides, they've gone to lunch." (At this point I could hear Cal muttering under his breath, "This is my last day here. I can't spend all day at this!")

Eventually Cleaves agreed to be taken home while Cal went for his truck. He struggled up onto my passenger seat, and Shirley sat in the back beside the folding chair. As we headed back, there was Fred by Con's house, having hobbled that far down with his cane.

"Oh my good Lord!" exclaimed Shirley as we stopped and let Fred into the van, where he balanced precariously on the folding chair.

We got Cleaves safely back to his house. I was going to take Fred and Shirley back to their house, but Fred said, "Where you going now?" When I said the wharf, he said, "Well, let's go!"

Cal had brought his truck down and pulled it up perpendicular to Cleaves' car on some hard ground. He had attached a heavy rope from the front strut of Cleaves' car to his trailer hitch, and with me at the wheel, rather easily lifted the car back onto the road, where I carefully backed it out of harm's way.

Thanking Cal profusely, I left him there to coil up his rope. Shirley drove Fred home in Cleaves' car, then returned it to his yard, and I went back to the house. There was a sense of a small adventure successfully completed, and even Cleaves smiled at the outcome, as if he had already begun to see it as a humorous story.

Ten minutes later, as I was preparing a list of errands to do in Glovertown, I heard Cal drive up to our gate on his quad. He knocked at the back door, and with a sheepish smile said, "I don't suppose you could do the same thing for me now that we just did for Cleaves."

"You're kidding."

"Nope, I got stuck in that soft sand trying to back out, same as Cleaves. Guess I'll have to take the bus to get her out."

"I'll be right down."

Sure enough, for some reason he hadn't backed directly out, but had pulled forward down into the sand at the wharf. The bus was already there, backed up to the head of the incline about sixty feet from the truck. There was no sign of Cal in the truck or the bus, so I walked back up to his house and shed and called for him, but no answer. I began to think perhaps he had had another heart attack and lay on the floor of the bus, or had fallen off the wharf into the water, where his big body would be floating belly-up and that this would become the Tragedy of the Summer. But as I walked down to the wharf again, he came walking up toward the bus with a big smile and a large coil of heavy nylon rope. "Had to go next door to his shed to get some rope."

I mentioned to Cal that I had some experience driving a school bus if he wanted to steer the truck, but he said, "No, she's pretty erratic to drive. Sometimes *I* can't even drive her. The other day I put on the brakes and nothing happened. She's got real low gears, though. I don't think she'll do over sixty. You get in the truck."

I guided him as he backed the bus up a few yards, and then we hitched up the rope to the truck. As we did, he said, "Cleaves kept talking about getting some people together to lift his car. What he doesn't realize is that there *aren't* no people anymore."

"But that's the way they used to do everything, getting together and pushing or lifting with brute force."

"Yep—they used to. And that's why we're all beat up in the way we is. Hell, I'm almost sixty—be fifty-nine later this month."

I felt at that moment we had bonded.

On the first try, with me giving it a little gas, the truck began to slide off into the ditch. Cal repositioned the bus, backing it onto a small rocky outcrop to the right, and this time, with the truck in neutral, she came up far enough so that I could back her out onto the hard ground.

"Well, this story will be all over the town within a few hours," I said.

He had put such force on the rope that his knot slipped, and it took him twenty minutes with a spade to wrest it loose again.

"I could cut it with a knife, but I hates to give up on anything. Especially when someone tells me I can't do something. Then I can't give up no matter what."

He did it, though, and while we stood there talking comfortably, I asked him if I could help him with anything or if he could think of anything else I could ask for to get people in trouble, just let me know. It was now two o'clock.

Later, I stopped in to tell Cleaves what had happened. He told me there never had been a road down to the wharf before. When they put the lumber mill in, they filled it with rocks, but kids would come down and throw rocks into the harbour, so they put sand on top of it.

"It's fallin' in, though, and there's no one to fix it. It'll all go to ruin."

Ettie concurred, "We're all going to ruin, too."

"Gee, thanks," I said. "This is what I came in here for—a bit of good news to cheer me up."

We were having drinks with Carol on her bridge Tuesday evening about 5:30 p.m. when she got a call, came out, and said, "All right, Bob, you are on duty. That was Jennifer. It seems Simon's dislocated his shoulder again. She needs you down at the Hiscocks' wharf ASAP."

Simon, it appears, has dislocated his left shoulder at least ten times, the initial occasions being the result of skateboard accidents. This time it occurred when, having jumped off the wharf for a swim, he reached behind his back with his left hand to grab the wharf piling and his left shoulder popped out. Somehow he managed to get up on the wharf and into the house to call Jennifer. Though she is a surgeon, she had never had to deal with this kind of situation in the field. All of Simon's previous dislocations occurred in St. John's, where he was taken to hospital, went under anesthetic, and the shoulder was put back in place.

She called an orthopedic surgeon she knew in St. John's, who described to her the technique we were now going to try, one that resembled something out of a frontier western movie or some medieval medical practice akin to torture.

What we had to do, her colleague said, was to get Simon to lie flat on his stomach on the surface of the wharf with the dislocated arm hanging straight down over the edge. Then Jennifer was to tie a cloth rope around that wrist and attach it to a bucket, which she would gradually fill with water. The idea was that at some point Simon's muscles would no longer be able to support the weight and would relax, popping the shoulder back in its socket again.

It sounded bizarre, and it was. For one thing, when I arrived, I could see that Simon was in great pain. He was dressed only in green swim trunks and was gingerly cradling his left arm with his right, as if it were a wounded animal. I could see the knob of his upper arm bone retreating under his skin a few inches behind the shoulder socket, and the distortion was intensified by his posture, crouched over in pain, so that he looked like a young hunchback. Jennifer, diffident in manner by nature, seemed even more so in this untried situation and unwonted setting, but having inherited her father Wulf Stender's German genes, she was determined to try it.

We had a hard time getting Simon in position, for any movement seemed to cause him more intense pain, even just lowering himself and turning his body, let alone extending his hurt arm. It took several minutes to get him into position, by which time he was shivering, not with cold, he said, but with pain. Jennifer tied a rag around his wrist and the other end to a red plastic five-gallon naval beef bucket. Then she filled up a smaller bailing bucket and began pouring it into the big one. Simon was game, but it was clear he was in excruciating pain. I think we all thought this was bizarre and probably futile, but at the moment we had no other option. Simon cursed and groaned and we could see his muscles remained tense. Finally, after five or ten minutes of this, he said, "I can't takes it no more."

With no evidence that it was working, we stopped. At this point Joel Fish showed up with Val and their kids in the van. They had been at Sandy Pond, and a friend had found them and told them about Simon. Joel, though also a surgeon, had had no orthopedic training, and although he was unquestionably strong enough to pull the shoulder back in place, he was reluctant to try it, either because he was unsure just how to do it and/or he saw that Simon had already experienced too much pain. Instead he decided he would drive him to Gander. So we put a towel over Simon's shoulders and got him in the van, while I ran back to the house for some Percocet, carisoprodol, and the rest of a bottle of Glenfiddich. Since Simon had never taken drugs, Joel didn't want to risk it, so I just gave him a couple of swigs of scotch. I offered to let him take the bottle with him, but Joel, a true Torontonian, said, "Oh no, I can't have an open bottle in the van," so he just gave Simon one more for the road and they took off. Then Val turned to me and said, "You look cute standing in the road holding your whiskey bottle and plastic jars of drugs."

Joel and Simon got back sometime after midnight, and Simon, his arm in a sling, stayed the next several days with the Fishes, because, as he put it, "if I'm alone, I can cook, I can eat, but I can't wash dishes."

It rained hard all last Wednesday. In the evening I cooked a large ribeye steak on Carol's grill in the rain, while she made onions and mushrooms with vinegar and honey served with baked potatoes and red wine, followed by her fresh-picked strawberries and vanilla ice cream. It was the most delicious dinner we've had in a long time, though I got soaked starting the grill in the rain.

Carol met Bill when she was fifteen, married him when she was nineteen, and has never been with anyone else. Kathy and I went home in the rain and read for a very short time in my childhood bed, and then lay listening to the rain on the aps leaves and fell asleep while it rained steadily through the night.

Ever since Sean found out I played the piano, he has been looking for one for me ("Got to have a piano, b'y! Otherwise, what's the point of knowin' how to play?") and one for his Burnside house. After several weeks of looking he found one that "should do for you" and one for himself.

Sean's piano is a beautiful antique—a circa 1880 upright built by, oddly enough, the "Tennessee Piano Company of London." The cabinet is made of burled walnut with inlaid flowers on the front, original ivory keys, and an ingenious and delicate music stand Sean calls "the wipers." It consists of a lattice of flat sticks that can swivel back and forth and cleverly folds up and swings up and over into the top of the cabinet. Sean found it in the basement of an outport Anglican church. It has a nice bright tone ("almost honky-tonk"), though Sean insists "it's not half the piano yours is."

The one he found for me is a much larger instrument, a 1912

Boston-made Emerson upright with a dark mahogany cabinet, very plain, simple panels, and lines that seem to anticipate the Art Deco style of the thirties. It has the original ivories, except for eleven in the middle range, which he had to replace with plastic tips. It came from "an old house in the East End of the city" and weighs "about eight hundred pounds." He paid $400 for the piano and $200 to have it professionally moved to his garage.

On Friday morning we loaded the pianos from Sean's garage onto a U-Haul truck Sean had rented the previous evening. We had asked for a fourteen-foot truck, but they gave us a twenty-four-footer, a monster big enough to move a three-bedroom house.

With two of us lifting at the ends and another friend of Sean's slipping a dolly under them, we had little trouble loading the pianos aboard via the wide loading ramp and tying them down at the front of the cavernous truck hold. We then proceeded to partially fill the truck with a new mattress and springs, a large sectional sofa, an electric range, framed pictures, desks, and other items for Sean's new house in Burnside.

We set off in light rain about 1 p.m. with Sean at the wheel. The truck was hardly new—the odometer said 203,000 miles, but we guessed it was probably 1,203,000 miles. One taillight was out, one tire didn't look good, and the rugged roads from their house to the Trans-Canada Highway led us to expect a rough ride, but once we got on the highway and drove out of the rain, she smoothed out and we made the trip without incident in a respectable four and a half hours.

When we arrived in Burnside, about 5:45, we drove to Sean's house and unloaded the furniture and other items in the newly finished upstairs master bedroom. Then, with Sean's builder, Wayne Martin, assisting us, we backed the truck up to the front door and the piano rolled directly into the house with little trouble.

By then it was about 6:30, and we both felt good about how things were going. I said that if it were earlier, I might be up to trying to unload mine tonight, but there were too many problems and possible hitches. First, there was no way to back the truck up to the front door, or even to put the ramp into the yard. We would have to roll the piano across the uneven ground of the yard and then find some way to lift or roll it up onto the wooden stoop, a direct thirty-six-inch elevation from the front, as the flimsy steps were of no use. Earlier in the week I had replaced most of the stoop planks, which were punky, and shored up the framing, which was doubtful at best, hoping it would sustain the eight-hundred-pound weight for a few minutes at least without collapsing.

But there was no choice. We could probably have brought it in more easily through the back door and into the kitchen. But she would never have made the turn into the narrow hallway, or out of it. Even if we tried bringing it in the front based on a paper footprint I made of Sean's measurements of the base at sixty by twenty-six inches, we would have only one and a half inches to spare, making the turn from the entrance into the front parlor, and that only with the inner door taken off. ("Plenty of room, b'y!")

Given that it was now close to seven o'clock and we had the truck till four the next day, all these uncertainties dampened my ambition, and I was content to let the piano rest in the truck overnight. But Sean had other ideas. Though he seems submissive and diffident compared to Diane, there is a hard stubbornness in him, and he was bound and determined to "hear that piano played in your parlor tonight." What happened next over the following hour was pure Newfoundland at its best.

Sean left me with the truck, saying he was going off "to scare up a yaffle of boys." Ten minutes later he showed up with Wayne Martin, who had put in a full day at Sean's house and had been recovering from a bad back; Wayne Oldford and his son Graham (who had been working on their own house next door all day); Wins Vivian and his cousin Don; and Keith Bonnell, recently back from teaching Arabic students English in "Qatter." With me, that made eight. (Cyril also showed up, but since he had strained his back lifting Con out of his wheelchair, he said he would just "supervise.")

There was suddenly a momentum in the air, created by the appearance of so many willing if not completely able bodies, and before I knew it, they had sheets of plywood strewn across the yard, then had rolled the piano down off the truck ramp and up to the base of the front stoop. On Sean's sudden "One—two—three—LIFT!"—we raised it, one hundred pounds to a man, up onto the stoop. I went inside to maneuver it and did not realize until later that, with the piano and at least four men, the stoop was probably supporting nearly fifteen hundred pounds. (If it collapsed and the frame snapped, twenty tons of steel string tension would be released like shrapnel.) A few adjustments, though, and then, like a sudden birth, it was in the room! We had done it! Of course we had done it—we could have done anything that night. We could have manhandled a trap skiff ashore, or pulled a barn across a field, or raised up a home to put it on pilings or launched it across the bay. We could have dragged sledges of turns out of the woods with man harnesses, or hundreds of seal carcasses across the ice. Although none of us except Cyril were from Burnside, we were all Newfoundlanders that night, b'y, and together we could do anything.

Or so it seemed. There was what psychiatrists call a "flow" in events, that sense of being caught up in an effort that requires the full use of one's faculties in pursuit of a common goal. It produces a sense of optimistic inevitability, and of surpassing one's own abilities and limits. It is probably the best and surest form of happiness, and it has been the fundamental and universal experience of all Newfoundlanders from the beginning.

In any case, the feeling followed us into the front room, where the piano was lifted off its dolly and set down against the inside hall wall. The top front panel and bottom panel were replaced and the bench set before it.

Kathy brought out wine, whiskey, and rum, and all but Wayne's son stayed to have a drink. (Linda, of course, had shown up with Cyril and took center stage on the couch in a blouse and skirt, a glass of white wine in her hand.) I was going to join them, but Sean, the undisputed impresario here, said, "Now I wants to hear what it sounds like in here—play us something." I demurred, having brought up mostly music I did not know, nor had I gotten acquainted with the instrument, but I knew I had no choice. I said, "I have to play from music, you know, and only if you keep talking."

I opened up an old and musty compilation of Chopin pieces and played the first piece, the *Raindrop* Prelude no. 15 in D-flat Minor, a serendipitous choice. It's an easy piece but impressive-sounding, and it shows off a good bass, which this piano has in spades. In fact, it has a big sound, an enormous sound, really. It filled that small room and made it seem smaller. Shortly, all talk stopped and the "flow" carried over to my playing. I carried the piece, or rather, the piano carried the piece, as we had carried it. I could not have botched it even if I had tried. I could tell I had them in thrall, and at one point during the minor bridge, I found myself smiling from inside. I took my time, for I owned whatever time there was now. The entire events of the day had given it to me. I could've gone on all evening, but I knew this was just enough. When I finished and the last D-flat chord echoed away deep in the bowels of the instrument's cabinet, there was silence, and then applause, and bravos. I looked at Sean, and he looked at me with approval and satisfaction. We had done it. It was here. If, as he says, a piano warms a room, this one possessed it.

I would later think that the sound was actually too big: the soft pedal does not seem to lower the sound that much, so that pianissimos are not really possible. On the other hand, I realized how much I had been *pretending* I had a real piano at home, how the action and sound of a true, large piano like this gives the lie to digital instruments, so that the difference is like that between a blow-up doll and a live, flesh-and-blood woman. Like the latter, this machine has its own unique personality, its own quirks, excuses, demands, and sensuous virtues. It requires knowing and adapting oneself to its capabilities. It says, *I have much to give you, but only on my own terms. Accept what I am, learn to play me as I am, and I will smother you with pleasure and fulfillment.*

Or so it seemed. At any rate, I now took my chair and joined the others in drinking and storytelling. I held forth, in fact, giving a detailed and embroidered account of the incident at the wharf the other day with Cleaves' car and Calbert's truck. Again, I was still in the flow, and told it superbly, allowing animated comments and interjections, but keeping the helm, as it were, of the narrative. I had put on, for the moving, an old paint-spattered plaid wool jacket, and at one point Keith Bonnell said to me, "You look like you belongs here now! You looks more like a Burnsider than the rest of us. You could be Cleaves' twin brudder!"

A few days later I walked over to see Jim Moss's daughter Audrey and her husband Dan, who had flown in from Calgary, but they had gone out, probably to Eastport to bring Jessie back to her house to stay, now that there would be other women staying in the house with her.

The next morning the phone rang. It was Christine.

"Bob, have you heard any news this morning?"

"No."

"I've got some bad news for you. Jessie died last night."

It seems that Audrey and Dan brought Jessie back to the house about nine thirty or ten. They stayed up talking for a couple of hours. Jessie had "a good evening"—and they went to bed, with Jessie staying downstairs. A few hours later, Audrey heard her mom groaning and went down to find her sheet had come off. She put it back on, but sometime later it came off again. Audrey could see her mom was congested. She asked her if she was sick and she said yes, so she called the ambulance, but by the time they got there she was gone. This was about 3:15 a.m. They tried to revive her, but there was no pulse.

"It was as if she just come home to die," Christine said.

The other day I was talking to Cyril about having our house foundation fixed. Cyril suggested I see Ben Burry in Eastport. "He does that grunt work. He can crawl into a space no bigger than this," he said, holding his hands about ten inches apart.

So I called him and he said he would stop by the next day to look at the foundation. Terry Matthews told me that Ben was not a good student and used to skip classes at the Eastport school. "Uncle Con taught him, and one day Ben and a friend ran out of class. Con chased them into the cemetery, where the boys hid behind gravestones. Con called out, 'Ben—Ben Burry! You're sixteen. You don't have to go to school anymore, you know.' This was a revelation to Ben. He left and never went into a classroom again."

Ben is an odd-looking fellow, like someone you might have met on the American frontier a hundred and fifty years ago, his face deeply sunken, with deeply sunken but clear blue, red-rimmed eyes, a short reddish blond beard, and a wiry, muscular body. But he seems to know his business, and Jennifer Stender, for whom he has been doing foundation renovations this summer, says he is a good worker. "Of all the people we have hired to do work this summer, he is the only one who showed up when he said he was going to show up and did what he said he was going to do."

Ben told me how he originally "got into the business," which sounded like a Newfoundland version of the "Seven Chinese Brothers" folktale. He is, in fact, the youngest—or at least the smallest—of seven brothers.

"Now, see, I was just a little tyke, and Da would send me in under the house to the tightest corner with a chisel and an ax. I'd burrow back there, see, and chip away at the rock until there was enough space for the next-biggest brother to come in and burrow some more."

Burry—name as destiny.

He has a somewhat generic approach to old houses and did not seem to need to look much underneath the house, although when he did, he was impressed at how well, if jury-rigged, supported it has been, with wooden posts every four feet across the span instead of every six or even eight, which was more common. He claims the wooden posts "harden" over time, regardless of the wood they're made of, so that "when you tries to cut one with an ax, it's like cutting stone—you'll be at it a long time."

This is his basic approach: "What I does first, you see, is to crib up the house. Not much, just enough to get her level. I finds the high point—usually a back corner in a house on sloping ground like yours is—then bring the rest of the corners up to her. Now I can do as much or as little as you want. I can just shove some posts in there on concrete blocks, but in five or six years you'll notice her starting to drift again. What I like to do—what I'd do if this were my house—and I'm not telling you what to do—is to get under there and scrape out all the mud. They probably went down to rock when they built this—but on a sloping lot, erosion causes mud to accumulate—so what I like to do is scrape out all the mud, put down plastic as a vapor barrier (I can put insulation under the floor too, if you want)—then I pours the footing, see, under the perimeter—then I can put a full concrete wall under the house, or just a set of concrete posts, and then you can skirt it all around with boards, adding a perforated board every three or four boards for ventilation. Then, my son, you'll have a guaranteed, warrantied foundation that will last, and you can go ahead to do anything you want to the house, and she'll stand."

I told him he could do the work after we left in September, which pleased him.

"I like to do my work in the fall and winter—I don't like the summer. In fact, I don't much like doing the work itself. I'd rather have a life doing something else than crawling around under houses like a rat, but you know . . ."

We parted with a handshake and a mutual agreement to "work something out."

The battle of the building divas has begun in earnest. Shirley and Diane have been vying for Wayne Martin's attentions all summer, him having promised his services to both. With some final items to take care of at Diane's house, and her having gone back to St. John's, he's been working on Shirley's new house in earnest, having finished pouring and framing the walkout basement. When I remarked to Diane that Shirley can be pretty adamant, Diane said, "Well, she can just be adamant. I can be pretty damn adamant, too!"

Linda had made only encouraging and complimentary remarks about Shirley's new house, so I was surprised the other day when, after their large picture windows were installed, she said, "I can't stands it. It shouldn't be allowed!" I gave her a puzzled look, and she explained: "Now Shirley will know everything that's going on in Burnside before I will!"

Cleaves returned home last evening from another eleven days in hospital. After supper we went over to visit and found him at the kitchen table poring over a grid of pills with Joan as she explained his new meds regimen to him.

Cleaves seemed weaker than when he left, but in good spirits and glad to be home. After a while Wayne showed up with his father Willis, who now, at ninety-four, despite walking with a cane, is clearly in the best shape of any of the Oldford brothers, sitting down in a rocker, and crossing his legs dapperly, wearing a green BUILD WITH BRICK cap.

The next morning I rose at seven, started the stove, dressed, and was at this journal by seven thirty, just as the sounds of hammering began next door. The skyline of Burnside is changing rapidly, with the roof trusses on Shirley's new house having just arrived, and Willis's Wayne and his boys starting to raise their second-story walls.

On the second-story deck, against the open background of the Bloody Bay Hills, sitting ramrod-straight in his rocker, his cane across his knees, looking like an elderly chain-gang boss with a shotgun, was Willis. He had climbed up a ladder to get there!

At midday I stopped in at Cleaves', where he, Ettie, and Willis were having a supper of pan-fried cod. Willis was going on about lumbering in the old days. He got animated and excited, in a way I hadn't seen before. He said that one winter he and a buddy went eight or nine miles up the Terra Nova River and hauled out 320 cords of sticks, "in six-, nine-, and eighteen-foot lengths," in dog-drawn sledges down to the water. "Some of them hills was so steep I unharnessed the dogs and set 'em to one side, afraid I might run 'em over. I was worried about the dogs, see, not myself. So I sat up there, using a short stick in front of me as a brake, you see, and drove 'em right down to the water."

I asked Cleaves if he had told Willis about finding Old Sport's harness. He brightened, and said to Willis, "He found Old Sport's harness in the house!"

"Eh?"

"Sport's harness. He found he up in one of the sheds."

"Oh. Yes," said Willis, his voice warming to the memory. "I remember drowning Sport. Took him down to the shore, tied one end of a rope to his neck and a rock to the other, and threw it in. But he wouldn't go to the bottom because the rock was on the ledge, so I reached in and threw her over, and then she went. I could see him going round and round on the bottom."

He told this with a kind of morbid glee, but then added, by way of explanation if not apology: "He was old, see? Couldn't work no more.

And we couldn't afford to feed he. He couldn't work no more," said the ninety-four-year-old man, and looked to Cleaves for confirmation, but Cleaves said nothing.

I cooked lamb shanks for supper, and had Terry Matthews, his girlfriend Sheila, and Linda over to share them. Linda, wearing boots, had just picked one and a half gallons of big beautiful raspberries along the road by Anthony Ralph's place.

"I swear he just waits for me to come down and get on my hands and knees with my arse stuck up in the air. I said to him, 'Ant'ny, you just waits for me to come down and stick my arse into the air for you to look at, don'tcha?' and all he did was choke and go *"Hrump."* He watches me and he disappears into the house and a couple hours later Maxine comes out looking pleased as punch and all nice to me and offers me tea. I think she looks forward to me coming down to pick berries."

I got up at 6 a.m. yesterday to go out fishing with Ken Hollett. We used handlines with one-hook jiggers, a hook with squid bait, and a squid lure. Ken hooked two cod, and I got two rock cod. The cod are glutted this month and Ken got them on the jigger, but the rock cod were taking bait, especially just below the cliffs of Bloody Bay Point. We could've gotten our limit on those, but there is a widespread prejudice among Newfoundlanders against eating rock cod. When we got back, Ken's wife Sandra squinched up her nose and said, "Ew—rock cod!"

"Did you ever eat it?" I asked.

"No."

Rock cod are darker and slightly greyer than cod and not as firm, and the meat has small dark flecks in it. The head and eyes are bigger, and in general it's not as handsome a fish. Still, it was lovely to be out on the water, even if I haven't managed to get a "real" cod all summer.

A few days later, however, I had an idea. This summer I had brought up my electric smoker and thought, well, if I can't catch any cod, perhaps I could smoke them. I discovered that although Burnsiders were fond of smoked mackerel and other oily fish, they apparently had never tried smoking cod. I smoked a dozen or so of the cod fillets I had been given by Ken and others, and then dropped them off at the givers' house. They were an instant hit.

The next day I smoked three packages of large fillets for Joel Fish. Because of their size, they were moister than the others and probably won't last as long, but Joel was quite pleased and assured me they wouldn't have the chance to "go off." Henry, Ken's son, asked me, if they caught some mackerel today, would I smoke some for them? Word got around, and within a week I seem to have established myself as the village smoker, providing a community service for a "commission" of about 30 percent. Piscine usury, no doubt, but they all seem quite willing to pay it.

Last Sunday was the Transfiguration of the Lord, and Father Paul Thoms gave a simple but moving sermon on moments of transfiguration in our lives. He began by talking about how the weather had transfigured from cold and wet to this glorious morning, how "little fishes in the sea are being transfigured into those big fish you goes out to get this month, the government permitting, and the berries on the hills being transfigured from the small green ones to the big blue ones you picks and takes home and makes blueberry pie or jam to have with the fish yer caught."

He is learning how to preach here.

After the service I wanted to try out the oars Ev Saunders had made for me. I took them and the oarlocks to the boat and went for a row. The wind had died, the sun was lowering onto the Bloody Bay Hills. I attached the killick to the painter and pushed the boat out, stern first, the full fifty-foot length of the anchor rope, where it sat, glistening in the water, like a picture. All at once, at that short distance, my thoughts that I should have gotten a more maintenance-free, safer, and perhaps larger boat, dissipated like mist. Watching her riding there at anchor, her curves and lines, her grey and white paint cleaving to the wood, that beautiful fit of craft to medium, I saw her for the first time for what she was: a surpassingly lovely aesthetic object that was also useful. I realized I could appreciate her that way, as I could not an aluminum or fiberglass boat, and suddenly I did not want to put a motor on her, especially not a large one. It would have been like putting a motor on a horse.

I took a shower at Carol's and rewarded myself with a fried cod dinner at the Killick restaurant in Salvage. On the way back I stopped in to see Harold, Sue, and Simon. They offered me a glass of wine and talked about the Newfoundland music scene in the 1970s:

"Figgy Duff was booed off the stage by local audiences," said Harold. "They didn't want to hear their music in a new interpretation. They wanted country and western."

Then Sue quoted Ivan Illich on seeing to explain Jim's character, saying how the eye is either an instrument for bringing an object into contact with you, or a neutral transparent eyeball for contemplation, and that Jim and the old Flat Islanders used it as the former, and we, the educated ones, as the latter.

"Now, Jim," said Sue, "when he wanted to recollect something, would make eye contact with you, and he would stare and stare until he pulled it out of you. Now, when we are trying to remember something, we break eye contact, we look off to one side, like this, and go into someplace inside. This is why Jim needed to have me stand with him on the stage and hold my hand while he was singing. Not because he was shy (he wasn't, except in a crowd), but because he needed an audience to sing to. He would sing to you or me, but he couldn't sing to a vague audience, the ones he couldn't see from the stage.

"A whole world passed away with Jim, a whole worldview, a way of thinking and seeing we have no access to now. I don't have the words for it, but I sensed it in his presence. It was very sophisticated in its own way, and Jim preserved that by remaining illiterate."

She spoke of Jim's sense of history: "They had no sense of their ancestors coming from England, settling in Conception Bay, and coming to Flat Island. They had always been there. They could tell you of their fathers and grandfathers, and the boats they sailed, maybe three or four generations back, and then it was all the dim Dreamtime."

Kathy flew home last weekend, just as the food fishery opened here. Men (and women) are pulling in fish like there's no tomorrow, and big ones, twenty-five pounds and more. Even ninety-four-year-old Willis went out Thursday evening in oilskins and got his fish before heading back to Toronto last night. It's good to see men and boys in their yellow and orange oilskins standing at the splitting tables on the wharves filleting the fish they had caught off Ship Island just hours before, an image roughly congruent with that of their ancestors.

Thursday night, about 10 p.m., I walked in the dark down to the Oldford wharf and out onto the nail-less planks. It was a calm, mild night, and a honey gibbous moon was rising over the tickle as a congeries of sounds carried over the water to my ears like voices from the past: children hidden in the darkness of the tickle bridge; adults calling after them; gulls out in the cove; a car turning here and there on the gravel roads. I felt it was a moment of high summer, and that the season, like the first of the blueberry bushes, had turned.

A couple of mornings ago Everett Saunders stopped by to say that he could fit the sculling oar on my boat if I wanted, so I rowed the boat around to his wharf. He had made an oak template for the oar hole, used it to cut out a hole in the stern, then screwed the template over it. Then he took me out for a sculling lesson.

One stands while sculling, he showed me, with the left hand holding the sculling handle and the right around the end of the oar. The oar blade is held underwater, flat to the surface, and the oar twisted back and forth in a manner similar to a fish's tail, but in a position perpendicular to that—more like a whale's. One corrects the direction by pushing harder on the side opposite from the direction one wants to go in—just as one does when rowing with a pair of regular oars. The hole is on the port side of the stern, just to the right of the transom. Everett, a perfectionist, said that the ten-foot oar should be about a foot longer. After a while I got the motion if not the hang of it, and now I just need to practice. Everett said the old-timers could scull with the left hand alone, keeping the boat up into the wind while jigging with the other.

When we came ashore, I said I wanted to settle up with him for the oars, but he said, "Oh no, b'y, don't you worry about that. I's glad to do it for you."

Last night I had my first Burnside dream. I dreamt that all of the Oldfords were hibernating in the fall: Fred, Betty, Cleaves, Ettie, even Albert, all simply lying down one day on the floor of Cleaves' basement, on blankets or simple pallets, going to sleep for the winter, like bears, with not so much as a by-your-leave, as if they were dead. They did it as a traditional part of their life here, as if it were something they all did on a specific date, which they all somehow knew without speaking of it. In the dream I tried to get Fred to confirm that this was, in fact, what happened, not merely a fine rumor I was wishing into fact, but he was maddeningly evasive and irritated that I wanted such certainty. He kept gesturing, striking on stoves and other objects, speaking in half phrases and growls, confirming nothing.

Rowing out in my skiff to the eastern point of the island this afternoon, I thought I had finally hooked my first "real" (i.e., not a rock) cod, but it dropped off the squid lure just as I was about to bring it in over the gunnel. I wonder if I am fated never to catch this symbol of traditional Newfoundland culture.

Nonetheless, people continue to give me fish. Harold gave me a couple of fillets. Albert came in with Craig, Ryan, and Bethany. They had gathered a bucket of squid earlier that morning and gave me two, which I've cut into rings and am marinating in lemon juice and chives for tonight's supper.

Joan brought Cleaves down to the wharf, and using two canes, he hobbled out on the loose planks to watch his family clean the fish.

"Not a very good seat," he grumbled when Joan brought out a rusted vinyl kitchen chair from the store for him to sit on.

"I'll trade you the fish box I'm on for it if you like," Joan said.

Albert split the biggest fish they got, maybe thirty inches long and over twenty pounds. His son Craig gutted it and Albert bent its head backwards over the edge of the splitting table, cracking it off. Then, with a broad-bladed knife, he flattened the fish out on its back and cut through the ribs on each side and through the base of the backbone, then ripped out the bones, leaving the characteristic shape of a split cod.

I finally finished nailing down the new roll roofing on the west side of the ladder shed this morning. I hope it rains to test it before I go. I am ready to go. The yellowlegs are back, poking along the landwash as they did that first August I was here, eleven years ago, signaling the end of summer.

There were a lot of squid in the cove yesterday morning. Some were beached on Harold's landwash, pulsing colors and making loud intermittent sounds, gulping as if breathing air. More were gathered on the bottom next to the Oldfords' wharf: golden-red encrusted creatures against an emerald and gold background.

I have been thinking that perhaps a month or so is the right amount of time to spend up here, a stretch that has always left me feeling that I was just arriving finally and how great it would be to be able to stay on. But a sort of jadedness has come over me the last few days, the sense of being at loose ends. Perhaps it was just the return of humidity and the nippers last evening. In any case, with a good night's sleep, a cool front coming in overnight, that clear early autumn light, and the blessed view out the parlor window of the aps trunks half lit by the early sun, their eastern halves like bars of light; the sea of fireweed beyond, shifting paler now as the blossoms burn out and narrow at the top and the first of the wispy white seedpods curl out like smoke and begin to fill the air with as sure a sign of fall as the yellowlegs' descending, three-note call; and the blue beginning of the bay beyond, moving in serene, glittering splendor—then the old feeling rushes back anew, a sense that I am only beginning to touch the wonders of this place, and all I wish for now is enough summers, enough miles, enough years.

This is my last full day here. I plan to leave around midday tomorrow and take a leisurely day and a half to get to Port aux Basques. Yesterday morning, about seven, I started up Everett's engine on my skiff and took it down to Ship Island, the last bit of land before Ireland, about ten miles east-northeast of Burnside. In a light southwest breeze it took me about forty minutes to reach the island, but I saw no boats all the way out, and as I approached the island, the swells, though low, grew muscular and, I felt, admonitory. The bay islands are much more dramatic than the shoreline around Burnside: great upended slabs and humps of shale, schist, and granite, almost as if they had grown from dark crystals, and topped with buzz-cut forests, green groundcover, and screaming gulls.

Ship Island is the most imposing hump of all. I managed to round its southern point. From there I could see the light on Puffin Island and Flat Island to the north. I had brought along a handline and a bucket of squid for bait and had intended to jig one more time in the hopes of getting a true cod before I left, but suddenly I felt a profound sense of exposure and vulnerability, of being *far from home*. So I didn't cut the motor but headed back, bouncing slightly in the headwind. The 6 hp motor zipped the boat along, but I could see one might wish to have some additional power in rougher seas or stronger winds.

I motored back to Everett's wharf without incident and walked back to the house, stopping at Cleaves' to tell him about my adventure at Ship Island. He was furious.

"What the hell was you thinking, b'y! You've got no business being out there in that *teeny* boat, and all by yerself, too! You could have disappeared and no one would ever have found you! What would we have told Katty? What was you *thinking?*"

I had never seen him so mad. I apologized meekly, saying I *wasn't* thinking, and slinked out of their house. It wasn't until I was back in our house that I realized he was so angry because he was genuinely concerned about me, that I was worth such castigation. I felt like a sinner who had been chastised by a preacher, at once remorseful but also pleased to feel I was worth his damnation.

That evening, apparently back in Cleaves' good graces, I watched the CBC news with him and Ettie, which ended with a feature on an elderly St. John's couple. She had a PhD and had taught at MUN for decades. He had had a career in government and politics. When they both retired ten years ago, they made a pact that they would never cook again, and they have been taking their meals at the Newfoundland Hotel ever since. Now she is in the early stages of Alzheimer's, but he still brings her to the hotel every day, wanting to have her with him as long as he can. When it was over Cleaves turned to me and said, "That's a nice story. See, he takes care of her," and Ettie nodded in agreement.

Monday, March 12, 2007
CLEAVES DEAD AT 91

Word came that Cleaves died yesterday. He was ninety-one. He and Ettie had both suffered from bad colds lately, and his heart just didn't have the strength to fight it.

SUMMER 2007

WE HARDLY RECOGNIZE THE TOWN ANYMORE WITH ALL THE new houses. Shirley and Phil's is finished now, as is Wayne Oldford's. Diane and Sean's was done last year. A new log house is being framed on the point across from Gus Oldford's house by Gordon Oldford, the manager of the wood pulp mill in Grand Falls. Mark and Fraser's small house seems overwhelmed by these new edifices, and I can't help but wonder whether and for how long they will remain once they return.

Ron Crocker has reacted to Burnside's "building boom" by expanding his store out the back, mostly with hardware supplies. He says the new "castles" will need these. His father, Lonz, is more cynical. He said to me, "I'll have a job for you next year, my son, after we're bringing in a Walmarts!"

How quiet the streets of the town have become since the Canada Day weekend crowds left! It is all bicycles and pedestrians now. Joan Oldford is staying in Cleaves' house for the remainder of the week. She told Kathy that in his last year Cleaves "told more stories about himself than he had all of his life. He became nicer, too." She said he had more schooling than Fred and that he was especially interested in history and geography. He was very proud that he could track Mark and Fraser's travels on the globe, and only wished to stay alive until they got back.

"He still liked to read westerns and was always into books. I never knew Mom to read much, but in the last year I would find her reading to him, which was quite unusual. Around Christmas, though, he gave up on books and said he wasn't interested in reading or being read to anymore. He was only interested in living and dying, and he was ready to go. But he was sharp right up to the end. He had a first-rate mind in a beaten-up body, and in the end he just didn't have the strength to fight anymore.

"He was always interested in people, figuring them out and where they came from. Even when he told stories, it was more out of curiosity, trying to understand the meaning of things, whereas Uncle Fred was more of a performer. Dad loved to work. He did all sorts of things in his life. But it was never about how much he got paid—he just loved the work."

Later that afternoon Kathy came back from visiting Ettie, Joan, and Terry with a smile on her face. She said that Terry, who has always been very laid-back and easygoing about most things, is becoming "the new Cleaves." For example, Joan and Shirley are organizing a town-wide yard sale, and when Joan talked about bringing up things from her house in St. John's, Terry said, in a very Cleaves-like tone of voice, "You can't do that! You just got your boat out of Dad's shop. You're not bringing anything more into there."

Well, someone's got to step in, eh?

Yesterday I spent a couple of hours out in the skiff, photographing three of the larger icebergs that have come into the bay. I will not even begin to try to describe them in words this time. In fact, it seems to be part of the nature of icebergs that they are indescribable—their shapes are suggestive, like dreams, or Rorschachs. They have a bulk and a certain majesty about them, which commands all due respect, as if they were visiting gods. Part of it is fear, the sense that you do not want to offend or show disrespect in their presence, for they might show their displeasure and literally turn on you.

Josh Oldford and his girlfriend Angela were out kayaking the day before. "We were passing the largest berg when I said to Angela, 'Wouldn't it be something if we could see it turn over?' and no sooner had I said it than it *did*! The back half cracked and dropped off and the front half rolled over right in front of us! It was the most exciting thing I've ever seen in my life."

But they are also whimsical and alive. The smallest of the three icebergs was about eight feet high and fifty feet long. I came up close to one end of it and a gull standing on the other end took off, and I *swear* the berg *rocked*, dipping several feet at one end before rising again. I was astonished to think that something that large could be so delicately balanced that a bird taking off from one end could make it dip at the other end.

I motored out to the second berg, the most impressive of the three, and ate my lunch several hundred feet upwind from it. At one point I heard a loud *ka-slump!* that seemed to come from its mass, though I could not see anything happening. When I told Everett Saunders about it, he said that large air pockets sometimes form inside icebergs and become compressed by subsequent ice layers. When the bergs melt, these air pockets can explode—sort of a mega version of the little explosions that take place when you put a piece of iceberg ice into a cocktail.

I took photographs of its peaks and slopes against a brilliant sky full of ranks of marching cumulus clouds. At times it was hard to tell the difference between the bergs and the clouds.

There is no separate word for iceberg in French.

Ettie said she used to work for Bert Burden and his mother, "before Laura came," doing housework and caring for Bert's mother after she broke her hip.

"They didn't take her to hospital then—they just brought her home to be cared for. That was the summer I had Terry, and I had to leave him there with Joan, who was fifteen, while I went to care for her. I had to turn her, you know, to keep her from getting bedsores, and I hurt my back and spent considerable time in hospital myself that summer. She was a nice woman, though. Her husband, Bert's father, had Alzheimer's, though we didn't call it that then—we just said he was off his head. He would do things like steal a teacup from the school and hide it under their porch. Or we'd find him just standing up against the wall, crying."

Joan said that Laura came from Glovertown, and the only time she ever saw her express emotion was when she talked about her past. "That was her life and she had lost it, taking care of Bert and his mother."

The next morning Linda called to say she was having her garden party at noon: "It's supposed to be a nice warm day. Cyril cut the grass, and who knows when we'll get another one."

I like that these are such impromptu communal affairs, though some people are put out by the lack of time to prepare something. I decided to make deviled eggs, using the *Joy of Cooking* recipe, which instructs me to spoon out the cooked yolks and "moisten them pleasantly" with a mixture of French dressing, soft butter, paprika, lemon juice, pepper, Tabasco sauce, parsley, and basil. They were superb.

At the party Linda was wearing a white sheath dress slit up on one side, with her wild black curly hair pulled back. When I told her that Joan had recently called her "the erotic factor of Burnside," she was delighted. At fifty-four she still likes to flaunt her body to make men uncomfortable. Yet that evening when she played the organ at the Eucharist service, with her hair pinned up, a shawl thrown over her shoulders, and a grim, severe look on her face as she tried valiantly to coax a discernible melody out of that old, battered box of a harmonium, she looked ever so grandmotherly.

As we came out of the church, she took my arm and, pressing it, said, "Now, look—did you ever imagine on your Cape Cod that one day you would all be sitting here in Squid Tickle looking out at the water?" It was largely a rhetorical question, but I knew what she meant, and as I stopped and looked out across the shallow, gold-braided water, I realized that she had recognized a moment, a distillation of the life we live here, and it made me stop and recognize it, too.

By the time Kathy and I got back to the house, a great wind had come up from the south. We sat in the lee of the front stoop under a blanket sipping our tea, reading our books, feeling "not too shabby" as we looked through the pillars of the aps in the front yard, across the road to the garden of fireweed beyond Cleaves' house, to the wide glimpse of the bay.

After a while I lay down in the hammock strung between two of the aps trunks, draping one hand over the edge and rocking myself back and forth as I watched the tops of the trees swaying gently.

When I said that we were lucky to have these trees, Kathy said, "Have? Are they ours? Do we own them?"

I knew what she meant: trees are such presences, so alive and kinetic in their stationariness that it is hard to think of owning, or possessing, them. Rather, we live in their aura. They include us. I could feel why the Druids revered trees. I lay there, gently rocking, supported by two of their sturdy, smooth trunks, beneath the green rotunda they formed.

Just as we were about to go inside to make supper, Cyril and Linda roared by on Cyril's motorcycle, Linda's arms wrapped around his chest. She waved as they went by, and for some reason I thought of the commandment in the Eucharist service to give up the sinful life, to resolve to live by God's commandments, and I wanted to ask Linda if she had "renounced the devil and his abominations."

We decided to sleep out in the screen tent—a perfect evening for it, cool, bugless, the sky full of brilliance. We read indoors until about ten thirty, then went out into the tent, where, in homage to *The Joy of Cooking*, we "moistened ourselves pleasantly" as the great wind blew all night, stirring the stars above us.

The next day we met Ken Hollett's mother Grace (née Hiscock), who was born on Coward's Island, part of the Flat Islands archipelago. She is the oldest of the four Hiscock siblings and was a teenager when her family resettled on the mainland, and more than anyone else I have met, retains the most detailed memories of life there. She moved dishes around on the table to show us the relationship between Flat, North, and Coward's Islands. "Coward's, like Flat, was actually two islands separated by a tickle, which the men built a bridge over."

She said they skated regularly on the salt ice "after it froze up good"—though it was "a bit rough." They often walked to church on Flat Island on the ice, going to North Island and then to the main island. He husband, Harry Hollett, said, "You would carry a stick with you, holding it flat in front of you, so that if you fell through the ice the stick would keep you from going all the way in."

Though Ettie was born in 1922 and has no personal memory of the 1912 fire that burned down the town, she remembers her mother saying how they all escaped on their boats, "her carrying only a red blouse and a black skirt."

Cleaves' mother, Minnie, was carrying her sewing machine down to the wharf when another woman came after her shouting, "You forgot your baby!" and so she went back to get Willis, who was only an infant (and is likely now the last living survivor of the 1912 fire).

On Tuesday evening, we went over to Christine's; she had invited us and Scott and Emily and Carol over for a supper of ham and pot-roasted moose meat with potatoes, carrots, and peas. Howard was sitting on the deck when I arrived. His head was bent and he was wearing dark glasses. He muttered a low "How's you, b'y" and I noticed he was stanching cuts on his chin with a piece of Kleenex; apparently he had just shaved, and none too adeptly.

He claimed that his father, John—always referred to as "Mr. Moss"—was a much better storyteller than his brother Jim, and although he was "a gentle man," he once showed his mettle when a boat he was on was boarded by some inspectors from the Department of Fisheries and Oceans, known as DFO. It turns out John's boat didn't have the proper tags for the mesh size they used, and the inspectors said they'd have to confiscate the catch. John raised an oar over his shoulder and said, "Now, is you going to let us go or take us in? Make up your mind, we haven't got all day."

"What happened?" I asked.

"Oh, they had him put tags on the next day."

I thought afterwards of Howard's life here. He is the only working fisherman left in Burnside. For most of the year he is isolated, with no local men his age he can talk to. His sons and their families have immigrated to Alberta, and he has no "hobbies."

On Monday afternoon I nailed some three and a half bundles of asphalt shingles over the old roll roofing on the woodshed. In the evening Ken Hollett and I took our boats out for some fishing in light rain. We tried our luck in Stock Cove, at Brown's Store Islet, Athwart Islet, and at the back of Squid Island. Ken got one small fish and I hooked a sculpin, but it was lovely just being out on the water in small boats with a warm wind off the land, exchanging chatter, surrounded by the hills and islands where outlines were softened and silvered by the mist and rain.

On Tuesday we got a phone call from Fraser. She and Mark are in Catalina, on the south shore of the Bonavista Peninsula, waiting for the weather to turn so they can round the cape into the bay. They plan to spend a couple of weeks in the waters around Terra Nova National Park, expecting to arrive in Burnside on the eighteenth of August so as to avoid most of the summer crowd. Nonetheless, they have notified the people of Burnside of their arrival, hoping, as Fraser put it, that "people might be interested in seeing a boat that was built here come in. I know I would."

They have applied to lease some of the land on the back side of Squid Island and use it as a base of operations for "outfitting Arctic expeditions." Presumably they will build a new house there.

"I don't know, though. We might be able to live in our old house."

"In the off-season, anyway," I offered.

"Yes."

The next day I stopped at Mary and Char's to give them a copy of my new book, *The Iambics of Newfoundland*. Their son Wayne was having supper with them, and he mentioned that Woody Oldford's son Wayne was due to get here tonight, bringing a U-Haul full of furniture down from Toronto. This prompted a lot of joking about the number of Waynes in Burnside: "Woody's Wayne," Willis's Wayne," and "Char's Wayne."

Char's Wayne said, "Dad got a call yesterday from Sears saying they had a mattress at the Eastport pharmacy for Wayne Oldford and they'd wished he'd come and get it as it was taking up a lot of room. Now, Mom, I could've gotten a mattress for you, just gone over there and scribbled my name and carried it off."

He said that Willis's Wayne was a "sullen" kid who, when he came here summers, was forced to stay onshore with Linda and Shirley, "while we were all out in boats on the water. He wasn't allowed to be with us, see?

"Then, one year Willis's Wayne was teaching statistics at MUN and my daughter Sarah was an undergraduate there, so I had her go up to Wayne's office one afternoon and say, 'I'm looking for my father. His name is Wayne Oldford.' Willis's Wayne told me later, 'My jaw just dropped. I was stunned and I just sat there trying to calculate, 'What's her age? Where was I then? and with whom?'"

Emily Hapgood called this morning to say they "have been wanting to have you both over before you was gone" and asked us to a barbecue that evening. So, after taking solar showers, we walked over about five thirty and sat with them on the deck. The breeze had turned easterly and was cool coming off the tickle. Scott was grilling chicken legs and thighs, some of which he would later take next door to his parents, Alma and Eldon. Scott told me he and Em usually fix one meal a day for them.

Em is one of those spunky, energetic, no-nonsense yet fun-loving outport women. Stomping on a wasp or a "stout" on the deck, she said, "Sorry, bug, yous got to go." When I asked them how they met, Em said they went on their first date to a movie, "which was a comedy"—beat—"and it's been a comedy ever since." When I put my Panama hat on her head to shield her eyes from the sun, she immediately set it at a rakish angle and asked Scott to take a picture of her holding a drink.

Everyone commented on what an extraordinary, lovely evening it was, especially after we ate and went back out on the deck, where the sun had lowered into a thin veil of clouds shining on the water like a sheet of silver fish scales. Em said it was a rare evening when the weather was this temperate but relatively bugless.

Scott said that his grandfather Nate Ralph came over from Flat

Island about the same time as Jim and John Moss, 1957 or 1958. "He didn't bring his house over—just beat it up and brought over parts of it for lumber, I guess, and burnt down the rest. No, he just got the house that you're now in. Now, Jim and Uncle John floated theirs over, and as soon as they got them pulled up on the shore, Grandfather Nate sent me down to tell them to come up to the house to have a bite to eat. I was only three or four at the time, and I don't remember it, but I must've done it."

It was as if the serenity of the evening had cast its mantle over the entire town. The wind was slight, though enough to keep down the nippers. The water was fairly calm, and yet there were no boats out on it. Arctic terns hovered like small annunciations over the waters of the cove, then dropped with a slight scream to the surface for minnows. Across the cove small conversations could be clearly heard. Albert's son Craig and his two boys, Ryan and Nathan, came out onto the Oldford wharf (the small boys in brightly colored life jackets) as if they were contemplating going out on a ride, but then thought better of it and went back in. From Scott and Emily's deck, it still looked like "the old Burnside," with none of the new architectural intrusions visible, and we walked home, content and full of affection for this place and one another, and took in the last of the clothes off the line as darkness descended.

On Tuesday night we received an invitation to Willis's Wayne and Nancy's new house on what Cyril now calls "the Gold Coast."

Wayne showed us black-and-white photos of Burnside that he had scanned onto his computer. Burnside forty years ago was virtually treeless, with extensive potato patches everywhere, and fences to keep the sheep out. The most striking picture, however, was a photo of the four Oldford brothers in tight dark jackets, taken some time in the 1930s when the boys were in their twenties and teens. Willis looks, as he always does, just the same—gaunt and joyless; Fred and Con's features are recognizable in embryo; but Cleaves is not only thin and almost unrecognizable, but his hair, blond and boyish, appears like a flaming ethereal pillar, probably from a gust of wind at the moment of exposure. He looks like Eraserhead about to undergo rapture.

Most flowers here are like seasonal signposts marking phases, or seasons, of the summer. But the fireweed is like a ticking clock that we feel speaks to us personally. The bloom usually begins in late July, starting at the wide bottom of the floral spike, and burns its way upward, like a sparkler in reverse, marking on its daily upward climb how much time we have left here. The first bloom signals that August is coming, and then becomes August's clock, marking off the days of the month like X's on a calendar. When the spike has consumed itself, August will be gone and so will we. The blooms are now in their third quarter, the lower half having rolled itself into those long, thin seed tubes, though these have not yet begun to unfurl and smoke their way into the air. The remaining unopened buds at the tops of the spikes are like snow on top of mountain peaks, remnants of the season that is quickly coming to an end. Meanwhile they cast their beauty everywhere, creating pink pools of peace across the landscape.

Today we began our preparations for leaving in earnest. Everett came over in the morning and helped me haul my boat out of the water and into our yard.

    The best stories always come after joint efforts like this, and Everett, looking at Cleaves' apple trees across the road, reminisced about being a boy on Coward's Island and stealing apples from the tree of a man on Flat Island who would shoot a shotgun after them.

    "Well, of course, he didn't *point* it at us."

    I said it seemed that stealing apples was a pretty ingrained tradition around here.

"Oh yes, and carrots, too. We'd stand outside a garden and throw loops over at them to see if we could snag them."

"And what did you do with all the apples and carrots after you had them?"

He gave a little noncommittal smile and nod of his head to convey that *that*, of course, wasn't the point.

Everett's family was the last to leave Coward's Island, in 1956, moving to Flat Island for two years before everybody left for the mainland. That was in 1958, when I was learning to drive in West Virginia.

I went to Glovertown this morning to get boat muffs (clamps) and fogging spray for the boat motor, and on the way back I stopped at Darren Lane's house on the highway in St. Chad's to give him a copy of my book. I was curious to know his reaction to my having devoted an entire chapter to him.

He was not there but his parents were, and when I told his mother who I was, her face lit up: "Oh my son, the CBC called Darren yesterday, and they wants to interview him!"

I could see that their faces swelled with pride. Darren and his girlfriend had a baby girl over the weekend—though his mother said she couldn't remember its name. His father, Dara, told me that his mother was the sister of Arthur Stevens Ralph, so that he is connected to our house by marriage, which explains why they "kept it up" after Arthur Stevens became sick.

They are obviously proud of Darren, their only son, and said that he and Bert were "very close. He was handling a chain saw and a boat when he was seven. We never had no trouble with him—it was like he was born a man."

I gave them an autographed copy of my book, which his mother held to her breast as if it were a small child. "Come again," said Dara. "Come again anytime. Bring anyone you like. They're all welcome," his father said as I left.

The next morning, as I was hanging up some clothes, two men in a pickup pulled up and walked into the yard, one tall and stocky with short blondish hair, the other short and pudgy with a thick black mustache. I recognize the first man immediately. He's got a bit of a paunch now, at thirty-two, and three or four of his top front teeth are missing, but the smile is unmistakable.

"Mr. Lane, I presume."

"You knows me," he said, sticking out his meaty hand.

"I met your folks the other day. They said you got an interesting phone call from St. John's."

"That I did."

"You going to do it?"

"Yep—on Monday."

I mentioned Bert, and said I missed him.

"You're not the only one."

"Much appreciated," he said as they left.

"Just returning the favor," I said.

"Right on."

August 18. Word had gotten around that Mark and Fraser are due in on the *Joshua* at 2 p.m. When the time came, we took Ettie down to the ferry wharf with us. At 1:45 there were only a half dozen or so people there. Shirley had called the CBC and the *Telegram* to let them know but was told that their reporters didn't work on weekends. At precisely 2 p.m. the *Joshua* rounded the point of Squid Tickle Island under sail, accompanied by a flotilla of a half dozen local boats, and by the time they pulled up to the wharf, a crowd of about thirty had gathered. We gave Ettie and Oldford cousin Amy Noel horns to blow, took pictures and waved as Fraser steered the boat in from the cabin and Mark, in the bow, threw a line to Fred, saying, "Fred, do you think you remember how to tie up a boat?"

It was a moving homecoming after nine years and seventy-five thousand miles of sailing, with much hugging with the remaining cadre of old people. They invited everyone aboard, including many people they had never met. Fraser said, "I guess I better bring out a cake," and she dashed into the cabin and brought out an English holiday cake with fruit and nuts that she had baked, cut it up, and went around with a tray serving people.

The first thing Mark said to me was, "Sure is a long way from Cape Cod, eh?" We managed to talk a bit among the crowd and I said I hoped we'd see them later—though I wondered if there'd be time, as we planned to leave early the next morning.

It sprinkled off and on throughout the rest of the afternoon, and we were feeling increasingly frustrated and pressured by how much we still had to do when, about 6 p.m., Mark and Fraser came striding down the road in rubber boots, Mark announcing that "we knows you're busy, but were going to visit anyway."

And that broke it. I suddenly felt how absurd it was to refuse what the day and the place hands you, so we invited them in for wine and talked for nearly two hours. As Kathy said, we had forgotten how good it was to be with them. They were genuinely glad to be back, and yet you could see they were profoundly hurt, not just by all the losses and changes in Burnside, but, having traveled around the world, by the sense that the earth was everywhere wounded ("The coral reefs are gone, b'y—the glaciers are done—they're *gone*, b'y!"), and an awareness of how hard it will be to keep quiet about what they had seen in their travels ("Canadians," Fraser said in frustration, "seem to think they are exempt from environmental blame"), to resist expressing their ecological rage.

But they have somehow managed to keep a saving sense of humor and compassion. Mark said, "You know, as I grow older, I divide the world into people I respect and people I don't. I don't mean people I agree with, for that would be a vanishingly small number."

He stated again that he and Fraser had made a conscious decision, when they first came to Burnside, to spend all their spare time and energy getting to know the old people, and they were glad they did—but this must now leave them deeply isolated, as virtually all of the people they were closest to are gone:

"I remember Uncle Jim standing on the point of Squid Island as we started out," said Mark, "waving his blue sweater back and forth over his head in farewell, and all through the years away I kept thinking, how could it not be the same when we returned?"

They have plans, of course, but I think they really don't know what they will do, knowing finally that there is no place on earth they can go to escape the things they hate—mostly the corrosive effects of money on culture and community.

SUMMER 2009

THE FOLLOWING SUMMER WE DIDN'T GET TO BURNSIDE. A major renovation to our house on Cape Cod required our presence there. When we arrived this year, we learned that the rapid exodus of young people from Newfoundland over the past two decades appears to be slowing, and even reversing, creating a resurgence of in-migration to the island. The main reasons for this are twofold:

First, many of those who left the province in the past decade to work in the oil sands of northern Alberta made good money and bought houses or rented apartments, but with the cost of living skyrocketing out there, they have realized they are not better off making thirty-five to forty dollars an hour as carpenters or laborers out west than they are making twenty dollars an hour in Newfoundland.

Second, the recent discovery of vast nickel mines in Labrador and the development of offshore oil drilling off the Avalon Peninsula have resulted in a dramatic rise in Newfoundland's economy, transforming it from a "have-not" to a "have" province for the first time in decades. This, plus a rise in Newfoundland's birth rate in the past few years, has resulted in a small net gain in the province's population, stopping its lengthy slide at just above the 500,000 mark.

All of this has had its effect on Burnside, and on Howard and Christine Moss in particular. Their older son Michael is still in Calgary and now has four children. Their younger boy Christopher is in Fort McMurray and has two children, but Howard tells me that both are planning to return with their families to Newfoundland when they sell their houses in Alberta, though they will likely settle in the St. John's area rather than Burnside. Still, Howard cannot repress his gladness that they are "coming home."

On our third day back, I ran into Wayne Oldford at Ron's store.

Me: "How's your dad?"

Wayne: "Dead."

Willis Oldford, last February in Toronto at the age of ninety-seven. Still, Wayne said "his death was unexpected. When he reached ninety-five, I was sure he'd see a hundred."

Ettie Oldford has just come back from four weeks in Gander hospital. It started with an infection in one of her fingers and traveled quickly throughout her body. They pumped various antibiotics into her and she seems to have pulled through, though she is still quite weak.

We went to visit her at her winter apartment in Eastport Saturday evening. She was lying on her bed but seemed in good spirits and was very talkative. ("I've come back a long way, my dears.") Kathy climbed in bed with her and I sat on her walker. She still tears up when she talks about Cleaves. We reminisced with her, looking at all the photos of him on the walls and dresser. When Kathy kidded her about going out with a new man, she teared up and hugged her and said, "No, my dear, no other man—only him."

"Too bad," said Kathy. "I was going to leave you mine."

"When he was so sick and I had to take him to the bathroom, and

I cleaned him, he said, 'You're a good woman,' which was the most direct and heartfelt expression of affection I ever heard him make." She repeated his words—"You're a good woman"—and I thought that with the possible exception of Jim and Jessie, who were incapable of dourness, Cleaves and Ettie might have had the happiest marriage in Burnside. She kept touching us with her hands as she talked, as if to reassure herself we were really back. But then, she was a Lane, not an Oldford.

Ron has expanded his store yet again. He now calls it "Crocker's Mall," having added basic carpentry, electrical, and plumbing stock. Unfortunately, as his store has expanded, his physical capabilities have contracted. More than anyone else in town, Ron has aged considerably over the past two years. There is more grey in his hair and beard, but it is not just his appearance. He walks with a cane. His hands and fingers are swollen up, like his dad's, with rheumatoid arthritis. He says that he can't bend his toes: "The feet stays straight out like that, and you know you can't walk if you can't bend your toes." It's a genetic condition, he says. In any case, he hasn't even put his boat in this year. "Can't. And if I could, and Dad or me fell overboard, the other one wouldn't have the strength to pull him out."

Lonz, on the other hand, seems unchanged, no slower than before, and still as prone to endless monologues on any subject that strikes his fancy: one, the price of fish ("Somebody's making money from it"), and two, well, the price of fish.

Ron was about to "run Essie home" when I got there.

"Oh, is Essie still around?"

"Oh sure, she's recovered again."

"From what?"

"Oh, you knows—a chemical imbalance in her brain"—here he points to his head—"Around Christmas, her doctor started taking her off her pills one by one so she wouldn't be so stunned, but one day here in the store she just flipped out, like that, so they put her in the hospital and put her on new meds and now she's better than ever, flitting around here like a bee. Cost two thousand dollars a month for those pills."

"Wow."

"Well, mine cost twelve hundred dollars a month. But I says, 'I don't care what they cost, Doc, as long as they work.'"

Albert Oldford retired this spring from teaching in Port Blandford. He and Pat are planning to move back to Burnside year-round. They celebrated their fortieth anniversary on Saturday night at the village's Annual Senior Supper and Dance held at the old school. There were at least six different kinds of fish and brewis—some with scrunchions and some without, some made with salt fish, some with fresh, some bowls with just fish, and others with bread, boiled potatoes, and cups of scrunchions and salt fat to ladle onto the fish—plus a dozen or so sweet desserts.

There were handmade place mats honoring Albert and Pat, and everyone spooned their glasses and plates until the couple kissed. Then all eyes turned to Fred to deliver the initial toast. Though visibly diminished, he nevertheless managed to struggle to his feet with his cane, took a slip of paper from his shirt pocket, and began to recite a verse about "codfish hot and codfish cold . . ." but then he stopped and seemed to get lost. For a minute or so there was an awkward silence, and the room began to murmur nervously: "Has he lost it?" . . . "Is he having a stroke?" . . .

Then, like Robert Frost at John F. Kennedy's inauguration, he reached down into his great mind and pulled out this story:

"Well, you see, Flo and Ralph were childhood lovers, all tru school, and then one day Flo and her family moved away. Ralph went to the minister and said, 'Fadder, I don't knows what to do, I miss Flo so much.'

"'Well,' says Father Joe, 'why don't you write her a letter?'

"'Oh Fadder,' he says, 'you knows I'm no good with letters.'

"'Well then, my son, why don't you send her a poem? You was always good with verse. Tell her how much you miss her. Oh, and Ralph—be sure you mention the Lord in it.'

"So Ralph went home and got pen and paper, and the next day he sent her this:

"My dearest Flo, I miss you to bits
Especially in your nightie—
And when the moon flits across your tits—
Lord—God—Almighty!"

The place exploded in an uproar, with shouts of "Way to go, Fred!" and "He's still got it!" Cyril said that the remarkable thing is that he's never heard Fred repeat himself, a statement I heard confirmed by several others.

The "younger" crowd—Emily, Christine, Linda, Shirley—seemed like women of an earlier era: they did not only all of the cooking and serving, but the cleaning up as well, while the men drank rum at the tables, or went out to the back bridge for a smoke. But when the dancing started, it was mostly the women who got out and danced like teenagers on the floor, their energy and wildness pumped up by one another. It was the contrast between the intensely regimented gender roles of women in the kitchen and their wild letting-loose on the dance floor that intrigued me. Once, Mary Oldford (now quite weak) and Char got up to do a slow dance. Kathy and I switched partners with them. Mary looked to be in pain and I found myself having to hold her up.

"I bet you were quite a dancer in your day, my dear."

"Oh, that were many a year ago."

"Yes, but you look like you enjoyed dancing."

"That I did, that I did."

Carol Hiscock arrived at her cabin the following weekend. With her was Frank Lane, a long-term family friend who apparently had always had a soft spot for Carol and who had helped her through the trauma of Bill's death. We walked over to see her late yesterday afternoon. Frank, who stays in a trailer next to the Hiscock House, has been caring for Carol during her grief and bout with throat cancer over the past two years, and now lives with her in her cabin. He was dressed, as usual, in a pair of Bermuda shorts, but, in deference to our company, had slipped on a short-sleeved shirt, sparking Carol to quip, "You got a nice chest there, Frank. You can show it off if you like."

Frank had some stories about the fire of 1912 and its aftermath, and about resettlement from Flat Island.

"Old Gus Oldford—did you ever know Old Gus? No, I guess not—Young Gus is now eighty-three. Anyway, Old Gus used to tell how after the fire one of his brothers said, 'Why don't we call it Smutville?' ["smut," a term which, according to the *DNE*, means "charred trees still standing after a fire"] But the local minister put the kibosh on that and had it changed to Burnside."

Frank said that when the Flat Islanders came to Burnside in the 1950s, many of the people in the town simply gave them some land or sold it to them cheap. "My grandfather sold the land where Albert Morgan put his house in 1957 for five dollars. Nate Ralph bought Joe Oldford's property for five hundred dollars, but it had a house on it."

Yesterday afternoon the annual church tea and bake sale was held at the old school. Despite rainy weather, there seemed to be a record crowd. Kathy helped to man the door, and I used the opportunity to meet with those I hadn't seen yet. We also met the couple who bought Mark and Fraser's old house. After the Carpenters returned to Burnside two summers ago, they bought a piece of Megan Chiperzak's land on a rise in

Hollett's Tickle with a commanding view of the bay. They had built another house there by themselves, using local materials, but much grander than the one we had stayed in. They apparently have decided to make Burnside their permanent home. Their earlier resolve not to exploit or publicize their discoveries seems to have softened, and shortly before we arrived this summer, they had left for Greenland in the *Joshua* to scout out potential destinations for a proposed Arctic tour business based in Burnside. In any case, it looks like we shall miss seeing them again.

Lying in the hammock slung between the tall white shafts of the aps trunks, tinted light green by the rustling leaves of the canopy above and reflecting the speckled light like water reflections on a boat hull, I realize the complexity of my attitude toward these trees. On the one hand, they have stature, dignity, heft, presence. At least twenty of the trunks have a girth of over six inches, and several approach, or exceed, a foot. They are, if not sacred, then indispensable, the most valuable part of the entire property. I find them an endless source of meditation and sensuous delight, at all times of the day and night, through multiple senses. They seem to span the entire spectrum of individuality. The tall, straight, smooth, firm trunks stand proud and apart from one another, like separate goddesses showing off their verdant hair.

Yet at the same time I am aware that beneath the ground they are all connected, genetically identical, one organism really, like underground fungal mycelia. Each year the trees send out underground runners in an attempt to colonize the rest of the property. Some of these runners are as thick as my arm, and tunnel, like pale, hard, static white worms, directly beneath the house, slowly upheaving it, coming up from under the deck and foundation, seeking, as it were, to usurp our very presence here.

Each summer I attack these runners and shoots, lopping them off with clippers, shearing them away with scythes and brush trimmers, slicing into the thickest exposed roots in an attempt to cut off the supply routes that feed these outpost insurgents.

But the runners and shoots are rapacious and opportunistic, growing larger and expanding faster the further away they are from the main trunks. If they are left uncut for more than a single season (as they have been these last two years), they will exceed my own height. I cut them down, haul them away in the old wheelbarrow, and toss them over the fence onto Crown land to the west.

On Thursday, with Everett Saunders' help, I put my boat in the water and motored it around to Carol Hiscock's wharf, where she has offered to let me set a mooring. I found Frank Lane there in his usual Bermuda shorts attire, doing some work in Carol's garden. I asked him if I could pick his brains about creating a mooring. He laughed and said, "That won't take long. I'm a city boy. I was born here but left when I was four. I don't know much about boats."

"But you have one."

"Yes."

So he spent the next hour explaining and helping me set up a mooring. He suggested putting it on a line stretching west of the wharf. "You're pretty protected from westerly winds here, but an easterly blow is what will whack your boat up." Basically, we set an anchor about a hundred feet out from the wharf, using a heavy line. Then we tied the boat to the wharf with the bowline at the second post in and secured the mooring line tight through the sculling hole, leaving the bow three or four feet off the wharf. Then, untying the bowline, we could swing the boat over to the end of the wharf, gaining several feet and enabling us to step aboard. Simple, but it works.

After we got the lines in place, Frank said we should attach a buoy to the anchor. I found a piece of wood to use as a temporary float and got in the stern with it. Frank took the oars and started to row backwards to the anchor, but we didn't move.

"Uh, Frank. I think we have to untie the bowline first."

"Jesus," he laughed, getting up to undo it. "Now, you knows you can't use this for material in your book. If you does, I swear I'll hunt you down and put the Newfoundland curse on you, b'y, and you don't want that!"

"I'll change the names, Frank."

"No, Jesus, you can't use the situation or somebody will track it down."

I swore silence.

A spell of fine dry weather followed, and this morning I spoke to Todd Turner—the tall, lanky contractor whose crew is building Howard's new shed and constructing new bridges for both him and Dan and Audrey Moss, who have been spending summers in Jim and Jessie's house. I've reluctantly come to the conclusion that reshingling the back side of our roof is too large and risky a job for me to try by myself. The weather is another factor, since you can't count on more than a day or two here without rain, though it looks now as if we might be in for a stretch of clear days. Todd said he'd come over and look at it in the next couple of days.

An hour or so later, as I was sitting on the front stoop, a small beige coupe came down the road, turned toward the tickle, braked, backed up spitting gravel, then roared up the road, swerved in front of our van, and skidded to a stop. Then, like a large clown getting out of a tiny clown car, the unmistakable form of Darren Lane emerged from it, flipped the gate latch, and swaggered into the yard. I rose to greet him:

"Mr. Lane, I presume," I said, extending my hand.

"None other," he replied, grasping it.

In his black baseball cap, red T-shirt, slightly chubby but muscular body, short cropped blond hair, and perpetual slight grin, he looks, except for the missing front teeth, like a Red Sox reliever.

I think he thinks it is incumbent upon himself to stop in and visit me once a year, ever since I put him in my first book, and has come to feel somewhat proprietorial about me. He and his two buddies are "straight out" with work these days and are about to start a house in Charlottetown.

He seems a happy man, or an overgrown kid, and wants you to know it.

"Of the eighteen guys in my high school class, seventeen of them are out in Fort McMurray. I'm the only one left. They say, 'Darren, b'y, why don't yous come out here—lots of money to be made.' I say, 'Yes, I'm earning thirty thousand dollars a year or whatever here—I could go out there and make one hundred thousand—but I've got a car, a quad, three bikes, the Ski-Doo, a roof over my head, a cabin, a wharf, a boat, rabbits, partridges, and moose to get, a bit of trout and fish. What more does I need?' And I says to them, 'Hey, buddy, why don't you come back here for a visit?'

"And they say, 'Oh, I can't, b'y.'

"'Why not?'

"'Oh, I got a twenty-four-thousand-dollar SUV, a ten-thousand-dollar bike, cable, a big flat-screen, and a hundred-and-fifty-thousand-dollar mortgage to pay.'"

"So who's the richer?" I expect him to say, but he doesn't, only "So we makes our choices."

"Ever spend a winter here?" he asks. "It's rough. I've had five feet of snow on my roof. But it's always been that way. There are people setting around on the dole, yes b'y, but there's always work here if you wants it. I hate to hear the phone ring in the evening, I does. I have a hard time saying no."

"Well then, I won't ask you."

"What?"

When I told Darren about how Cleaves lectured me for going out to Ship Island in my small skiff, he said, "See, you took to Cleaves the way

I took to Bert. The Old Ones are all gone now. The others, the ones now in their fifties and sixties, they might have been born in the old time, but they grew up different. They don't have the same stories."

We agreed that the people here enjoyed their life for the most part. But where I might've gone on about the connection between a difficult and a satisfactory life and the lack of the critical element of choice, he simply said, "This was all they knew. They didn't know anything else." I demurred, citing all the men who went away to find work when the fishing gave out, but who always came back, he simply said, "If I ever has to leave here, it'll be some hard."

"So Darren, if you're so busy, how come you're loafing around the yard here with the likes of me?"

"Oh, this is my off time. I takes a half hour every now and then to step back and put things in perspective."

It clouded up in the late afternoon, but by six the easterly wind had dropped and it began to clear. I went out with Ken in his boat to fish near Baker's Loaf and Stock Cove. He got one fish, which he cleaned and gave me. As usual, I didn't catch anything; but it was a beautiful evening not to catch fish. We came upon a skiff with an old man and a young woman jigging.

"Any fish?" called Ken.

"A?" said the man.

"Any luck?"

"A?"

"Arn?"

"Oh—scattered."

The sun had just set behind the hills, and there were two minke whales feeding in the cove, their large black silhouettes slicing the calm water, turning and sinking under again like a silent, giant table-saw blade.

We both knew it was late and we weren't getting any more fish, but Ken wanted me to catch one. So we jigged for a while more until I finally said, "Let's call it an evening."

We got back to the wharf a little after nine, a pale afterglow still in the sky, where the nippers were waiting for us. I entered our whalebone-latched gate carrying the two small fish fillets Ken had given me, and for a moment I felt I was inhabiting Nate Ralph's space, returning with his wheelbarrow full of fish, returning to Blanche's supper and his pipe.

I decided to smoke some fish yesterday, using the electric smoker I brought up from home on this trip. I walked up to Ron's to get some lemon juice, garlic, and onion powder for the brine. Ron said it was he who had pointed Mark and Fraser toward Megan's land, where they have built their new house:

"I told Mark, nothing's been done with the land for two years and she might, just might, be willing to sell. Well, he was after her for two months, and she finally give in. Now Mark refers to me as 'my realtor.' I teases Mark all the time about being a 'furriner.' I can talk to Fraser for hours on end as one of me own, but Mark's always a furriner."

"But Fraser's a Brit."

"Doesn't matter—it's Mark was the furriner."

"I know Mark likes to claim he's from Nova Scotia."

"I don't care if he was born right here in the store. He'd still be a furriner."

At the end of the day I got Todd Turner and his crew to come over and look at the back roof. They smiled when they saw it, agreeing that it was "a bit rough" with a number of shingles gone, but Todd said he'd seen "plenty like that, and they don't leak a drop. I think you could build one of these steep roofs without *any* shingles and she'd never leak."

I went inside the house, leaving Todd and his boys to figure out the cost of reshingling the back side of the roof. Less than ten minutes later I heard Todd shout, "Bob! Bob b'y! Come out here!"

I went out into the backyard and turned to see Todd straddling the ridge of the roof. It's a small, narrow chimney, what they call a "five-brick chimney"—five bricks arranged in a square, forming an unlined flue five by five inches.

With his right hand resting on the top of the chimney, he casually asked, "So, Bob, does you plan to use this chimney in the future?"

I assumed he was going to tell me I needed to clean the built-up creosote, which was the cause of the many chimney fires in the town.

"Yes," I replied.

Then, without further words, he gave the top of the chimney a gentle push with one hand, and the entire protruding top of the chimney fell off the gable end and landed on the ground with a soft *thunk!*, all the bricks coming apart as if they had never seen mortar.

"Well," I said, "maybe not."

In any case, Todd said, "Don't worry. We'll take care of you" (the sweetest of words), adding that he'd do up an estimate for me tomorrow.

Later that evening Ken stopped by with his kids, Henry and Amelia, and told me of the adventure they had had the day before. On Saturday Ken had made an excursion to Flat Island in his boat, following Cyril in his. With Cyril were Linda, Sean, and Diane with Eli, and Josie. In Ken's boat were Sandra, Amelia, and Henry. A breeze had picked up during the morning, and Ken's boat is "a little tippy," but they made it to Flat Island all right.

"You should see the berries out there," said Ken. "There are four kinds—gooseberries, blueberries, raspberries, and currants—some good."

They headed back in late afternoon, and although there were

swells, they were not in open water when it happened—an unpredictable confluence of factors, a mini perfect storm. First, there was about a foot of water in his hold. Second, the gas tank, Sandra, and the two kids were all on one side. And lastly, they took a rogue swell broadside.

"I could feel the wheel trying to turn in my hands when the boat suddenly went up on her beam. I thought if I held onto her she might capsize, so I let go and Sandra and I were tossed out into the water. The kids were tucked down, that's what kept them in. Then the boat righted itself and, with the motor still running, started veering away with the kids in it. Cyril was ahead of us and didn't see what had happened, and so there we were, bobbing in the water, watching the two boats veering away from us, headed towards Spain. But Henry, he pushed the kill button like I taught them to and began bailing. They were about as far away as from here to, oh, the tickle bridge." (He was smiling broadly as he told all this.) "Well, it just seemed funny, us in the water and the two boats veering away from us. I thought, 'Well, this is it.'"

Later that evening the story was told and retold. Diane said she had actually seen the boat go up on its beam end but didn't see Ken and Sandra get tossed out.

"We looked back after a bit," she said, "and there was Ken's boat, heading towards Bessie's Island. I said, 'Cyril, I don't think there are any adults in that boat.' At first we thought they were all hunkered down in the hold, but then we saw the red life jackets bobbing about some four hundred yards behind us. 'Oh my God!' I shouted. 'There's Ken and Sandra!' and Cyril zoomed his boat around. We headed to Ken's boat first, and when we saw that the kids were secure, we headed over to pick up Ken and Sandra. It was hard getting them in the boat, and Sandra was a bit panicked about the kids, but I thought, 'If I lose her, I'll have to take care of her kids,' so I just hauled away and got her up. It all happened so fast."

"No," said Ken, "the water didn't feel cold at all. The adrenaline, you know. Plus, it's the best time of year to get thrown in the water. The kids were actually fine—stayed with us in the boat coming back. I guess I'm going to have to get a bigger one. This one's just too tippy. But it all came out all right, so I guess it's just lore now. In the end I lost my glasses, my boots come off, and my pride was nowhere to be seen."

Kathy and I had supper with Linda, Cyril, and Shirley on Thursday evening. Here we heard the full story of Cyril's father, whose parents both died early, his mother in childbirth, his father four years later in the Great War. Cyril's father was taken in by his father's parents:

"This was Bad Grandfather, who beat my father all the time. His grandmother didn't figure much. Dad's mother's parents were real nice people, but Bad Grandfather got him as the paternal grandparent because there was money in it. You see, the government paid you a certain amount to raise an orphan of a veteran. Bad Grandfather would always be waiting for him when he came home, right behind the door, and then whip him on the neck when he came in. So one night, when he was sixteen, Dad comes up to the door and stops. Then he opens the door quick, dashes in and ducks. Bad Grandfather misses him, and Da runs in, jumps up on the stove, turns around and leaps on him, pinning him. Bad Grandfather never touched him again."

Then Shirley and Linda talked about their girlhood here. Linda came to Burnside when she was ten, when her dad started teaching in Eastport. The only other kids around then were Char's Wayne, Scott Hapgood, and Joan Oldford.

"What about Cyril?"

"Oh," said Linda mischievously, "we didn't have much truck with those down the harbour and beyond."

One Christmas, however, she and Shirley went mummering down Hollett's Tickle, dressed in disguise. "We stopped in at a house down beyond the Butts, one of them that come over from Flat Island. Well, they offered us something to drink. We didn't know what it was, but we figured it was syrup, and in any case it would've been impolite to refuse. Well, since we were in disguise, they must have thought we were adults, because what they give us was moonshine! My son, we barely made it home; we staggered up Bradley's Hill, then veered apart, then crashed together and slid back down the hill. It was all ice, you see. It was a long time before we had another drink after that!"

On Thursday the wind picked up again and blew hard all day, though it remained mild and clear. Late in the afternoon we threw blankets and pillows on the hammock and spent an hour or so reading and slowly rocking in the wind while the tall straight trunks of the aps tapered like spars on a fully rigged schooner and the leaves shouted down on us.

On our last Sunday in Burnside I played the evening service, after picking out hymns with Joan. I had asked Char ahead of time if I could ring the bells before the service.

"You go right ahead, my son. We used to have five seniors who would take turns ringing the bells—Cleaves, Henry, Gordon, Brock, and myself. Well, then, after a while, most of them couldn't climb the stairs anymore, and when Henry died and I was left sole sexton, I said, 'Darned if I'm going to climb the stairs anymore.'"

I went over to the church in the afternoon to practice and opened up the bell tower shutters. At 6:15 I rang the bell for five minutes and closed all the shutters again before it stopped ringing. Several people in the church and around town told me how much they enjoyed hearing the bells. I went up to Ena, Henry's widow, after the services and said, "I hope Henry wouldn't have minded my ringing the bells."

She smiled and then laughed, "Oh, he couldn't hear him!"

I played "Abide with Me" for the closing hymn. A woman came up to me afterwards and said, "I'm so glad you played that hymn. Most people wouldn't have had the courage."

"Why not?"

"Because it's a funeral hymn."

SUMMER 2010

I ARRIVED IN BURNSIDE ABOUT 5:30 P.M. IT SEEMED CURIOUSLY familiar and unmomentous to be here now. I unlatched the gate and entered the yard, which was billowing in the wind with long grass, soft, new aspen shoots, and thousands of tall buttercups.

Hard to believe the changes in the landscape here, architectural and personal, over the previous half dozen years or so, beginning with Jim's death in 2004. Since we were last here in Burnside, the changes have been chthonic.

The first blow came last October, when I received an email from my friend Penny in St. John's, containing a short news story in the *Gander Beacon*. It reported that Mark Carpenter of Burnside had been missing from his home and the RCMP (Royal Canadian Mounted Police) had been searching for him.

I made calls to friends in Burnside, but little was known or said.

A few weeks later I called Albert Oldford to ask him if he had checked our house for leaks after the torrential rains they had there earlier in the fall. After a couple of minutes of small talk in which he told me that "the boys" had finished all the contract work on his new house and he was doing the rest of it himself, he said, "So, b'y, did you hear the latest news about—Carpenter?"

No, I hadn't.

"They found Mark's body this morning—on the beach right below his house. It was Ralph Oldford that found him. He walks that shore a lot, saw the gulls up ahead, and there he was. He was wearing a pack of some sort—must've filled it with rocks and just walked in. He'd been on the bottom for a while, but we had a big storm the day before that rattled things up. Oh yes, b'y, we've had some terrible storms this fall. It's a sad, sad story."

Suicide notes were found by the police before Mark's body was found. Would reading them help to understand his state of mind before taking his own life? When I finally talked to Fraser on the phone, I said to her that whatever demons Mark lived with, he did much good in the world, and that's how we will remember him.

On New Year's Eve some more horrendous news came from Carol Hiscock in St. John's. Just after Christmas, Sandra Tilley, Ken's wife, was walking up her stairs, felt suddenly unwell, and collapsed backwards. She was dead ten days short of turning forty-two. Apparently she had some form of heart problem, but whatever the cause, it is another fracture in what once seemed such an integrated community.

In February Carol called with more Burnside news. That week Ettie Oldford died of a heart attack in Eastport at eighty-seven. It was hardly a surprise, but we are still, as Kathy put it, bereft. Another large light has gone out in Burnside, one of the last of the true Old Ones left.

In April Fred Oldford died, and a few days later an email arrived from Sean Tiller, addressed to "Cher amis," telling us that he was "a man in crisis," that Diane had informed him that she wanted a separation, and that he realized he would be spending less time in Burnside, though his "heart is there."

Ah Burnside! Now that I am back here, I'm discovering more changes. Eldon Hapgood has been moved into a "home" in Glovertown, and there may be more I don't yet know about. Ron says Char is now the oldest of the old people left, and "when he goes, my da will be." But Lonz may not make it; he had a heart attack this spring and has congestive heart failure, which has sent him back to hospital several times.

Derrick Bowring also died this spring. Char told me that the family is coming up later this summer to scatter his ashes out in the reach, and there will be a memorial stained-glass window placed in the porch of St. Alban's.

"But the family never came to church, did they?"

"No," replied Char, "but every Christmas Betty Hunter, our secretary, would get a card from him with a five-hundred-dollar check for the parish."

It is remarkable how many of the old folks die in late winter or early spring. It is as if they hold on, hoping to see spring, and when the winter lets go, so do they.

Wayne Oldford ("Willis's Wayne") arrived by car from Toronto this week. I invited him to drop by for a beer after supper, which he did, and we sat talking for nearly two hours.

He plans to have a monument to his father placed up in the old cemetery between Willis's first two wives. "It'll say, 'Call Before You Dig,'" he said, and smiled.

"The roads here used to be full of sheep shit. There were even a few schooners, though it was never a fishing village like Salvage."

"I understand they settled here because there was arable land."

"Well, shit, b'y, they came from Salvage, for chrissake. Anything was going to look *arable* compared to that place!"

Wayne showed me a beat-up, coverless copy of a collection of stories about Buffalo Bill, published in 1907 by a Colonel Sprouse, which had been his father Willis's copy. Wayne said that he (Willis) had read the book to his lumber crew in the woods around the campfire. Wayne held it up to his nose and said he could smell the smoke.

The book was entitled *Buffalo Bill and the Magic Button*. I said to him, "I didn't know Buffalo Bill ate hallucinogenic mushrooms."

"Sure," he replied without missing a beat. "Haven't you ever heard about Buffalo Bill and the Peyote Kid?"

The following week I drove to the St. John's airport to pick up Kathy. She descended the stairway, her head cocked with those large brown eyes and that sheepish smile I love so much.

"Will you marry me?" she said.

"Were you watching that Valentine's Day movie on the plane where everybody asks that?"

I realized how essential she is to my being here even when she's not here.

When we arrived back in Burnside, we encountered Wayne and Joan walking down to the old cemetery. We joined them and Wayne pointed out the stone for Eli Oldford, Wayne's great-great-grandfather. He confirmed that Eli was the first man to settle in Squid Tickle and that both he and one of his four sons, William, died young. In both cases, according to Wayne, "it was something stupid." In one case one of them was showing how strong he was by lifting a barrel full of fish and "something burst." The other, Joan thought, was rowing from Salvage to Burnside on a dare and had a heart attack, but Wayne said, "No, it was when he was in a wrestling match."

So the women died earnestly, in childbirth, of TB, flu, or exhaustion, while the men died of boasting.

The Hollett clan arrived in force on Friday evening. Seeing several cars at Ken's house, we drove over and found them all cutting up carrots.

Val Fish was outside with Henry, who was examining ants on the ground.

"Did I ever tell you the story about your dad and the chocolate-covered grasshoppers?" she said to him.

Henry, showing only tepid interest, shook his head no, and Val began telling the story with great energy and affect, at the same time rubbing Henry's back as he stood against the railing. The story involved Ken and his friend Herman:

"One time," Val began, "when Ken went to Greece, he promised Herman he would bring him back some chocolate-covered grasshoppers, which were quite a delicacy. And did he remember? No, he did not! So when he returned home, he caught some Newfoundland grasshoppers, killed them, melted some chocolate bars, covered them and let cool, and brought them to Herman. Herman was suspicious, but his dad came in and picked one up and ate it. Ken laughed so hard he could hardly talk."

It was a great story, but it was more the way she told it, with such great strength and love, rubbing Henry's skinny, motherless back, taking him out of himself and his confused grief for a few minutes. I loved her for what she did, what she was able to do for him.

The next morning we got a call from Julie Oldford telling us that her mother, Linda, had decided to hold her annual garden party at noon. Nothing shows the readiness of the townspeople to have a party at the drop of a hat more than the fact that two hours later forty to fifty people showed up at Linda's yard with prepared food ranging from salads to ribs to salt beef to fish and brewis to Kraft dinners to hamburgers, etc. In the midst of it all Linda sat in her white hat and party dress, holding court like the Queen of the May, as if she'd had the whole thing catered, which, in a way, she had.

At one point Phil Pomeroy's sister Beth went ass over backwards in her chair, unhurt, but precipitating much talk about who was wearing underwear and who wasn't.

Linda: "When I looked over, all's I could see was your salad going over."

Beth: "Well that's good, if that's all you could see!"

"Dad," said Josh, "we ought to get T-shirts, ones that say 'I Survived Linda's Garden Party.'"

Linda said that when her father Con died a year ago, she was so busy taking care of everything and everyone that she never took time to grieve, and then one morning a few months later she was taking a shower and "it all just hit me like a ton of bricks and I stayed in bed for two days and just had Cyril bring me comfort food from my childhood."

Cyril's personality is in many ways the opposite of Linda's, not just in his quiet demeanor, but also in his genuine curiosity about what others are saying, whereas Linda tends to acknowledge another's comment with a noncommittal "It's all good," then return to her line of speaking. For example, Cyril quite admires the ability of the old people to remember with great accuracy whatever is told to them. I began to explain the old Roman orators' strategy of creating mental rooms and houses into which they could place, or file, parts of a long speech. Linda's eyes were politely glazed over, but I could see Cyril had become animated and thirsty for more.

Then, on Tuesday evening, I got a call from Ken asking me if I'd like to go out fishing with him in the morning. I was reluctant at first, having accepted the likelihood that I was fated never to catch a "real" cod, and had made my peace with it by becoming the village smoker.

It began inauspiciously. After some telephone tag with Ken Tuesday night, I was unsure if he would really call me in the morning. I woke a little after six, saw that the day was calm, and debated whether to call him again or just go out in my own boat and take my chances. I finally called a little before 6:30 and left a message. He called back at 6:40, said "Thirty minutes," and hung up.

Ken's mother Grace had shown up to babysit Henry and Amelia, as well as the two daughters of Ken's friend Geoff. The tide was high, within a foot of the top of the wharf, but mirror-calm. Whatever happened, I knew this would be my last outing for fish this year. We motored out of the still mostly sleeping village about 7:30. As we cleared the ferry channel, we were passed by Joel Fish and his elder daughter Jessica, who went roaring by at full throttle. "Hotdogger!" I yelled.

Nevertheless, we joined them on the far side of Brown's Store Islet, where they were catching a few. Ken caught a couple, Geoff one, and I got a sculpin—again—a useless, grotesquely beautiful and variably colored fish. Ken had to keep backing us up, or motoring a trolling speed, to keep us over the ledge. I could see he was getting into an antsy mood as he pointed to the chart, saying, "There's some rocks where we might get some," or "They were getting some down off this point at Baker's Loaf last week." I was afraid to suggest something for fear he would head off just because it was a new spot.

"Where would you like to go?" he finally said.

"How about where the fish are?"

Because it was such a calm day, he and Joel finally decided we should head down to Ship Island. Ken discovered that he had forgotten to charge his cell phone and commented, "If you break down here and there's a westerly blow, you'd better start brushing up on your French."

But even on the east side of Ship Island's cracked, sheer cliff walls, the water was calm. The sky and water turned all silver, so that it felt as if we were in some dream landscape or seascape, dreaming perhaps of fish. Ken's chart only went as far east as Flat Island.

"What if you go beyond that?" asked Geoff.

"You fall off."

Joel and Jessica were only about fifty yards off. It was so calm it was like talking to them in the same room. Then they both began catching big ones with their rods. Jessica became very excited, giggly and laughing almost hysterically. She pulled in one she called "a dinosaur"—a fifteen- or sixteen-pounder, shouting to us, "Can someone come over here and help me pull this in?"

"Sure—if I can have half the fish," I replied.

"No problem—I don't even like fish!"

"Oh, thanks for adding insult to injury."

We were frustrated, being so close to them and not getting any fish. Ken suggested I might want to try a rod. "I'll try anything," I said, and was about to cast when Ken hooked a big one.

"Forget the rods," he said, and we all tossed our jiggers overboard again. Then Ken and Geoff began to pull them, good-sized ones, three- or four-pounders at least. Some were gut-hooked, and so felt larger than they were, but with no fight in them. With fish being hauled in all around me, I could not believe it was going to be another summer with everyone but me catching cod, of me being, at best, an object of charity.

Then, there it was—not just a tightening on the line, but an underwater thrashing, a palpable resistance as I pulled in the green monofilament line hand over hand, praying that I wouldn't lose it. And then, coming up out of the clear, green, dark, translucent waters, was the fish—a beauty, perhaps two feet long, speckled like a gift, its large dark eyes filled with that look of surprise and catastrophe, clearly hooked through the mouth. It was too big to put in the smaller box with the other fish, so we transferred them all to a larger box and filled it with water.

And then we were on a roll—each of us pulling in a fish every few minutes—eight, nine, ten, eleven—Ken bleeding the fish as they came aboard by slashing their throats. I was pleased to see Joel motoring over near us.

"No fish here, b'y," I said. "Go away!"

Ken caught one nearly as big as mine. Then I got a medium-sized fish and a mackerel on one of the smaller lures in one drop. I felt gifted, as if we had found a vein and were following it.

"Come to papa," I said as I hooked my third one—twelve, thirteen, fourteen. The fifteenth and last one was small but gut-hooked, so we had to take him, or at any rate we did, more to avoid "displeasing the gods," as Ken put it, than DFO.

Then we set for home with purpose, hardly a word passing among us. It was fine. I kept looking at the blue-topped fish box, knowing what was in it, knowing that some, many, were mine. When we entered the harbour, it began to sprinkle lightly, and the smooth surface of the water began moving again. It took two of us to lift the fish box up onto the wharf. It was ten o'clock and the kids had just gotten up. When Ken announced that we had caught fish, they all raced down over the rocks and groundcover out onto the wharf. We followed them and began the work of cleaning the fish.

It is hard to explain what I felt. It was more, and more immediate, than just the satisfaction and relief of finally landing a fish after all the seasons of rock cod and sculpin (and pretending that rock cod was just as good as real cod)—more than the thrill of hooking the actual fish, invisible at first, but pulling back, making contact, acknowledging the connection now between us. It was like being plugged, hooked into a current of life, one that had been all around me, one that had been the essence of this place, long before I started coming here, one I had seen so many livyers[*] and CFAs, even strangers, be a part of but which, until now, I had been denied, separated from, observing only. I felt I had taken Communion for the first time—"Take, eat, this is my body"—or, more vulgarly, as if I had finally lost my virginity, and therefore, as with every other male's sexual initiation, needn't worry about the next one.

So with the kids crowded on the wharf, dangling their unbaited

---

[*] Newfoundland permanent residents, or native Newfoundlanders

hooks down among the conners and sculpins feeding on the silver cod carcasses on the bottom, we sluiced the cutting table and began cleaning the fish. I cleaned my three and felt I was getting pretty good at it. But after Geoff went up to the house to use the bathroom, Ken looked at me and said, "That was painful to watch."

"Oh?" (*Was I that bad?*)

"I like Geoff, but he's one of the most uncoordinated people I know."

The sprinkles that had dimpled the water surface that morning turned into steady rain, driving the children indoors by the time we finished. I drove home triumphantly soaked and smelly, regally covered in fish guts and blood.

I realize, of course, that in participating in traditional activities like fishing and berrying, Kathy and I are simply playing at the old life here, not just because we are CFAs, but because none of the old people here ever had, in their working years, the leisure we have and the freedom of choice we have, of what to do and when to do it. There must be a name for this in the history of any place with a local behavioral and material culture, when the old, hard, unrelieved working life is largely gone, or rather, has sunk into its soil, leaving a rich, felt legacy for others, descendants or appropriators, to savor and enjoy vicariously or residually, inhabiting the same spaces—houses, gardens, roads, meadows, wood paths, sheds and stores, wharves, orchards—feeding on the ghosts of their labors.

On Tuesday evening we paid a visit to Wayne, Nancy, and Graham Oldford at their new house and got Wayne's version of his childhood and teenage visits to Burnside, presented in the form of a sardonic rant:

"I just gets so Christ's-sake sick of having going on about how Burnside is God's paradise on earth, how the sunsets are the most beautiful anywhere, how the goddamn sun never sets anywhere else, how folksy and adorable everything was, when the truth is people lived from hand to mouth here, and there was nothing to do.

"It's not true that I didn't want to go out on a boat fishing. I did—but it was always raining, or Dad says we can't go because there's too much wind or there's not enough wind or the wind is from the east or the south or sideways.

"Sure, I was up for doing things, but what was there to do? Linda and Shirley would say, 'Let's play Feature Value.'

"'Sure,' I'd say. 'That sounds good. What is "Feature Value"?' And then they'd pull out a Sears or Eaton's catalogue and begin flipping pages, and every few pages there'd be a yellow sticker with 'Feature Value' on it and they'd say whoever sees it first slaps their hand on it and shouts 'Feature Value!'

"'That's *it*?' I'd say. 'What kind of a game is that?'

"'Well then,' they'd say, 'we've got a horse.'

"'That's more like it,' I says. 'Where's it to?'

"'Oh, it's not here now.'

"'Not here? Why not?'

"'Well, we lets them out on the roads in summer.'

"Jesus Christ, what kind of a horse is that, running around somewhere in Eastport. What kind of a horse is it you can't look at, let alone a ride? It's an absent horse!

"This was before electricity or TV. We had to read the Bible in the evening—by kerosene lamp. I'd say, 'Dad—we don't do this at home, why does we have to do it here?'

"And there was sheep shit on the roads everywhere and drying fish smelling up the yards with maggots dropping off them. Oh yeah, it was great fun."

"But obviously something stuck," I said. "You came back."

"Oh, of course, I value the history of the place and the culture, the sense of community, though that was about keeping each other from starving more than going over and asking a buddy if he like to watch TV with you."

We were surprised to learn that Wayne keeps an extensive website of old Oldford photos and bios, has a full-page printout that explains the long and complex "lineage" of the magnificent rack of caribou antlers hanging in the large room over the scale model of his family's schooner. He doesn't have a boat, and I've never seen him picking berries.

On Monday, our last day in Burnside, it seemed that the whole town decided to come visit. First, Christine popped in and Kathy gave her a bar of French soap. I thought she was going to weep. "I don't think Ron carries that," I said.

Then Char and Mary walked into the yard. Kathy got Char a whiskey with water and put out cheese and chips with Ritz crackers. Mary kept commenting on how good the "biscuits" were—she had never tasted them before.

Char Oldford is related to the Hapgoods in Squid Tickle through his grandmother, who lived in Eldon's house across the tickle. "There was a narrow wooden bridge over the tickle then," he said, "big enough to walk across, but not to drive a car through—'course there weren't any vehicles then.

"Anyhow, I remembers how if it were a fine day, Grandmother and Charlotte Ann, both in their long dresses, would meet on the bridge and dance a little jig together."

He never knew his grandfather, who died young, "p'isened on the ice. They never found out who did it, or why—probably someone wanted his job." Mary kept remarking, with obvious pleasure, how "your house looks the same. Nothing has changed."

I'm not completely sure why, but in spite of the shocking losses and diminutions among the villagers, this has been in many ways the most gratifying summer yet in Burnside. Maybe I have absorbed something of the fatalistic attitude of the old Newfoundlanders, though "fatalistic" seems too dramatic a word—acceptance then, not resignation, acceptance that recognizes what one cannot help, but remains open to the gifts of life.

In the summers that followed, Squid Tickle did not escape the costs of the human condition. There has been more sickness, infirmity, death, loss, separation, dislocation, divorce, and loneliness; betrayal, selfishness, and pettiness, unintended or intentionally cruel. But there was still fish to be caught and split and dried, berries to be picked and jammed, gardens to be cultivated, weddings and births, family gatherings and pig roasts, kids (still mostly boys) paddling kayaks and canoes and rowing dories in the water and bicycling up and down the hill to Ron's, wildflowers to be picked, the slow magenta burning of the fireweed, rivers of stars by night, fir-pointed ridges, islands and headlands slipping by you as you motor into the arms and up the reaches of the bay, stories of times past and those gone, the sudden vital catch and twist of your line, letting you know it is something you have never caught before, and the silver-bleached filleted carcasses of cod lying on the bottom around the wharf, nibbled by armies of conners and crabs.

I don't think any one thing accounts for this (though catching my first cod was probably a turning point), maybe not even the accumulation of experiences. Perhaps I just don't need anything more from Burnside, and so it gives me more. Whatever the reasons, this summer has seemed a high tide in my life here.

SUMMER 2011

THE OTHER EVENING WHEN KEN AND I WERE OUT IN HIS BOAT, with about five fish in the bucket, swimming in a couple of inches of blood-colored water, one of the larger fish suddenly went into a sustained flurry, thrashing its tail against the bottom and raising its big head up against the side of the bin, like a salmon thrashing upstream, in a clear effort to escape its confines and its fate. There was such mute desperation and pleading in its large round eyes, such puzzled astonishment in its open, gulping mouth, that, had I been by myself, or even had it been unquestionably my fish, I might have let it go. Instead I bore it, and waited for it to subside back down into a commodity.

You can't deny, nor do you really want to deny, someone like Ken—he is so uncannily gentle, funny, un-self-absorbed, curious about the world, lightly analytical, good-natured, and seemingly healthy, mentally and physically, especially for someone who had such a hole ripped out of his and his children's life when Sandra died. Perhaps it bespeaks the value of not having too examined a life. It's not that he denies anything that has happened to him—he just doesn't seem to take it personally and sees it more as a series of practical problems. For example: He is in the process of buying and moving into a new house in St. John's. He says he has no "attachments" to the old house, but rather talks about how the new house is in a neighborhood where most of his friends are, and is on the bus route so he won't have to drive the kids to school. His aunt Carol, of course, sees it as a perfectly natural need to get out of that house: "Every day he has to go up and down that staircase where Sandra fell backwards into his arms, dead."

A second day of gorgeous weather—cool westerly winds, clear or nearly clear skies, temperatures in the low 20s Celsius.

I left my smoker with Albert to use over the winter. The following summer I asked him if he had used it.

"Oh yes, b'y. She worked fine. But when I went to Gander to pick up some more wood chips, all they had was mosquito-flavored chips." Only later did I remember him slightly smirking as he said this. So locals play the CFAs by playing on their own stereotypes.

Yesterday, as I was driving around town delivering some packages of smoked cod, I passed Ev Saunders' wharf and noticed a man and a woman standing there.

"Can I help you?"

"Are you Laurie McLean?" the woman asked.

"Pardon?"

"Are you Laurie—the archaeologist?"

"No," I replied, "but he might be up at the museum."

"No, we looked there."

"Well, he's not at his house—I was just there."

"Do you think he might be willing to take some people out on the boat tomorrow? We got a whole campground of visitors."

"I don't know—you'd have to ask him."

"We'll have to try calling him."

A pause—then the woman pointed to the tickle bridge and said, "Is that a covered bridge?"

"Pardon?"

"Is that what they call a covered bridge?"

"No, ma'am, but you can put a cover on it if you like. I don't think anyone would object."

She looked a little nonplussed, but persisted: "Is that a cute little bridge?"

"Pardon?"

"Is that what you'd call a cute little bridge?"

Then the man said, "I don't think *he'd* ever call it a cute little bridge."

"Well," I conceded, "it *is* a nice little bridge."

Then the woman gave him a look and said, "*See?*"

"Well, good luck," I said, and drove off.

As I dozed in the dreaming summer of the country's heartland, beneath the green dome of the aspen grove, it occurred to me that these trees, planted so firmly in the yard of the house built for the first Oldford woman in Burnside, could stand for the family itself, all sharing similar genetic material, all physically connected by material ties that nourish one another, all supporting one another so that, although shallow-rooted, they withstand even fierce winds, rain, and snow.

The other day, I was talking with Simon Hiscock about all the new houses in Burnside and people who seem to have a need to do everything on a larger scale. Simon said, "Yes, they've got to have a bigger boat and a bigger wharf than anyone else, and then they'll tells you how they had to go out twenty-five miles—past Ship Island—to get their fish, and, of course, it's bigger than anyone else's fish and they cook it up on a grill that's also bigger than anyone else's."

SUMMER 2012

IT WOULD BE DIFFICULT TO PINPOINT EXACTLY WHEN OUR relationship to Burnside and its inhabitants began to change. There was, I think, an unspoken, perhaps even an unconscious recognition that our summer sojourns in Squid Tickle were, if not over with, then not to be endless.

My feelings about this were contradictory and inconsistent. In many ways I continued to act as if we would be coming here forever, pursuing Ben Burry, Wayne Martin, Todd Turner, and Darren Lane for estimates on placing the house on a concrete foundation.

I have spent most of the day in our cool, sun-dappled front yard, scraping, sanding, vacuuming, and wiping down the interior of the boat, even taking off the screwed-down floorboards in the cubby; listening to the CBC's *Sunday Edition* and greeting people as they came by, whether or not I knew them.

At the end of the afternoon I put a primer coat on the inside, and if we get one more good day, as we are supposed to, I'll put the last coat on tomorrow. I have realized, with some surprise, that much, if not most, of the pleasure I get from the boat is simply from looking at it, moored in the water, moving in the wind with the grace of a thoroughbred.

After I washed up, I walked down to the Hiscocks' wharf, where Simon and his older brother Will, a lawyer in St. John's, were cleaning a batch of fish they had gotten that morning. Simon's shoulder seems to have improved, and he had recently been offered a job as a part-time "observer" with the Department of Fisheries and Oceans, going out with commercial fishing boats to make sure quotas and fishing gear regulations were adhered to.

I realize that I have gathered many artifacts from my youth here in this house: my childhood bedroom furniture; my 1958 Motorola stereo with detachable speakers, and many of my earliest LPs; the teacups and saucers and the soup bowls from the sailing camp mess hall where I worked during college summers—and with these, other artifacts of an even more distant era: the 1912 Emerson upright grand, the Thor wringer washer, the Fawcett cookstove, old Newfoundland maps and calendars, the hand pump, the wooden boat, etc.—not to mention all the artifacts in the sheds.

Was it my intention to rescue all these things from oblivion? If so, what a precarious sanctuary I've given them! It would not take much to push me out of here: the back roof has already fallen in once, and the top of the chimney was pushed over with one hand. The storm windows are held together with spit and twigs. Two of the shed doors have already rotted away. The outhouse sinks further down each year—this may be the last season I can get the door off the latch. I am surprised every time the boat motor starts. Sod builds more palpably up over the house sills each year, as the aps suckers, some of them as thick as my arm, undermine the Rube Goldberg foundation under the house. The clapboards are in dire need of replacement and repainting. The washer has a leak somewhere that I have not been able to locate. And what if the water should fail? The cistern itself is probably secure, but what if the plastic line cracks somewhere underground? What if the primitive septic system should fail, or the toilet itself crash through the rotted floor? What if the foundation actually does rot out?

Yet every year, for the most part, things continue to work, as if under a magic spell. Perhaps it will be like the carriage in Oliver Wendell Holmes' poem "The Wonderful One-Hoss Shay," which works until everything goes at once, and there is nothing left but a pile of dust and paint flecks, as if it had all been a dream.

Yesterday morning Kathy and I took the boat out for a row around the harbour and through the tickle—a glorious day where the hills to the west seemed like undiscovered lands you wanted to explore. The signature landscape of most of Newfoundland, and particularly this part, is a low line of undulating hills rimming a body of water, a gentle aspect of varying degrees, where no peak stands out against the other, but each rise seems to flow smoothly into the next like sea swells. This is unlike the landscape of the American West, which fosters individual achievement or mastery at the expense of others.

Char Oldford is an affable, favorite-uncle kind of man with his little clipped mustache, silver hair, and potbelly. He has accepted gracefully his role as the community's oldest citizen (he was grand marshal at the one hundredth anniversary of the Great Fire of 1912 parade in May), and is in fact the last remaining full-time resident of his generation.

He talked about going to the Labrador himself as a young man in the late 1930s, where, in a good season, they could catch up to one thousand quintals of fish in the traps. "Some years the black flies would be thick as bees. This was in the days before bug hats, and we couldn't even swipe ourselves because we were cleaning fish. The catch was divided when we got back—half to the ship's owner and half to the crew. Each man made his own fish and then the whole load was taken to St. John's."

Eventually he got up with one heave of his legs ("I gots to shake my legs out now"), gracefully accepted Kathy's gift of blueberries and smoked fish, and trundled down contentedly through our yard gate and into history.

Todd Turner stopped by a little after eight this morning to look at the house and suggest approaches for its stabilization. He feels the foundation is rotting and needs to be replaced—probably within the next ten years. He estimated it would take "a week's pay, or a few thousand dollars," for men to jack up the main house and put it on pressure-treated posts—depending, of course, on what they find—but definitely less than five thousand dollars.

It seemed more exhausting to close up the house this time, though we didn't run into any hitches. My feet felt partially numb after standing on the ladder rungs for hours putting in the storm windows. This may have precipitated a long but ultimately good talk on our final night here, during which Kathy expressed her "limited desire to spend more time here."

SUMMER 2013

SINCE I ARRIVED IN BURNSIDE TEN DAYS AGO, NO ONE HAS invited me to dinner, or even up onto their deck for a drink. Individually, everyone is generous and friendly enough, but the gatherings here are mostly clan gatherings and I am not part of any clan here. I feel like Simon, who told me that when he was a boy of twelve, his family didn't have a boat.

"Dad would maybe rent one for a couple of weeks, but most of the time I spent sitting at the end of our wharf hoping somebody would offer to take me out fishing. But nobody did—ever—nobody—except Matchim [Joan Oldford's ex]. I knows he doesn't enjoy a very good reputation in this town because of the way he treated Joan, but whenever somebody starts ragging on Clar, I reminds them that he was the only one who ever took me fishing."

More likely, and more disturbingly, my sense of isolation may stem from the sense that, with the gradual but inexorable disappearance of the old people, I've come to the end of the mystery of this place, the end of the endless stories about this place, that sense of being in a constant and endlessly fascinating narrative that has brought me back here summer after summer. Perhaps it is, at last, coming to seem not just familiar but (say it) *ordinary*. This place is still beautiful, distinctive, and dramatic, but it has become prosaic, past, predictable, known. I still have the desire to write about it, but I will write about it in the past tense.

Yesterday, a damp, drizzly morning, I played the 9 a.m. service on the old harmonium, which grows more and more asthmatic every year, losing another stop, it seems, each season, and which that last Sunday lost its low A-flat key, which I had to glue back on. But I managed to pull another performance out of it and was greeted warmly afterwards by several of the dozen or so congregants, and so felt *connection* for an hour or so before the sense of isolation set in again. Not even the sight of Val Fish, who arrived in Burnside yesterday, riding toward me on her bicycle trailing a train of sunlight behind her—lovely and smiling as always, wearing her straw boater with a black velvet band, carrying a plastic container of blueberries, with a dozen or so stalks of rhubarb, planted up at the Big House by her grandfather, sticking out of the pocket of her light, quilted jacket like a quiver of arrows, shouting "Bob!" and giving me a big hug—dispelled it for long.

Again, I think this funk may come, in part, from the dispiriting sense that this place, which has held so much for me for so long, now seems to hold so little. And that, rather than coming from any deep shift in me, may come from the specific, prosaic fact that no one here explicitly invited me over for dinner or even a drink, or simply to talk—the way that Jessie and Jim, or Ettie and Cleaves, or Alma and Eldon, or Howard did. Burnside seems a closed world to me this year, and therefore one, I realize, I could easily let go of.

On Thursday, August 8, 2013, I picked up Kathy at the St. John's airport on a 9 a.m. arrival from Toronto. When I woke with her the next morning in my childhood bed, yesterday's mood of isolation was gone, and I felt more rested and relaxed than at any time since I arrived here a few weeks ago. Mostly, of course, it is just having her here again, not just her constant presence and affection, not even the standing in the community that her presence here gives me—but also, and perhaps most significantly, her *sociability*, her ability to make these streets and the people who walk or drive them alive for me—from the two burly young Newfoundland men who manhandled our defunct freezer off the road and up onto the truck yesterday morning as Kathy lifted the front window and shouted out, "You guys are fantastic!," to meeting Donna Rockwood, Shirley's sister, and her two grandkids, just back from her son David's wedding in Halifax to a young woman named Laura, to stopping Howard and Christine in their red pickup and getting big hugs from both of them. I am, somehow, now part of a *couple* that people want to stop and talk with. She is both my buffer between and entrance into this place.

The wind has blown strong and unabated since around midnight on Monday—nearly sixty hours—though it shifted from north to southwest and the temperature has risen over twenty-five degrees Fahrenheit during that time. The roar of it in the high branches of the aps gives a substantial feeling to the day. I love this temperate exposure to seemingly inexhaustible resources of wind. It is like riding the swells of the ocean with their great sense of excess. It makes eating a meal an adventure, clouds and sun racing one another across the sky. We have to hold onto things: our hats, the deck umbrella, newspapers, books, and our thoughts. Kathy jokingly suggested the people here cut down the trees so they won't have to hear the wind, but unsheltered exposure, such as they had on the water, would be even worse. If the wind is spirit, then the leaves of the aps are shouting hallelujahs of inspiration and praise as it passes through them, thousands upon thousands of bright green ovate leaves, each one chanting a small song, but each part of the greater motion and song of the multitude, stirred and swayed by the same spirit.

The trees sing in so many keys, sometimes handing off their clatter from one bough to another, sometimes making three- or four-part fugues moving at different levels, and, most thrillingly of all, moving the whole mass of limbs and leaves at once, like the organ chords in the last movement of Saint-Saëns's Third Symphony. Kathy says that in such a wind, if a man fell overboard . . .

Yesterday morning I walked over to the post office. When I got to the door, I heard, "Be wid you in a minute, Bob." I turned to see Howard on a ladder, painting the side of his plywood store with a roller, and Christine, in boots, holding the bottom of the ladder, with the shale slabs and masses of gold seaweed exposed at low tide. What a scene for a painter: the ochre red shed, the splattered steel ladder, the steel grey rocks and golden tresses, Christine in her blue boots, and a single black crow on a nearby rock, looking on. In Squid Tickle the mail waits for the essential tasks to be done.

This has certainly been, for me, the most mercurial of summers in Burnside. The pall of doubt, confusion, distance, and gloom that settled over me when I first arrived began to dissipate once Kathy arrived, and then dissolved completely in the last week or so in a flood of visitations, mostly accompanied by apologies and a wave of friendliness and warmth. Still, the sense that something crucial is missing remains, though I am sanguine about it now. I have come to realize and accept that the story may, in fact, be over.

SUMMER 2015

I AM LEARNING TO LET GO OF THINGS.

This morning I told Albert that, seeing as we no longer have a chimney or a working stove, he is welcome to any or all of the birch and spruce junks in the woodshed. "Some of the birch is getting a little punky, but the spruce is still solid," I told him.

Since I was last here two summers ago, the year-round population has continued, slowly but steadily, to decline. Lonz Crocker died last August just shy of his eighty-eighth birthday. That leaves Char as the last of the Old Ones still living year-round in Squid Tickle.

One afternoon I stopped in to see him. At ninety-two, he is still mentally sharp and ambulatory. I thought how hard, how isolating, it must be for him to look around and see no one—*no one*—who remembers what he remembers, but he expresses no self-pity. When I asked him how he was getting on, he simply said, "Oh, I'm pretty well—my hip gives me some problems and my doctor says my liver isn't what it should be, but it's better than it was."

Everything seems to be for sale: Maxine Chaytor told me that Ron has had the store and his adjacent house up for sale for a year now, asking $400,000. He's had "a couple of inquiries" and plans to build a smaller house on an adjacent piece of land he already owns. Soon there will be no store, and likely no post office.

I had forgotten what a heartbreakingly beautiful place this can be when the sun comes out after nine days of damp, cold, blustery weather, as it finally did yesterday evening about four thirty. The sudden brilliance and clarity filled me with a sense of grace and possibility that there might be more life here yet to come.

This morning it had cleared by 9 a.m. and there have been boats and trailers heading to the ferry wharf all day. Soft westerlies lift the layered ranks of aspen leaves into a chorus and the blue pearl of water beyond Cleaves' garden offers itself to me like a promise hidden but kept.

But this waiting sucks. It is still ten days before Kathy returns. On the phone last night, she told me that Paul and Linda McCartney were married for nearly thirty years, and in all that time he was only away from her for three nights. We're not that compulsive. Two or three days apart now and then is fine—maybe even a week for a good cause or a worthwhile project. But I cannot think of any good reason for us to be apart for a whole month!

When I finally drove to St. John's to pick up Kathy at the airport, she appeared, as she always does, magically, at the top of the ARRIVALS escalator, as if she had just been hiding there during this past month. She flashed her wonderful smile, lighting up the terminal, as if she had just been handed some marvelous present she neither expected nor thought she deserved.

When we got back to Burnside, she patted me beside her on the couch and we had the Talk. It was expected and pretty straightforward, like an accomplished fact that just needed to be spoken. Basically, her time with this place (the house, Burnside, Newfoundland) is over. She is ready to leave, for good, but is not sad about it, is actually excited by the idea of new destinations and possibilities to explore. Like me, she feels she has given our time here what she has to give and received what it has to offer her. I said that, intellectually, I was heading in the same direction to the same place, but that it was just going to take me longer to get there, since I was more emotionally attached from the beginning. We are, if not on the same page, at least in the same book—I'm just reading more slowly.

We've been over the reasons for this and didn't need to rehash them. Mostly, it is the loss of most of the people with whom we've had a real connection here, especially the old people—Jim and Jessie, Fred, Bert and Laura, Cleaves and Ettie—but also the impracticality of, or lack of motivation for, putting any more time, effort, and money into the house. It was as if the decision had already been made before we began to address it, and only needed to be articulated.

So, just like that, and surprisingly simply, we realized that this would be our last summer in Squid Tickle. The question of the day has become: What do we want to take back home? Surprisingly, there seems to be very little: a couple of prints, a few old tools, some books, my old LPs, maps, fishing line and jiggers—not much, b'y, not much.

That evening about seven, as we sat on the front stoop sipping a scotch and a hot toddy, the diminishing light seemed to gather in intensity as it declined, throwing a transformative glow across the scene—and as it did, the house (and all of its past) also seemed to gain in intensity. Yet at the same time it lost substance, became less something real and more something remembered, or imagined. I felt I was witnessing something larger and deeper than what I was seeing, something growing out of my long relationship with this particular scene.

Then it was time to go in.

The next day I stopped at Albert's and told him we "might" sell the house "in a couple of years," and that if we did, we would probably offer it to someone in his family (the Squid Tickle Oldfords) first. He accepted the news noncommittally, smiled, and said, "You know what the first question's going to be, don't you?"

I said we'd come up with that.

When I got back to the house, Kathy was sitting on the front stoop with Joan, Shirley, and Phil, as if they were all lifelong friends. I joined them, sharing our joint knowledge of Burnside and its people. Their visions were, of course, much deeper and connected than ours. Their memories were more like speedboats, which we trailed behind in our rowing skiff. In some ways, the conversation that doesn't beg to be recorded is the best of all, holding most strongly the elements of belonging.

Oh, but this place still sparks and feeds my imagination, dumping ideas into my head pell-mell, like the sunlight and leaf shadows dancing across my writing lap desk. I had thought, like Kathy, that I was essentially "done" with it, then consciously withheld myself and began divesting from it physically and psychologically. But it is no-go. However strongly I might feel or believe that I am done with this place, it seems that it is not yet done with *me*.

The night before our departure, we had dinner at Cleaves' house with Albert, Pat, and Terry. It was probably the best evening I've had all summer. Pat was more sociable and friendly toward us than she had ever been, and both Albert and Terry were at ease and talkative. (Terry had just finished mowing the grass *twice* that day, to keep the universal forces at bay.)

I felt more relaxed, more unselfconscious than I have ever felt in a Burnside conversation. I later realized it was because I wasn't listening with effort, wasn't trying to hang onto the words of the old people for a sense of meaning, significance, or difference. I wasn't trying to "fit in" or learn something. We talked about Terry's various duties at the school he teaches at in Marystown, his son Joey's travels with a hockey team, Albert and Pat's trips to Houston to visit their daughter Patty, etc.

Terry drank Jack Daniel's and Pepsi, Albert had some of my single malt scotch with ice. Kathy served ice cream and our fresh-picked blueberries, and Terry brought out nachos with red peppers and cheese that he had just baked in the oven.

It was that easy, undirected, unmemorable talk that friends make just for the pleasure of conversation. I was not "listening in" on an "exotic" conversation, but simply talking among contemporaries. Paradoxically, by unconsciously ceasing to try, and by acknowledging that our life in Burnside was coming to an end, I at last felt that I belonged here.

SUMMER 2017

May 25–June 5, 2017

IT IS LATE MAY, THE EARLIEST I HAVE EVER BEEN IN BURNSIDE, and the last. I made this short trip alone for the purpose of packing the van with the items from the house I wanted to keep, and to sign a realtor's contract with Gail Turner, the agent. Albert had offered me the use of his father's house for the two nights I planned to be in Burnside. I parked the van in Cleaves' driveway and walked across the street to look at the house, so naked among the bare aps branches and dead grass, with hundreds of tall, thin, spear-like aps shoots five to seven feet tall.

The next morning, as I was packing some final items from the house, I heard a shout through the door: "Is there a Bob Finch in this house?" It was Jim Rockwood, David's father.

David is now married with two kids in New Brunswick. It was good talking to Jim. He understood my deep feelings of loss but confirmed that it was the right thing to do.

As he left, I saw Ron Crocker shuffling across the yard to his empty store. He has "a spot" on his pancreas, too small for them to tell if it is cancer, but he is going to have chemo anyway. He has lost eighty-five pounds in twenty weeks. I told him that, despite his insults, I had always enjoyed his company. He leaned toward me and said, "There's an old Chinese proverb: KISS—MY—ARSE!"

After thirty years of being his non-live-in girlfriend, Essie Chaytor is now staying at the house and caring for him. He said he's had fourteen members of his family die of colon cancer in the past two years, all on his mother's side, all Flat Islanders, interrelated.

The light—the light! So bright, so clear, making everything transparent and ephemeral. Everywhere, everything and everyone is passing, disappearing.

What tokens of our life here am I bringing back with me? A couple of wooden lunch pails, some books, some fishing line and jiggers, a half dozen wooden shoe lasts, a white shawl, a homemade post digger, a twig besom—random objects that we have touched, used, wondered at—talismans of a life here no longer ours.

The last things I took were the photos we had pinned to the kitchen corkboard hung just inside the door to the back kitchen: photos of Kathy and me entertaining Jim and Jessie on our stoop, Kathy and Linda at Linda's garden party, me rowing Bert's skiff in the harbour . . .

But the one that got to me most was the one that showed us—a still-young couple (oh so young!) posing behind the newly rebuilt gate (now weathered grey) in our yard, looking out on the brink of a new adventure. When I later showed it to her, she said, "We look like Newfoundlanders there."

It is memory laid upon the present scene that unmans me—the deep sense of change and loss, and of shared delight, and I realize again that Kathy is at the center of every scene I remember, even when she was not present.

I woke about seven and drove to Port aux Basques, driving through the Codroy River Valley on the west coast that has greened into full spring since I stayed here (was it only a week ago?): the silvery water of the river flanked by gentle, sloping open fields (I saw Newfoundland ponies in one), and rising behind it, like presences lifting up the land, range upon range of snow-streaked dark hills, like sculpted stage sets, their tops secured by a blanket of mist, like clouds of fading memory.

It is a stunning, clear, sparkling day as the MV *Vision* pulls away from the ferry terminal at Port aux Basques, with bulging naked granite rock bulwarks to the left and snow-plated mountains to the east, fronted by a dark beige plain of tundra-like heath in between. The old port town keeps its traditional face to the sea—old houses, cemeteries, and turreted churches. I walk on the starboard deck from the bow to the stern, trying to keep up with the withdrawing island, but it outstrips me and leaves me alone, bereft, here on the waters of separation.

I have never seen it more beautiful.

ACKNOWLEDGMENTS

THE AUTHOR WOULD LIKE TO THANK THE JOHN SIMON GUG-genheim Memorial Foundation for a grant that made the completion of this book possible. Portions of this book appeared in an essay, "The Bell(s) of St. Alban's," in the Winter 2023 issue of the *Kenyon Review*.